Blacks in the White Elite

With deep appreciation to
the many ABC graduates, and
the ABC program, for their
help on this project.
　　　　　Richard L. Zweigenhaft
　　　　　November 3, 2003

With great admiration for ABC
and its graduates,

　　　　　G. William Domhoff
　　　　　Oct. 28, 2003

Blacks in the White Elite

Will the Progress Continue?

Richard L. Zweigenhaft and G. William Domhoff

ROWMAN & LITTLEFIELD PUBLISHERS, INC.
Lanham • Boulder • New York • Oxford

ROWMAN & LITTLEFIELD PUBLISHERS, INC.

Published in the United States of America
by Rowman & Littlefield Publishers, Inc.
A Member of the Rowman & Littlefield Publishing Group
4501 Forbes Boulevard, Suite 200, Lanham, Maryland 20706
www.rowmanlittlefield.com

PO Box 317
Oxford
OX2 9RU, UK

British Library Cataloguing in Publication Information Available

Library of Congress Cataloging-in-Publication Data

Zweigenhaft, Richard L.
 Blacks in the white elite : will the progress continue? / Richard L.
Zweigenhaft and G. William Domhoff.
  p. cm.
Rev. ed. of: Blacks in the white establishment? c1991.
Includes bibliographical references and index.
 ISBN 0-7425-1620-2 (cloth : alk. paper)—ISBN 0-7425-1621-0 (pbk. :
alk. paper)
 1. Social mobility—United States—Case studies. 2. Social
mobility—United States—Longitudinal studies. 3. African American
college graduates—Case studies. 4. African American college
graduates—Longitudinal studies. 5. Private schools—United
States—Case studies. I. Domhoff, G. William. II. Zweigenhaft, Richard
L. Blacks in the white establishment? III. Title.
 HN90.S65 Z94 2003
 305.5'13'0973—dc21
                                                        2002154391
Printed in the United States of America

♾️™ The paper used in this publication meets the minimum requirements of American
National Standard for Information Sciences—Permanence of Paper for Printed Library
Materials, ANSI/NISO Z39.48-1992.

Contents

Preface

This updated and extensively revised edition of *Blacks in the White Establishment? A Study of Race and Class in America* adds fifteen more years to the life stories of the key people we interviewed for the first edition, published in 1991. We also have added a new chapter on their children, many of whom are young adults going to college or starting their own careers. Thus, the study now has both a longitudinal and intergenerational perspective.

To emphasize our extensive updating and rethinking, we also have given this second edition a new title that better reflects its new orientation: *Blacks in the White Elite: Will the Progress Continue?* This title signals our belief that the educational and occupational advances made by African Americans, thanks to the civil rights movement, may be at a crucial juncture.

Due to the recent ascent of a number of African Americans to high-level positions in major corporations, we have expanded our discussion of blacks in the corporate elite to the point where it is now a separate chapter. At the same time, we extended our discussion of professionals, independent business owners, and government employees in our original chapter on careers. Finally, we have reframed our general analysis in the light of our new findings and the new ideas on the intersection of class, race, and identity developed in recent years by a wide range of social scientists.

We hope that the case studies and ideas in this new edition can be used to stimulate discussions about what remains a sensitive and complex issue in the United States: relations between African Americans and other Americans. Although we present an analysis of our findings, we do not try to provide definitive answers to the questions we pose. Instead, we provide alternative interpretations of the detailed personal stories that a small group of African Americans graciously shared with us concerning how it felt to move from low-income neighborhoods to exclusive private high schools and prestigious colleges, and then into the white occupational structure. They thereby provide readers with an opportunity to think about and discuss difficult issues such as race consciousness, subtle and covert forms of prejudice and discrimination, and intermarriage—issues that are often hard to talk about in any setting.

We are indebted to many people for the assistance they have given us throughout the fifteen years we have worked on this project, most especially A Better Chance (ABC) graduates who have generously shared their experiences and observations with us in interviews, letters, and emails. Rather than list the thirty-eight names of the original cohort, and the additional ABC alumni who have helped us for this second edition, we thank them collectively, but we do wish to give special thanks to Sylvester Monroe for allowing us to use his photographs on the cover. Many colleagues have provided invaluable feedback, both in the reviews they wrote of the first edition and, more recently, in response to questions we have asked of them as we worked on this updated edition. In particular, we wish to thank Randolph Carter of Equity and Justice for Education for the background information and leads concerning the many new scholarship programs that have developed over the past twenty-five years. We also thank Gene Baptiste, Bill Berkeley, Rod Harrison, John Iglehart, George Perry, Caroline Persell, and Robert Putnam for various assists along the way. Many employees of boarding schools have responded to our questions, including Timothy Bradley, Bobby Edwards, Michael Gary, Ellie Griffin, Pat Macpherson, and Christine Savini. The first author received a series of small research grants from the Dean's Research Fund at Guilford College for which he is grateful. He is also grateful to Libby Happel, Joan Seagraves Rees, and Sarah Rollins for their careful typing of transcripts of taped interviews, and to Letitia Hudson for her diligent assistance in locating ABC alumni on the Internet.

Most of all, we thank Rhonda F. Levine for numerous contributions to this second edition, including her role in encouraging us to write this updated edition, and in interesting Dean Birkenkamp, our fine editor at Rowman & Littlefield, in publishing it. She also read several drafts of the manuscript and added greatly to its focus and readability on the basis of her experience teaching a course in race and ethnic relations at Colgate University. The fact that she had used the first edition in her course over the past several years gave her special insight that helped us to make this new edition much more accessible for classroom use.

Blacks in the White Elite

1

From the Ghetto to the Elite

There are now a small but significant number of African Americans in top positions in American society. Overcoming great historical odds, they serve as executives in major corporations, presidents of high-status universities, and high-level appointees in the federal government. This book recounts the unique journeys of some of these men and women who were among the first to participate in an unusual scholarship program, A Better Chance, known by many simply as "ABC." Since the mid-1960s, the program has sent over ten thousand youngsters from low-income families (most of whom are black) to the most exclusive private high schools in the country, places like Groton, Miss Porter's, Choate, Foxcroft, Episcopal High, Miss Hewitt's, and dozens more. Thanks to this boost, they then went on to the most prestigious colleges in the country, including Harvard, Smith, Stanford, Wellesley, Dartmouth, Yale, and Wesleyan. This book retraces their paths from the ghetto to the elite in an attempt to understand the complex intertwining of class, race, and identity for African Americans.

Although the book tells the inspiring stories of young black women and men from low-income backgrounds, its primary focus is on race, class, and identity in the elite. By "elite" we mean the higher levels of the social ladder, where the upper class of corporate owners and executives, along with the upper middle class of highly educated professionals, make up about 15 percent of the population.[1]

Despite recent shifts in the racial composition of the occupational structure, the movement of African Americans into key leadership positions occurs at a lower rate than it does for other previously disadvantaged groups, and the pace may be slowing. For example, blacks are now fairly represented in sales and clerical occupations, a dramatic change from earlier decades, but they make up only 5.6 percent of officials and managers, and only 6.2 percent of professionals, even though they are 10 percent of the workforce.[2] Furthermore, the percentage of African Americans at elite private schools has barely changed in the past two decades, remaining between 5 and 6 percent, even while the percentage of minority or "multicultural" students has increased at most of these schools.[3] Similarly, the percentage of African Americans who receive MBAs, one of the key gateways to the corporate elite, also has remained constant at 6 to 7 percent.[4] Thus, this book is also an attempt to understand the extent to which the incorporation of African Americans into the middle and higher levels of American society will continue.

In addition, we use our findings to contribute to the ongoing discussion concerning the relative importance of race and class in shaping the identities of African Americans. Have these well-educated black Americans, with tastes and cultural styles similar to those of high-status whites, been incorporated into the groups we define as the elite, the owners and managers of large corporations, along with the doctors, lawyers, and other highly trained experts in the professions? Have the graduates become less race conscious and more class conscious, as a class-oriented theory might expect? Or have they become more race conscious, as a theory stressing the predominance of race over class would predict? Or have they perhaps become both more race conscious and more class conscious as a result of the emergence of a new situation for black Americans?

MOVING ON UP

An understanding of the lives of ABC students begins for us on a September day in 1966, when fifteen-year-old Sylvester Monroe said goodbye to a decaying tenement in the poorest neighborhood in Chicago, where he lived with his mother, his younger brother, and his five younger sisters. Known as Vest to his friends, his destination was St. George's School in Rhode Island, one of the most exclusive prep schools in America. Twenty years later, in 1986, when we first interviewed him in the downtown Washington, D.C., office where he then worked as a writer for *Newsweek*, he vividly remembered that trip and the greeting he received upon his arrival.

Monroe had never been out of Chicago before, so the airplane ride to Providence was a first for him, but what struck him most powerfully was how dark it was on the night bus ride from Providence to Newport. After all, he was used to a place where "the lights come on at night." Then, in his initial moments at St. George's, he received the first of many lessons about what was and was not acceptable in the elite world he was about to enter.

Taking one look at him, his future adviser asked, "Do you have any other clothes?" Smiling at the recollection, and recalling that he was a fringe member of a well-known gang, the Blackstone Rangers, Monroe remembered that "I had on a pair of black-and-white Stacy Adams wing-tipped shoes, a pair of high-waisted reversible pleated pants, a long-collared shirt, dark glasses, and a big hat." So he replied, "Yeah, just like this. Why?" And the adviser said, "Because that'll never do, particularly the shoes won't do for Sunday chapel." "So," Monroe continued, "the next day he put me in this Land Rover, and we drove off to the Anderson Knitting Mill in Fall River and he bought me a blue blazer, two pairs of gray flannel slacks, two suits, and a pair of black tie shoes to wear to Sunday chapel."[5]

Attire was just one of the many issues Vest Monroe confronted when he moved from the Robert Taylor Homes, a row of twenty-eight sixteen-story buildings that stretched for two miles and housed twenty thousand people, to a scenic New England prep school that caters primarily to the children of the American upper class. Indeed, St. George's is singled out by one sociologist as among the sixteen most exclusive of the many boarding schools that "serve the sociological function of differentiating the upper classes from the rest of the population."[6] Monroe would also learn about sports like crew, field hockey, and lacrosse, which he had never heard of back in Chicago, and he would learn the arcane language of prep schools, which includes terms like "prefects" and "forms."

Sylvester Monroe was not the only ABC student who found the world of elite prep schools to be full of surprises. Back in 1966, Cheryline Lewis was in her first year as an ABC student at the Abbott School (Abbott was later to merge with Andover). Cheryline, known as Cher, was baffled when one of her classmates told her that another classmate was Jewish. "What does that mean?" she asked. Her hometown of Richmond, Virginia, has one of the oldest Jewish communities in the country, but she grew up in a black neighborhood and attended all-black schools. The distinction between Jew and Gentile was not one that meant anything to her. "In Richmond," she said, "I knew white people and I knew black people." Now she knows Jewish people; in 1981 she married one. Most ABC students did not end up married to Jews, but it turned out that for many ABC students Jews have played important roles as their friends and mentors.

After graduating from Abbott and New York University, Cher Lewis worked for a few years in New York and then received an MBA from the Columbia Business School. By the time she finished business school, she was living with her future husband. They had met seven years earlier, while she was at NYU and he was studying sociology at Rutgers. They became friends and a few years later began dating seriously. By the time they married she was one of the highest-ranking black employees at Citibank, and he was an independent producer of radio shows.

At the time of our initial interview, twenty years after entering the ABC program as a girl from Richmond who didn't know what a Jew was, Cher Lewis found herself married to a successful Jewish businessman and living in an elegant Fifth Avenue apartment. With the help of a Haitian governess, she was busy raising her twin daughters. She had quit her job at the bank and was not sure what she was going to do next, though she doubted that she would work for a bank again. She was thinking of returning to her early love, writing. By 2001, when we interviewed her again, she and her husband were divorced, and she had just returned to New York City from six months in Italy where, as she put it, she "read, ate, and wrote." Her daughters, college students, are among the increasingly large number of biracial young adults.

OUR SAMPLE AND OUR METHODS

Sylvester Monroe and Cher Lewis were two of 430 students between the ages of thirteen and sixteen who had been selected to participate in the A Better Chance program in 1966. They are also two of thirty-eight men and women we interviewed between 1986 and 1988, when they were approaching forty or in their early forties. We have continued to interview many of them over the years, and by the time we conducted our most recent interviews, between 2000 and 2002, they were approaching fifty or in their early fifties. We therefore can track their lives from their first experiences as ABC students to an age where some of them are thinking about retirement. We also can report on the early experiences of their children, some of whom are now young adults.

In developing our interview sample, we searched carefully for individuals who might be considered "failures" or "dropouts," for we know that the successful are more likely to respond to an interview request. Then, too, we developed a "snowball" or chain referral sample using some of the tactics recommended to improve the quality of such samples with difficult-to-locate populations.[7] We are therefore confident that we have a representative sample and that we can estimate the percentage of graduates who fall into one of three categories: those of outstanding achievement, those of solid occupational accomplishments, and those who did not thrive either educationally, economically, or both, even though they were often satisfied with their adult lives. (For a detailed account of the sampling and methods used, see appendix 1.)

In addition to our interviews of these early ABC graduates, we also interviewed a few recent graduates, and we draw upon other studies of ABC students that are based on surveys, transcripts, and alumni records, which provide a general foundation for our in-depth portraits. We also draw upon interview and survey studies of black corporate executives. Recent statistics from private schools and government agencies provide context for our interview findings, as do autobiographies and biographies.

Although we were aware of the different theories regarding race and class in America when we began our study, we did not begin with a specific set of hypotheses to test. For this reason, our study draws in part on the open-ended qualitative research tradition within sociology and social psychology called "grounded theory." This tradition is more inductive in approach than traditional social science while being no less concerned with developing and testing new explanatory concepts.[8] Thus, in keeping with the purpose of grounded theory, we found some of our ideas as we conducted our interviews, and we assessed the interest of our findings partly on the basis of the surprise they caused us. We also interviewed at length on a given question only until we were satisfied that we were learning nothing new, and from that point on we stressed questions that had not been fully answered in early interviews, or had been rendered problematic or more interesting by earlier interviews. For example, our early interviews convinced us that we understood how the graduates felt about the program, so we spent more time in later interviews trying to understand their adult personal lives and the possible effects of racism on their careers.

THE A BETTER CHANCE PROGRAM

The ABC program was founded in 1963 by sixteen independent secondary schools, with assistance from Dartmouth College, the Merrill Foundation, and the Rockefeller Foundation. The program was a direct response to the ferment of the civil rights movement. As one of the private school headmasters who created the program later told us, "The revolutionary implications hit even us, we the headmasters. I mean, we knew history was moving fast." About 70 percent of the 430 students who joined the program in 1966, the first year it sent a large number of students to prep schools, were black; the other 30 percent included students of Hispanic, Asian, Native American, and Eskimo backgrounds. Other programs developed for disadvantaged students, such as Upward Bound, typically consist of after-school, weekend, or summer tutoring aimed at improving the students' performance in their own schools. In effect, they prepare the students for possible entry into the middle class. There are also a few government programs we will mention in a later chapter that bus African Americans each day to and from magnet schools in the city and suburban schools, such as a successful program in St. Louis. But the ABC program was unique in that it was the first program to take students away from their homes, their neighborhoods, and their local high schools for months and years at a time to attend the finest secondary schools in the country. These students are brought to live and study with students who come from the very top of the social structure, the rich and the super-rich. They are being prepped for possible entry into the upper class and the corporate elite.

To find these students, the ABC staff travels to low-income junior high schools throughout the United States to introduce the program to faculty, counselors, and the teenagers themselves. They also rely heavily on community resource people, including church leaders and community leaders, to help them identify promising prospects. Students are accepted on the basis of their grades, their test scores, the recommendations of teachers and counselors, and their written applications. If accepted, they are then "matched" with participating schools (a few public schools were added to the program in the late 1960s). The schools make the final decision whether to accept the students that ABC recommends. In a typical year since 1995, the program hands out about 16,000 applications, winnows those that come in to about 800, and then, after careful evaluation of each applicant, selects between 360 and 380 students to attend one of about 200 schools currently participating in the program.[9]

For example, in 1974, twelve-year-old Charlise Lyles was living in the projects in Cleveland, watching teenage Black Panthers with admiration, and doing poorly in school, where she spent most of her time daydreaming, looking out the window, or giving teachers a hard time. Then she turned in a short story to the "white hippie-turned-teacher" in her remedial English class that was so good she had to convince the teacher she really wrote it. The teacher arranged for Charlise to be tested, and within days she was moved to a higher-level class in English and then invited with four other students to a counselor's office, where he told them about the ABC program and urged them to work hard enough to win one of its scholarships. She decided to dedicate herself to her schoolwork, running for class president, and starring in school plays, and thereby earned a scholarship to nearby Hawkens Country Day School, high on a hill in a tony suburb. By 1981 she was an honors graduate in literature from Smith College and subsequently chose a career in journalism. Her book about her pre-prep years, *Do I Dare Disturb the Universe?*, which described the mixed feelings she had as she headed off to Hawkens, has been used in college courses on race and ethnicity, and is on the ABC recommended reading list for its new students.[10]

Before they headed off to prep school in the early years, the students attended an eight-week summer orientation program. The first year this program was held at Dartmouth; in subsequent summers there were also orientation programs at Mount Holyoke, Duke, Carleton, and Williams. The summer program was designed to help correct what were thought to be social, as well as academic, "deficiencies." As one of the headmasters of a participating school condescendingly put it, revealing the attitude many of the first black students would encounter, "They couldn't come to Andover or Northfield from Harlem in September and fit, because many of them didn't know a knife from a fork." Since the early 1990s, students have had the option of attending a briefer summer orientation (generally one to three days) with ABC staff members, usually including ABC alumni who live in the area.

In the glory days of the ABC program, from 1964 to 1975, when Vest Monroe and Cher Lewis were among its top students, more than one hundred schools across the country were participating (most called themselves "independent private schools," but, as we've noted, a few public schools also participated). However, like so many other successful advocacy organizations launched in response to the civil rights movement, the ABC program met with some hard times once the pressure from the streets cooled down. The government cut out most of its support, and the donations from corporations and foundations did not keep up with inflation. By the early 1990s, the financial situation for ABC was rather grim. So ABC had to cut back on the number of students and count on the prep schools for more of the scholarship support. By the late 1990s, however, the program was back in the chips, thanks to some new funding sources: individual contributions from wealthy African Americans and highly successful ABC alumni.

ABC described the year 2000 as "extraordinary," with more than $14.5 million in new commitments. ABC has also managed to establish relationships with highly visible African Americans in the entertainment industry. Since the 1990s, journalist Ed Bradley of CBS, one of the co-hosts of *60 Minutes*, has been the master of ceremonies at the annual awards luncheon. In 1994, Diana Ross joined the board of directors and established the Diana Ross Academic Achievement Award, presented annually to eight ABC students. In the summer of 2000, Ross and two other former members of the Supremes donated some of the proceeds from a twenty-three-city concert tour to the program.[11]

But the biggest celebrity supporter of all was none other than Oprah Winfrey, the second-wealthiest African American on the 2001 *Forbes* list of the four hundred richest Americans (she ranked number 280; Robert L. Johnson, who started the Black Entertainment Network, ranked number 172). As early as 1990, Oprah was a strong supporter of the ABC program. When she received America's Hope Award in September 1990, presented to an entertainer whose words and deeds "best demonstrate generosity and humanity," she designated

ABC to receive the $25,000 charitable gift.[12] Described as a "friend of the organization" throughout the 1990s, she became a very good friend indeed in 1997 when she became ABC's "National Spokesperson." Over the next three years, she contributed $2.3 million to the program. At the June 2000 awards luncheon, Oprah announced a $10 million gift, by far the largest in the program's history.[13] (For a more detailed treatment of the origins and history of the program, see appendix 2.)

In the late 1960s, only about 40 percent of the black students who completed high school went on to attend college.[14] In contrast, in the late 1960s and early 1970s, 99 percent of the graduates of the ABC program attended college, and many attended the best-known colleges and universities in the country.[15] Participation in the ABC program puts students on to a different educational track, one that is much more likely to lead to the best colleges, to graduate or professional schools, and to a life of economic comfort and security. Jesse Spikes, whose success as a corporate lawyer in Atlanta will be discussed in a later chapter, is one of the ABC students propelled on to an educational fast track that led to economic security. The eleventh and youngest child of a Georgia sharecropper and his wife, neither of his parents had more than a sixth-grade education, and none of his siblings graduated from high school. After completing the ABC program, he was accepted at Dartmouth on a full scholarship. He spent his sophomore year in France and part of his senior year in Nairobi, Kenya. Upon graduation from Dartmouth, he spent two years at Oxford as a Rhodes Scholar, then returned to the United States to attend Harvard Law School.

After working for a few years as a lawyer in Atlanta, Spikes was offered the chance to go to the Middle East as legal adviser for the Al Bahrain Arab African Bank. He spent four and a half years working for the bank as a legal adviser and special assistant to the chairman and managing director. Most of his time was spent on the road—and in this case "on the road" meant traveling from the Middle East to Europe or the United States. "I was just tired most of the time," he recalls, "and working seven days a week." In December 1985 he returned to Atlanta, where he now works in a large law firm.

Eric Coleman, another early ABC student, grew up in downtown New Haven, where he lived with his mother, his two brothers, and his sister. After attending the Pomfret School as an ABC student, he went to Columbia University and the University of Connecticut Law School. From 1983 through 1994, Coleman served in the Connecticut House of Representatives, and since then he has served in the Connecticut Senate (where he is now the assistant majority leader). As he told us in our 1986 interview with him, he tries to represent the interests of "women, minorities, small business owners, children, and workers." Just a few weeks before that interview, Coleman was arrested for his support of a striking union at Colt Firearms Company. Along with forty-four other protesters ("the Colt 45"), he was cheered by about four hundred members of Local 376 of the United Auto Workers as police escorted him to a patrol wagon.[16]

But has very much changed as far as the nature of the ABC students and the quality of their experience since the early years of the program? Not if Anthony Ducret is any indication. A 1995 graduate of Groton who went on to graduate from Wesleyan University in 1999, Anthony is the only son of a single mother who was on welfare in Houston, Texas. He was attending a magnet school in Houston when he heard about the A Better Chance program. Though he was hesitant to leave his mother, and she was reluctant to let him go so far away to school, he readily accepted when Groton offered a scholarship. When Anthony later read what we had written on the experiences of ABC students at prep schools twenty to twenty-five years earlier, he wrote that he felt like he was "reading an unauthorized autobiography." Recent information from ABC alumni who work in prep school environments, and from the ABC program, also suggests that many of the key issues encountered by current ABC students are the same ones faced in the late 1960s and early 1970s.

There are, however, some big changes since the 1960s. Many of the prep schools are now coed. At some schools, as many as 20–25 percent of the student body may be considered nonwhite if foreign students are included (as they sometimes are). This diversity includes a substantial percentage of middle-class black students. One survey of first-year and senior students at twenty prep schools found that the fathers of 70 percent of the black students were professionals (17 percent doctors, 14 percent lawyers, 8 percent professors, 25 percent school teachers, and 6 percent bankers), and that one-third of the families earned more than $75,000 per year.[17] Here, we should note, we are defining middle class based on education and income, as sociologists typically do. In the last chapter, we will discuss the importance of adding wealth to the equation.

The middle-class black students at prep schools today include sons and daughters of the early ABC students, who are given special consideration as "legacies," just like the descendants of rich whites who attend their parents' alma maters. Sylvester Monroe's son, for example, was a legacy student at St. George's, where he started at point guard on the varsity basketball team and was "the" senior prefect, not just "a" senior prefect, which is the equivalent of being class president. Now, after graduating with a major in marketing from Babson College in 1999, he and his former prep school roommate are in the process of taking over management responsibilities at a company owned by the roommate's family, which makes high-tech furniture for restaurants and coffeehouses.

THE PLAN OF THE BOOK

In this book, then, we use a longitudinal perspective to examine the ways in which a special educational program contributed to the occupational mobility and social identities of low-income African Americans who have been prepped to become part of the white elite. We attempt to uncover which experiences led to economic mobility for some students, including how quickly and thoroughly they acquired an upper-class style and identity. We look at their careers to determine the extent to which their work takes them into the white professional and business worlds, and the degree to which any of them have risen to top positions in the large corporations that play a preeminent role in American life. Finally, we explore whether they are able to pass on their newly acquired class standing to their children.

We examine these and related issues in chapters 2 through 8, primarily on the basis of our interviews with Vest Monroe, Cher Lewis, Jesse Spikes, Eric Coleman, and the other men and women with whom we have spoken over the years, almost all of them originally from low-income families. In chapter 2 we discuss their experiences in the summer orientation program, which was essential to the academic success of ABC in the early years, before either the ABC leaders or the private school administrators knew quite how the program and its students would fare. In chapter 3, we draw on their memories to examine their experiences at the private schools, which turned out to be different in many ways from what we expected. In chapter 4, we turn to their college careers, including where they went, their interactions with roommates and friends, and their academic performances. In chapter 5, we consider their social relationships with whites and with other African Americans, looking in particular at the different patterns in friendship, dating, and marriage. Chapter 6 focuses on occupational careers. We highlight the many achievements of ABC graduates in a wide range of occupations and professions, but we also note that some of them have not been upwardly mobile economically. At the end of the chapter we analyze the factors behind the differing educational and career paths.

Chapter 7 discusses the careers of those ABC graduates who rose to the top in the corporate world, either as executives or corporate lawyers. This chapter also incorporates research by others to provide a wider perspective on the upward mobility of African Americans to the highest corporate levels, including information on the seven men who became CEOs of some of the largest corporations in the United States between 1987 and 2001. Chapter 8 presents information on the educational and occupational careers of those children of ABC graduates who are now young adults, with a particular interest in whether they attended public or private secondary schools before going on to college, and we discuss both the similarities and the differences between their educational experiences and those of their ABC parents.

Finally, in chapter 9, we return to the more general questions about occupational mobility, race, and identity that we posed at the outset of this chapter. We explain the overall success of the ABC program in terms of the way in which it provided its students with the elite cultural and social capital that is usually available only to those with great economic resources. Drawing on our interviews over the years, we also discuss the relative importance of race and class in the social identities of ABC graduates. Then we combine our results with those of other researchers to discuss two different views concerning the likelihood that black progress will continue, with progress defined as continuing occupational mobility into the managerial and professional elites previously reserved for whites through processes of discrimination and exclusion. Whereas the first view argues that progress will continue because African Americans are now able to obtain the educational training and job skills that are valued by the job market, the second view maintains that the progress in recent decades could be in the process of grinding to a halt because the necessary "political mediation" generated by the civil rights movement and government legislation has declined since the early 1980s. Based on our evidence, we add a new dimension to the debate by showing that the decrease in government support has been counterbalanced to some degree by a wide range of "corporate-mediated" educational organizations, such as the ABC program, that produce a small but steady stream of upwardly mobile African Americans who can compete for professional and corporate positions.

We end chapter 9 by noting a dilemma that highlights the ironic tensions between individual and group mobility. The civil rights movement and programs like ABC generated the possibility for individual mobility into previously all-white professions and corporate positions, thereby showing what is possible when African Americans are given the same opportunities as the children of white elites. At the same time, however, the presence of just a few African Americans in previously white-dominated elite positions may provide stability to the social system as a whole, thereby decreasing the likelihood of the kind of collective action that created the opportunities for individual mobility in the first place.

NOTES

1. This figure is based on the model used in Dennis Gilbert, *The American Class Structure: A New Synthesis*, 5th ed. (Belmont, Calif.: Wadsworth, 1998), in which the

highest class, referred to as the "capitalist class" (those whose income "derives largely from a return on assets," including "investors, heirs and executives") is estimated to be about 1 percent of the population, and the upper middle class ("well-paid, university-trained managers and professionals") is estimated at about 14 percent (pp. 17–18).

2. These figures are from the Equal Employment Opportunity Commission and the Bureau of Labor Statistics. See Tyrone A. Forman, "The Social Psychological Costs of Racial Segmentation: A Study of African Americans' Well-Being," paper presented at the annual meetings of the American Sociological Association, Chicago, August 19, 2002.

3. According to the National Association of Independent Schools, in 1991 the percentage of African Americans in private schools was 5.3 percent, and in 2002 it was 5.4 percent (phone interview with Gene Baptiste, May 31, 2002). For data on elite private schools in New York City, see Randal C. Archibold, "Minority Growth Slips at Top Private Schools," *New York Times*, December 12, 1999, A1 (as of that time 8.6 percent of the students at those schools were black, a figure that was essentially the same as it had been in 1990, and lower than it had been in 1980, when it was 10 percent). Data we have collected from various boarding schools indicate that for the most part the numbers of African American students have remained about the same since the early 1990s. At Choate, for example, the percentage of students of African descent (most of whom are African Americans) has been between 5 and 6.7 percent for the past eight years. At Exeter, for the past decade between 6 and 8 percent of the students have been African Americans (in the fall of 1992, it was 6.1 percent, and in the fall of 2002 it was 7.7 percent).

4. These data can be found on the Web site of the National Center for Education Statistics, nces.ed.gov/edstats. For evidence that the number of African Americans admitted into medical schools has declined since 1996 when court decisions and legislation began to dismantle affirmative action programs, see Jordan Cohen, Barbara Gabriel, and Charles Terrell, "The Case for Diversity in the Health Workforce," *Health Affairs* 21, no. 5 (2002): 90–102.

5. These events and the quotations used are drawn from our interview with Sylvester Monroe in Washington, D.C., on March 14, 1986. Monroe went on to write a moving account of his return to the projects in which he grew up ("The Brothers," *Newsweek*, March 23, 1987). A longer version subsequently appeared in book form; see Sylvester Monroe and Peter Goldman with Vern E. Smith, Terry E. Johnson, Monroe Anderson, and Jacques Chenet, *Brothers: Black and Poor—A True Story of Courage and Survival* (New York: William Morrow, 1988). Unless otherwise attributed, all quotations throughout the text are from interviews conducted by the first author between 1986 and 1988, in the summer of 1994, or between 2000 and 2002.

6. E. Digby Baltzell, *Philadelphia Gentlemen: The Making of a National Upper Class* (Glencoe, Ill.: Free Press, 1958), 293.

7. Patrick Biernacki and Dan Waldorf, "Snowball Sampling: Problems and Techniques of Chain Referral Sampling," *Sociological Methods and Research* 10, no. 2 (1981): 141–163.

8. Barney G. Glaser and Anselm L. Strauss, *The Discovery of Grounded Theory: Strategies for Qualitative Research* (Chicago: Aldine, 1967); Susan A. Ostrander,

"Upper-Class Women: Class Consciousness as Conduct and Meaning," in *Power Structure Research*, edited by G. William Domhoff (Beverly Hills, Calif.: Sage, 1980), 74–76; Anselm L. Strauss, *Qualitative Analysis for Social Scientists* (New York: Cambridge University Press, 1987).

9. These figures are drawn from a presentation given by Judith Griffin, the president of the A Better Chance Program, at the Brookings Foundation titled "Race in America: New Approaches to Bridging the Divide," May 7, 1999. The figures were very much the same in 1986. According to the ABC Annual Report for that year, there were 1,763 students in the "Applicant Pool," and 324 placed at participating schools.

10. Charlise Lyles, *Do I Dare Disturb the Universe? From the Projects to Prep School* (Boston: Faber and Faber, 1994).

11. "Diana Ross to Donate Proceeds from Tour to A Better Chance," *A Better Chance News* 2, no. 1 (Spring 2000): 1, 6.

12. "Oprah Winfrey: ABC's Good Friend," *Abecedarian: A Publication of A Better Chance, Inc.* 5, no. 1 (November 1990): 1.

13. "Oprah Winfrey 'Invests' $10 Million in A Better Chance," *A Better Chance News* 2, no. 2 (Fall 2000): 1–2

14. Alexander W. Astin, *Minorities in American Higher Education* (San Francisco: Jossey-Bass, 1982), 35. Also see Peter Cookson, Jr. and Caroline H. Persell, "English and American Residential Secondary Schools: A Comparative Study of the Reproduction of Social Elites," *Comparative Education Review* 29, no. 3 (1985): 296. On the basis of 1982 census data, Cookson and Persell report that only 33 percent of "all high school graduates" attended college after secondary school graduation.

15. The 99 percent figure is drawn from George Perry's study of ABC students from 1964–1972 ("A Better Chance: Evaluation of Student Attitudes and Academic Performance, 1964–1972," study funded by the Alfred P. Sloan Foundation, the Henry Luce Foundation, and the New York Community Trust, March 1973, ERIC Document 075556, p. 100). Cookson and Persell, "English and American Schools," report that "more than 95 percent of American boarding school graduates attend college after secondary school graduation . . . and two-thirds attend the most highly selective colleges in the country" (296).

16. Susan Howard, "3 Legislators among 45 Arrested in Colt Protest," *Hartford Courant*, May 14, 1986, Al.

17. Peter W. Cookson and Caroline Hodges Persell, "Race and Class in America's Elite Preparatory Boarding Schools: African Americans as the 'Outsiders Within,'" *Journal of Negro Education* 60, no. 2 (1991): 219–228.

2

The Summer Program: "This Is Your Spring Training, and That's Where Pennants and World Championships Are Won"

Bobette Reed Kahn, who graduated from the MacDuffie School, Williams College, and the Harvard Divinity School, remembers quite well her eight weeks at the 1966 summer transitional program at Mount Holyoke.

> When I hit Mount Holyoke, they provided little packages for us—toothbrush, toothpaste, a hardbound *Webster's Dictionary*, which I still have. They gave us all different kinds of things they thought were important to females, and not in a condescending way. They gave us all kinds of sanitary devices, and we appreciated that. Our resident person, our tutor, was in charge of making sure that each one of us was being educated in the proper way, but never in a group, never in a way that would really embarrass any one person. . . .
>
> They took us to Tanglewood, and what an incredible experience! Most of the girls had not been exposed to classical music so that was just a wonderful experience to have. . . .
>
> They did all kinds of things. Had I ever heard of field hockey? No. We all had to learn how to swim, we took ballet, they took us out to dinner and we had to order for ourselves. Most of us had never been to a restaurant, let alone order. We had one meal a week with dress-up, and afterwards we had demitasse—I'd never had coffee, let alone had demitasse—and we'd learn how to hold the cup.

When we first interviewed ABC graduates, more than twenty years after they had entered the program, they had vivid memories of their summers at Dartmouth, Mount Holyoke, Williams, Duke, or Carleton. Many referred to the summer program as being like "summer camp." Cher Lewis had attended traditional summer camps and had hated them all—she even came home early from one. However, she loved her summer at Mount Holyoke so much that she said it was "like a magic summer camp." When asked if they remembered enjoying the summer, almost all of those interviewed said without hesitation that they had, though many were quick to point out that they worked quite hard. Most smiled as they recalled specific aspects of the summer that had enchanted them. Some mentioned the thrill of seeing ballet for the first time. Others mentioned how much they enjoyed canoeing or being in the woods.

Beyond the niceties and small touches, the "primary mission and consuming concern," as it was phrased in a report written about the first summer program, was "to improve each student's chances for survival" at prep school. On the assumption that academic survival would depend especially on verbal and mathematical skills, the decision was made to focus intensively on English and math. Though adjustments were made for individual students as needed, the basic weekly class schedule included nine hours of English literature and composition, six hours of reading instruction, and nine hours of math.

The intensive academic work was supplemented by social and cultural activities, athletics, and weekend trips. One of the most important social activities was eating dinner with other students, faculty and their families, and invited guests. For these meals the male students wore jackets and ties, and the female students wore dresses. In addition, they were expected to follow the examples set by their faculty and resident advisers, which included such behaviors as using the proper silverware at the proper time and politely asking for things to be passed rather than reaching across the table. The decorum expected at the evening meal and the manner by which it was taught are reflected in the following account of an event that occurred during the 1966 summer program at Dartmouth: "Once, on the next to the last evening, the boys were surprised to find the tutors acting as waiters and responding with mock gravity to requests of every kind; there was, understandably, a little less decorum than at other evening meals, when tutors and faculty taught, by example mainly, the etiquette to be expected at their schools."[1]

The students were encouraged to engage in conversation with those around them. At times, the seating of students and their guests was based on mutual interests: "A scientist might sit with students interested in nuclear physics; a reporter with students active on school newspapers; a professional actor with those rehearsing for the ABC play; or a visiting headmaster with the students accepted by his school."[2]

Frequently, there were after-dinner talks by faculty or guests. One of the highlights that first summer at Dartmouth, 1964, when all fifty-five of the participants were male, was a dinner visit by Jackie Robinson, who told the students: "This is your spring training, and that's where pennants and world championships are won."[3]

During the 1964 summer program, the students attended Sunday evening concerts by the Community Symphony, and they saw performances of *As You*

Like It and *Rhinoceros* by the Dartmouth Repertory Theater. For much of the summer, the staff resisted pressure from the students to have a dance (on the grounds that they wanted the students to "learn to endure"); finally, ten days before the end of the program, the staff gave in. The dance, however, was not simply an occasion for a group of teenage boys to invite a group of teenage girls to dance to their favorite music in a gymnasium. It, too, became a lesson designed to prepare ABC students for the kinds of social events they would encounter as prep school students. As the summer report explains: "In capitulating, we gave the students both the privilege and responsibility for issuing invitations, meeting their guests, escorting them to dinner, the dance, Sunday breakfast and church. They were superb—as were their young ladies."[4]

Almost every weekend, the resident tutors took groups of six or seven students on outings. Some of these trips were to explore local mountains and lakes, some were to visit New England prep schools, and some were to work on a nearby farm. Typically, on one of the eight weekends, Saturday classes were cancelled to allow for longer trips to Quebec and Boston.

Athletics formed another important component of the summer program, but not the sports the students were used to playing. The staff purposely chose activities that were common to prep schools but that the ABC students were unlikely to have encountered. Every student received swimming instruction almost daily, and soccer, volleyball, canoeing, and rock climbing were among the other athletic activities. Jay Farrow, a graduate of Westtown School (and now the associate head there), left his home in Cleveland to participate in the summer orientation at Carleton College in Minnesota. He explained to an interviewer that he had never played, or even heard of, soccer: "Believe it or not—this is funny—I hadn't even heard of soccer. I couldn't spell soccer. I had no idea what soccer was."[5] Very few of the ABC students knew much, if anything, about rock climbing, which, according to the 1964 final report, took on special importance: "Perhaps of all the summer activities, the rock climbing was most symbolic of ABC spirit and goals. The apprehension, the ascent, the longing but not quite daring to turn back; and finally, the confidence and joy that [come] with doing a difficult task well."[6]

All these academic, social, cultural, and athletic events were part of a rigorous daily schedule modeled on the schedules the students would encounter at their prep schools. The day began early, and from the time the students awoke until the time they went to bed, they were kept busy with scheduled activities. The daily schedule shown in table 2.1 reveals all the features of what sociologists call a "total institution," one that controls every aspect of a person's life. One characteristic of a total institution is that "life is tightly scheduled."[7] A detailed study of private schools conducted in the early 1980s presents a typical schedule for private independent schools that is remarkably

Table 2.1. Daily Schedules, Dartmouth 1964 and Prep Schools 1980s

Daily Schedule Dartmouth, Summer 1964		Typical Schedule Prep Schools, 1980s	
Day began	6:50 a.m.	Rising bell	7:00 a.m
Breakfast	7:15	Breakfast	7:15
Class	8:00–8:50	Work period	7:55–8:10
Class	8:55–9:45	Class periods	8:20–9:55
Break	9:45–10:05	Chapel	10:00–10:10
Class	10:05–10:55	Recess	10:15–10:40
Class	11:00–11:50	Class periods	10:45–12:20
Lunch	11:55	Lunch	12:30 p.m.
Faculty appts.	1:00–2:00 p.m.	Class periods	1:20–3:15
Athletics	2:30–4:30	Athletics	3:15–5:20
Free time	4:30–5:30		
Dinner	6:15	Dinner	5:55
Study period	7:15–10:30	Study	7:00–10:00
Lights out	10:00–12:00	Day ended	10:00

similar to the one used by the ABC summer transitional program twenty years earlier.[8]

One of the ABC graduates in our study, Kenneth Pettis, a vice president of Bankers Trust in New York at the time of our initial interview in 1986, asserted that the structure of the summer transitional program was much more important than its content. In his view, the purpose of the summer program was "more to get us used to being away from home than anything else, and being supervised by people other than our parents." Comments such as this made us realize that these students were being initiated into a new "culture," which leads to the idea that the experience of being an ABC student might be thought of as an initiation into a new social identity. Such an initiation made it possible for the students to think of themselves as belonging to a new in-group, thereby helping them to overcome any doubts they might have about whether they belonged at a prep school.

At the same time, the summer program also gave them a sense of solidarity among themselves, which would help in relieving any feelings of guilt over leaving their peers behind. If other African Americans were involved, and if they could feel that they were proving a point for African Americans as a group, they would be less likely to feel they were breaking their collective identity. They were less likely to suffer conflict over allegedly "acting white" by taking school seriously. They could see themselves in a more political way, as "emissaries," which is one strategy that individual African American students use to do well in school and stay solid with their peer group.

The rigorous academic program, numerous cultural activities, and carefully planned schedule all contributed to an emphasis on the participants' worth. Cher Lewis, for example, mentioned how "special" she was made to feel by the attentiveness of the sophisticated and worldly college women who were tutoring the ABC girls the summer she spent at Mount Holyoke. In addition, knowledgeable, cultured, and even famous guests came to dinner. They were interested not only in telling the students about themselves, but also in hearing what the students had to say. Even the *New York Times* considered their activities fit to print. When the ABC boys from Dartmouth and the ABC girls from Mount Holyoke got together for their one social encounter at the end of the 1965 summer program, the *Times* covered it as if it were a significant society event:

> Dartmouth was the host this week-end to a delegation from Mount Holyoke at a college house party for teen-agers.
>
> For a 24-hour period beginning noon yesterday, the group, mostly eighth and ninth graders, enjoyed a respite from an eight-week course of concentrated study. The course was to acclimate them for the academic and social life at some of the most prestigious preparatory schools in the nation.
>
> The group dined in Thayer Hall and strolled around the picturesque campus with its hourly chimes from the tower of Baker Library.
>
> Last night the teen-agers danced until midnight to recorded music. This morning, before their final campus meal at noon, they worshipped in the Bema, a wooded glade nestled in a hollow between glacial boulders at the northeast edge of the campus. . . .
>
> A choir of ABC project girls softly practiced a hymn on the platform made of indigenous rock as birds twittered in the sheltering elm, hemlock, and birch trees. . . .
>
> In the choir, wearing black robes and white surplices, were girls from a dozen states. The girls included Gloria Shigg and Sarah Palmer of Darien, Ga.; Marian Hayes of Atlanta; Jacqueline Brownley of St. Louis and Maria Viera and Judy Kreijanovsky of New York.[9]

There was another side to the summer program, however. Many of those we interviewed stressed some of the difficult aspects, two in particular: first, the academic work was more rigorous and the expectations were higher than most of them had previously encountered; and, second, many, away from home for the first time, were homesick.

All these students had done quite well in their own schools, and some had done so without having to work especially hard. Suddenly they were surrounded by other students who had also excelled in their schools. Francisco Borges, who goes by Frank, the treasurer of the state of Connecticut from 1986 to 1993, and now the president and CEO of Landmark Partners, Inc., an investment managing firm, as well as the treasurer of the NAACP, has distinct memories of the academic demands at Dartmouth in the summer of 1966:

> The intensity of the competition was extraordinary. I have been in very competitive environments—prep school, obviously, college, law school. None of them

was as intense as the competitiveness that was there that summer for eight weeks. There were some of the brightest, sharpest, most capable students I'd ever run across. Having come out of a place where all of us were star students in our class, and all of a sudden you're sitting there in a room where everybody was a star, and, let me tell you, it was a struggle to keep up.

Not only were the students bright, but the staff was both capable and demanding. Borges recalled that small groups of students were assigned to counselors who gave them additional tutoring in the evening. His counselor was Robert Reich, at the time a graduate student and now a professor at Brandeis after serving in Bill Clinton's cabinet as secretary of labor. Reich, he recalls, "was a real tough son of a bitch . . . I was a royal pain in his ass."

In addition to being asked to work very hard, many ABC students were told they needed to do some remedial work to be able to compete successfully at the prep schools they were to attend. Harold Cushenberry, a superior court judge in Washington, D.C., recalled how his "ego was bruised" during the summer of 1965:

> I assume all of us who came were the cream of the crop from the environments that we came from, myself included from my segregated environment. I didn't realize how deficient my writing skills were, and that's what really plagued me early on. I never got any practice writing. We didn't do a lot of writing. I was used to going home and going through the encyclopedia and basically parroting what came out of the encyclopedia, as opposed to being given a short story to read and then composing something fairly quickly in a quiz. That was very difficult for me. My ego was bruised a great deal when I didn't do as well as I thought I would on the written material.

Cushenberry remembers struggling with his writing skills while others recollect their struggles with math; Bobette Reed Kahn recalls, "I was horrendously deficient in math. I was a wonderful straight A student who was really not a straight A student." Yet even if the students had not caught up (and most had not) by the time they started prep school, they knew what their academic deficiencies were, and they knew what they needed to work on. They were not overwhelmed by these realizations on top of all the other adjustments they had to make as they entered what could be daunting environments at overwhelmingly white, old money, prep schools.

The second difficult aspect of the summer program was not unique to these students. As in any summer camp that includes some youngsters who have never been away from home before, many of the ABC students very much missed their parents, their siblings, and their friends. Jesse Spikes missed his rural Georgia family so badly during the summer of 1965 that his best friend nicknamed him "Homesick." And unlike most children who go to summer camp, many of the ABC students had never before been outside the city limits of their hometowns. Calvin Dorsey, who at the time of our initial interview lived in Atlanta and worked for Cox Communications, recalled that when he left Clarksdale, Mississippi, for New York City on his way to attend the summer program at Williams College, he had never before spent a single night away from home. When he had to spend the night at a YMCA in New York City, he was "very, very afraid . . . because I had heard all these stories about New York." Bobette Reed Kahn, who lived in Cleveland, told us: "One of the biggest things about going to that summer program was that they sent you a plane ticket in the mail. And I said, 'I have to fly? Please, put me on a bus, put me on a train—I will not fly.' Thirteen years old and never been out of the city, and then all of a sudden you're put on a plane. I was scared, but my parents said, 'On the plane you go.'" She was "dreadfully homesick," but she recalls that everyone else was too, and they comforted one another.

Some students faced another problem, one that foreshadowed a difficulty many more would encounter after they had been at prep school for a while: explaining their new lives to their old friends at home. The negotiation of two very different identities is a potentially difficult problem that recurs as a topic throughout the book. One ABC graduate interviewed by a journalist, while thinking back to his summer experience at Dartmouth in 1965, recalled worrying about what his friends in Harlem would think when his picture appeared in a photograph that accompanied a *New York Times* article:

> I always wondered, knowing there were so many other people around me who were so much more talented than I was in so many ways, Why me? Why was I taken? You feel happy to get out, but guilty, too. You feel you don't deserve it. . . .
>
> When I was selected, they sent all of us up to Dartmouth that summer to prepare us for life in prep school. There were fifty of us altogether and the *New York Times Magazine* did an article about us. The article had a picture. I kept wondering whether my friends at home would see it. I kept wondering what they would think.[10]

Many of those we interviewed indicated that one reason they enjoyed the summer transitional program, despite the academic pressure or homesickness or worries about what their friends back home would think, was that they made new friends. Many stayed in touch with summer ABC friends who later attended nearby prep schools. In fact, having ABC friends at other prep schools was, for many students, of considerable importance. Though unable to see each other often, knowing other students, like themselves, who were struggling with the adjustment to academic and social life at prep school was comforting. In addition to exchanging letters, they periodically had occasion to see one another at athletic events, glee club concerts, or mixers. As Bobette Reed Kahn recalls: "There were two other [summer] programs in New England—one at Williams, one at Dartmouth. Dartmouth came down—all the boys came down—and spent a weekend with us, and we went up to Williams and spent a weekend up there. . . . When it came to the god-awful mixers that we all had to go to for three years, we had friends. There was a whole network of ABC kids, at least on the East Coast."

The network formed among ABC students was strengthened when ABC scheduled special events for all the ABC students in New England, as was occasionally done in the early years. Bobette Reed Kahn remembers that "ABC did something wonderful" in her second year at the MacDuffie School: "They invited us all to go to Dartmouth and spend Thanksgiving at Dartmouth. So there were tons of us from the East Coast, and we all got together at Dartmouth. They planned a program for us, an awful lot of it was entertainment, but we got to see each other. We got to form more friendships, and to continue friendships."

Many consider the summer program to have been the linchpin of the ABC program: after the students had been recruited and selected but before they went off to prep school, it provided a transitional experience that was crucial to ABC's early success. There was, therefore, much concern when the summer program had to be whittled down over the years due to financial constraints—from eight weeks to six weeks, and then to two weeks, and finally, beginning in the early 1990s, to optional orientation programs of just a few days (in the summer of 2002, approximately 75 percent of the incoming ABC students participated in one of six programs held in cities around the country).[11]

Fortunately, the summer program is less important now than it was in the early days of the program. For one thing, most of the schools have more black students than they did in the very first years of the program, and, therefore, when ABC students arrive at these schools, there are other African American students and ongoing organizations for students of color. Moreover, many schools now have administrators whose sole responsibility is to attend to the many issues that are related to diversity. The Milton Academy has two full-time people working on diversity issues, and for the past eight years has held an annual weeklong summer conference on diversity issues attended by prep school teachers and administrators from around the country. Craig Robinson, a 1991 ABC graduate of the Tabor Academy, who was on the admissions staff at Andover for five years before leaving to work for ABC in their New York office, was the driving force behind the creation of a new organization of prep school "diversity professionals." The new organization, called the Diversity Roundtable of the Ten Schools, includes a member of the admissions staff from each of ten prep schools known as "the Ten Schools" (Andover, Choate, Deerfield, Exeter, Hotchkiss, Loomis, Lawrenceville, Northfield Mount Hermon, St. Paul's, and Taft). The group is designed to provide support and ideas across these institutions as they work on diversity issues. In addition to Robinson, another of the founding members, Tim Bradley at Choate, is a 1972 ABC graduate who works in the admissions office of his alma mater. Michael Gary, a 1982 ABC alumnus of Pomfret, became the director of admission at Exeter in the summer of 2002. And, although most prep schools do not have very many African American faculty members, there are more now than there were in the late 1960s and early 1970s (some are ABC graduates), and a few schools (including the Milton Academy) have had African American headmasters.[12]

Even though there is less need for an intensive transition program now, the summer program played an essential role in the early decades of the program. It gave the students an idea of what to expect, offered any remedial training that was needed, and provided them with contacts at other prep schools. These contacts not only served to improve their social lives while they were in prep school, but, perhaps more importantly, they reveal that the summer program was a first step in providing ABC students with the kind of social networks that each new generation of upper-class people builds on the basis of its experiences in elite institutions from the church preschool to private elementary schools, summer camps, and, ultimately, the corporate boardroom. Thus, this seemingly "special" program really gave its participants only what the wealthy students at the prep schools already had and took for granted. It is the gradual accumulation of advantages at the top and disadvantages at the bottom of the social structure that are overlooked by those commentators who praise the "initiative" and "efforts" of our rich leaders and then blame the poor for their alleged personal failures.

In the early years, then, the intense summer program, combining intellectual work with social solidarity, was spring training for both the program and the students. It got them ready to win when it counted, in the pressure-cooker world of the elite prep school.

NOTES

1. Summer report, Dartmouth, 1966, 38.
2. Summer report, Dartmouth, 1964, 25.
3. Ibid.
4. Ibid., 25–26.
5. Jay Farrow was interviewed by Pat Macpherson, Alumni Coordinator at Westtown School. See Pat McPherson, Irene McHenry, and Sarah Sweeney-Denham,

Schooled in Diversity: Readings on Racial Diversity in Friends Schools (Philadelphia: Friends Council on Education, 2001).

6. Ibid., 27.

7. For the classic work on total institutions, see Erving Goffman, "On the Characteristics of Total Institutions," in his *Asylums: Essays on the Social Situation of Mental Patients and Other Inmates* (Garden City, N.Y.: Anchor Books, 1961), 1–124.

8. Peter W. Cookson, Jr. and Caroline Hodges Persell, *Preparing for Power: America's Elite Boarding Schools* (New York: Basic Books, 1985), 35–36.

9. John H. Fenton, "Dartmouth Greets 140 Studying in Talent Project," *New York Times*, August 16, 1965, 27.

10. Robert Sam Anson, *Best Intentions: The Education and Killing of Edmund Perry* (New York: Random House, 1987), 41.

11. "Student Orientation Programs," ABC 1991 Annual Report, p. 3, and subsequent newsletters. The information on the summer programs in 2002 was provided in emails (August 31 and September 1, 2002) from two ABC employees, Craig Robinson, vice president for programs, and Keith Wilkerson, program officer.

12. When Edwin P. Fredie became the headmaster at Milton in the fall of 1991, he was, according to the *New York Times*, "the first black to be named headmaster of one of the major American private schools." See Fox Butterfield, "At Milton, a Headmaster with a Difference," *New York Times*, January 10, 1993, Sec. 4A, pp. 37ff. See, also, Sylvester Monroe, "Diversity Comes to Elite Prep Schools," *Emerge* (October 1993): 50–53, and "Michael Gary Named Director of Admissions," *Exeter Bulletin* (Fall 2002): 2.

3

The Prep School Years

INTO THE CRUCIBLE

As ABC's black teenagers left their homes in New York, Philadelphia, Richmond, Atlanta, Chicago, and other American cities to live and learn among the children of the nation's wealthiest families, they faced a paradoxical situation. On the one hand, they encountered physical and economic comfort the likes of which they had never seen before. On the other hand, they were placed in environments in which it was often difficult to feel comfortable.

The spaciousness, the elegance, and, in some cases, the grandeur of America's prep schools confirmed the assumption held by many ABC students that by deciding to attend prep school they had chosen to enter another world. With the exception of the specific geographic location, the following description of the Lawrenceville School could apply to many American boarding schools: "The school is located on 330 magnificently landscaped acres of New Jersey countryside just five miles south of Princeton. Its physical plant—including a nine-hole golf course, mammoth field house and covered hockey rink, library of some 23,000 volumes, science building, arts center with 900-seat auditorium and professionally equipped stage—would be the envy of most colleges."[1]

Most colleges would be pleased to have Lawrenceville's endowment as well. Lawrenceville and the other fifteen prep schools that make up the select sixteen have a combined endowment of hundreds of millions of dollars, and their physical plants are valued at about the same amount. These schools continue to draw on gifts from alumni and other supporters to add new gyms, libraries, art buildings, planetariums, and dorms, and they often use internationally renowned architects to plan these buildings. "In effect," says one detailed sociological study of private schools, "the combined real estate holdings of American boarding schools represent a 'Prep National Park,' a preserve free from state and local taxes, where boarding school students are allowed to explore, backpack, horseback ride, rock climb, play, and temporarily escape from the pressures of adolescence and the total institution."[2]

Though most of the students are economically privileged, and attendance at these costly and often luxurious schools is part of the system that allows them to maintain (or enhance) their economic advantages, life in the prep school is not without its harsher side. These institutions place "relentless" pressure on students. For most prep school students, this pressure begins early in life, but it intensifies upon their arrival at boarding school. "From the cradle," the same study continues, "most prep school students are told 'to be somebody.' . . . From the moment they jump (or stumble through) the hurdles of admission to an elite school, they must prove their worth by mastering the curriculum, the student culture, and their own vulnerability. . . . We began to see boarding schools as crucibles, from which some students emerged as tempered steel and others were simply burnt to a crisp."[3]

These schools have become crucibles in order to serve an important function: to transform highly privileged individuals into "soldiers for their class." The schools are central to the socialization process that passes on upper-class values to children. As the students learn they are part of a larger privileged class, their individualism is melted down into "the solid metal of elite collectivism." The schools encourage not only the development of a collective identity but also the adoption of values that serve to legitimate privilege. Not everyone succeeds under such pressures; some students, become "prisoners of their class," trapped in a system they don't accept but can't escape; and some are destroyed by the prep school environment.[4] There are books on and by such casualties, and also accounts of those who decide to spend their money to help create a less class-based society.

One psychologist who has studied the psychological effects of all kinds of relocations provides some empirical evidence that the transition from living at home to living in a prep school is quite stressful for some students. Although he does not examine the demanding nature of the prep school environment per se, his point is that relocation as a process, whether to a prep school, a college, or a new city, creates a "tremendous amount of stress." Drawing on fifteen years of research and consulting, he estimates that 25 percent of the students who attend prep school have a "significant problem" adjusting to their new environment.[5] There can be no doubt that this transition is even more difficult for ABC students.

Not surprisingly, there is considerable evidence that prep school administrators and students have demonstrated many of the same prejudices found in the larger society over the years. The experiences of Jews and blacks at Andover are instructive because that school has long prided itself on educating "youth from every quarter," and it was one of the first boarding schools to accept black students. Unlike many histories of prep schools, the one written about Andover does not gloss over embarrassing or distasteful moments. It provides ample evidence that, for Jews and blacks at Andover, anti-Semitism and racism were likely to be part of their prep school experience. In the 1930s, for example, when about 3 percent of the student body was Jewish, the headmaster wrote to a colleague: "We shall never have a larger percentage, and I am trying to reduce it just a little. On the other hand some of them make first class students and real leaders, although very few of them are permitted to hold important social positions." Some Jewish students were given the "silent treatment" by the other students in their dormitory. Similarly, although Andover accepted black students relatively early, it did not accept very many, and they were not especially welcomed by the community. Prior to the 1950s, according to the school history, "the School had done little if anything for blacks." For example, in 1944, in response to a request from an alumnus that Andover accept more black students, the headmaster responded that there were currently two black students at the school, and that accepting more might "cause trouble."[6]

In the 1950s, according to a Choate graduate who was one of the few Jewish students at the time, the words "FUCK YOU, YOU KIKE" were written on his math book by one of his classmates. Choate was even more overt in its intolerance of blacks: "At Choate, during the Eisenhower years, racist remarks were as much a part of our daily lives as the chapel services which we were required to attend each night. In fact, at the first Sunday service I attended there, Seymour St. John, the school's headmaster and also its chaplain, began his sermon with a joke about 'Old Darky Joe' and his friend 'Moe.' The humor that the sons of America's (mostly Republican) elite shared with one another was considerably blunter."[7]

Julian Bond, a former Georgia legislator and now the chairman of the board of the NAACP, attended the George School in the mid-1950s. He remembers that his fellow students were not very concerned about hiding their prejudices. "You'd be sitting around a room and some kid gets a package from home and there'd be some cakes in it," Bond told an interviewer, "and he'd pass it around and miss somebody and the kid would say: 'What am I — a nigger or something' — Then he'd say, 'Oops! Bond's here!'"[8] Still, Bond was more upset by something an administrator said to him. He was dating a white girl, and, like other George School couples, they used to walk to Newtown, the town near the school. Bond recalls with some bitterness that the school dean asked him not to wear his much-loved George School jacket when he was walking into town with his girlfriend. Bond concluded that the George School in the 1950s was a "hotbed of racism."[9]

This, then, was the world ABC students entered in the mid- to late 1960s: comfortable, often luxurious physical environments that did not necessarily make students, especially black students, comfortable, and psychological environments that could be overtly bigoted.

GETTING THERE

How were ABC students placed in the particular schools they attended? The president of the ABC program from 1966 to 1974 describes the program as a "huge mail order operation." As he explained it to us in our 1987 interview:

> We would read the files—it would be like an admissions office—we'd have a team of people read the files. Each person had to put down some schools they thought the kid would work in best, and then somebody was assigned to sort of be the shepherd for that kid. Using the notes in the file, we would make mailings out to the schools, and the understanding was that the schools could turn down any kid that they didn't want and send him back and we would send them more, which was fine with us. We really wanted the schools not to feel they were being assigned kids.

Each school was aware that it was the only school to receive a particular ABC applicant's file and that it had a brief period to decide whether or not to take the student. If the school chose not to accept a student, his or her file was then sent to another school. Once accepted, most students attended the prep schools for three years, though some graduated after only two years; most, upon entering, did not need to repeat a year, though some did.

Even before they arrived at their prep schools, many ABC students had to deal with the kinds of problems that would soon set them apart from their more affluent white peers. First of all, many had to convince their parents to let them leave home to attend a school the parents had never heard of. Some of those we spoke with said that their parents thought they were too young to leave home, and they therefore had to enlist uncles, aunts, grandparents, or favorite teachers to help persuade their parents to let them go. One ABC graduate told us that her mother didn't want her to attend a girls' school because she feared that her daughter would become a lesbian. Within a few years after the program began, the ABC staff realized that in addition to providing an in-depth eight-week orientation for the young ABC students who were about to attend prep school, they needed to address the parents' concerns in a more structured and consistent fashion.

There were other problems as well. Jennifer Casey Pierre (who earned an MBA from Columbia, worked as an executive at R. J. Reynolds from 1981 through 1997, and subsequently worked for United Way) recalled in our first interview with her that the seemingly simple task of getting from her home in Baltimore to the Baldwin School outside Philadelphia was "a struggle." Her father had died when she was four, her mother had never obtained a driver's license, and none of her close relatives had a car. Her mother solved this problem by putting aside some money to pay "a guy who said he would be willing to drive us, and all my belongings, to the school."

Other ABC students encountered similar "struggles" that ABC and the prep schools didn't foresee. In the summer of 1969, Gordon Right, a thirteen-year-old who had won a scholarship to Groton through the ABC program, faced what appeared to him to be an insurmountable obstacle when he received a notice from Groton instructing him to bring various items with him when he arrived at school. The lengthy list included blankets, sports jackets (three of them), slacks, luggage, and towels. Gordon, who lived in Harlem with his blind mother, four younger brothers, and a sister, owned a pair of sneakers, a pair of dungarees, two shirts, two sets of underwear, and not much else. The state legislature had recently eliminated special grants that would have allowed families on welfare, like Gordon's family, some extra money to pay for unusual back-to-school costs. As a result, Gordon feared that he would not be able to attend Groton. "I never heard of Groton," he said late in the summer of 1969, "until a few months ago, then I was spending days preparing for the tests, then I won it, and then comes the clothes list. I figured I'd lose it all." But Gordon Right overcame this hurdle with the help of a group of sympathetic social workers who voted to provide $300 from their "brotherhood committee." He headed off to Groton with blankets, sports jackets, slacks, and even the required seven dozen name tags, ready to confront new challenges.[10]

Even after he had managed to acquire everything on Groton's list, Gordon Right may have felt quite intimidated when he saw what other students brought to school. One writer provides the following description of students arriving at Choate in the late 1960s: "The cars are pulling up to Hillhouse. Most are station wagons, some with zippy names like 'Et Cetera Too' stenciled on the driver's door, but there is a sprinkling of Cadillacs and Mustangs as well. From the cars the trunks and suitcases tumble, and the tennis rackets, the sports jackets temporarily suspended from wire hangers, bookcases, barbells, and chest-pulls, chairs too big to squeeze through dormitory doors, guitars and radios, phonographs and rifles, fans, tape recorders, and mothers in tailored suits."[11]

Many of the ABC graduates we interviewed were appropriately impressed when they first saw the schools they were to attend, though their reaction was not always unequivocal. Sylvester Monroe recalls that when he got his first glimpse of St. George's School in Newport, Rhode Island—the school was founded in 1896 on a scenic promontory overlooking the Atlantic Ocean—he was struck not only by the beauty of the place but by the looming presence of "this gothic chapel that to me looked like some medieval castle with dungeons." Monroe's ominous impression of his new school underscores how unfamiliar and threatening the boarding school could be for nervous young blacks from the inner cities.

By way of contrast, arriving at prep school was like "coming home" for many white students, especially those "legacy" students whose parents and grandparents had attended the same school. Compare the following recollection by a 1972 graduate of Groton with Monroe's image of a castle with dungeons: "When I first arrived at the school in the fall of 1967 and discovered the Georgian brick buildings arrayed around the lawn called the Circle, and the high-towered Gothic chapel, I felt oddly that I was coming home. I recognized the buildings—Hundred House, School House, Brooks House—from our family's dinner plates, and I knew the chapel from a watercolor that my father had painted as a boy in the class of '17 and later hung in my bedroom."[12]

BEING THERE

Early Memories

In response to our general question about how they liked being at Hotchkiss, or Milton, or Loomis, many responded by describing events that took place on the very first day they arrived—and in some cases, during the very first minutes after they arrived. Some of these memories concern clothes, as they had for Sylvester Monroe. Bobette Reed Kahn recalls that one of the first things she noticed was that "all the girls were wearing these wonderful clothes, and I wasn't." And Calvin Dorsey remembers, with both pain and amusement, that the airline had lost his luggage, and he therefore had to wear the same suit for three days. "Can you imagine? Unsure, trying to make a good impression, with no clothes and no money!"

Others remembered that the issue of race came up immediately. Bobette Reed Kahn, who like her father is very light-skinned, recounts that the day before she left for prep school, her father warned her that people were going to ask her: "What are you?" It did not take long for a prep school classmate to prove him right: "I got to MacDuffie early for some reason. I was the first one there. There were no other students there, and I kind of puttered around. It's scary anyway, but then when there's no one there and you're feeling lost in this place. . . . Finally, two other girls came and they were introduced to me, and we went down for lunch. And do you know the first thing they said to me? 'What are you?' I couldn't believe it. And then the next thing the girl said was, 'I've never been near anyone black except for my maid.' And, I thought, I'm going to have problems here. I'm going to have real problems here."

Bobette Reed Kahn's experience of being informed, not very subtly, that she was different in terms of both race and class was not typical, but neither was it unique. The girl who told Bobette that the only black she knew was a maid was both thoughtless and cruel, though it is possible that she did not intend to offend Bobette as much as she did.[13] Other students' memories leave no doubt about intent. One particularly ugly encounter also took place at a student's first meal at prep school:

> I remember the first night I went to dinner at school. To my right was an heiress to a cosmetics fortune. To my left was an heiress to a department-store fortune. Across the table from me was an heiress to an oil fortune. And they were all talking about the places they had been, the things they had bought, the vacations they were going to take, as if I wasn't even there. Finally, one of the girls—it was the department-store heiress—tapped me on the elbow and said, "You better be nice to me, because I'm paying for half your scholarship." I almost got sick to my stomach. I didn't say anything, I just got up from the table and walked out. It was two weeks before I could bring myself to go back into the dining hall.[14]

Another frequently occurring early memory involved the difficulties of the person's initial living situation. Many prep schools had never had black students before, and those in charge of assigning roommates often did not know where to put them. The schools differed in the policies they employed. Some schools assigned ABC students to room with other ABC students, while others would not allow ABC students to room together. Some placed ABC students with white students but sent letters to the white students beforehand alerting them to the fact that their roommate would be black, while other schools simply let the roommates discover this when the students met. Some schools simply placed the ABC students using the seemingly random assignment systems they had always used.

Some of the schools apparently tried to sidestep the question of roommates by giving the first black students single rooms. For some, like Ken Pettis, this worked out well: "My first year at Taft I lived in a single—a single for a freshman was very unusual. Not only that, but I was in a single on a floor that didn't have that many students on it. As a matter of fact, there were three of us on the floor (I had a single and they had a double right next door to me), and the three of us that were on the floor are all still in touch. One of them was just in my wedding. He has become a lifelong, very, very good friend of mine."

But for some, their earliest prep school memories of being isolated, different, and alone were exacerbated by physical isolation. For example, Cecily Robbins, an executive with the Big Sisters program in Washington, D.C., when we first interviewed her, and working with the National Mentoring Partnership when we interviewed her in May 2001, recalled her first semester at Walnut Hill: "My room happened to be sort of at one end of the hall. My next-door neighbor on one side was the infirmary and then there was the stairwell on the other side and the rest of the hall. Nobody had to walk by my room unless you were going into the infirmary. And I sort of would go upstairs and isolate myself."

One former ABC student recalls that her school told her there was no room for her to live on campus. Instead, arrangements had been made for her to live with a faculty member and his family. This did not work out well: "It was an incredibly regimented family, and I hated it. I used to try and get away from that family to have dinner on the campus, which was only two blocks away, and this caused some upsets. Actually, I preferred being on the campus and eating that grade C food to sitting and eating this wonderful food with this family that I hated." After complaining to the director of admissions, she was able to move onto campus the second semester, and "everything smoothed right out."

As these poignant examples clearly show, the initial days and weeks were trying times for most ABC students, reminding them they were black in a white world. Many also said that they were terribly homesick. Of course, many had been homesick during the summer transitional program, but in the summer they had been surrounded by others who were also homesick (and also black); furthermore, they knew the summer program would be over in a matter of weeks. At prep school the ABC student was often the only black or one of a few blacks, and he or she knew the semester would not end for months. Gail Warren, an Andover graduate who is now back in her hometown of Atlanta, remembered that she phoned her mother so often during her first semester at boarding school that her mother finally said, "Look, what do you think if I fly you home for a weekend? I think that would be less expensive than the phone bills we're getting."

Some students developed strategies for going home. While participating in the first summer program at Dartmouth, a homesick Jesse Spikes heard an ABC staff person tell a group of students that the program was still very much in the experimental stage, and that he wasn't even sure how the Southerners would adjust to the amount of snow they would encounter in New England. Jesse recalls saying to himself, "Aha. That's my answer. I'll just wait until the first big snow and I'll just freak out. And, at that, I'm relieved of the responsibility—it's not my fault, I just couldn't handle the weather. And I'll go home." But when the first big snow came, Jesse Spikes—by then playing halfback on the football team, doing well academically, and having made friends—had abandoned his plan. Sylvester Monroe had a different plan:

> I got there, I didn't want to be there. I had discussed this with my mother—my mother was a very wise lady, though not well-educated. She said to me: "Look. I think you ought to try it. You ought not to turn down this opportunity. If you see it and you don't like it, then come home."
>
> So I went with the intention of staying a couple of weeks and then coming home. I got out there, I had been there about two or three weeks, when I got sick. I had eaten something, got a stomach bug. I went into the infirmary because I couldn't keep anything down. I remember thinking, "This is it. This is terrific."
>
> So I called my mother and I said, "Hey, Mom, this place is terrible. It's made me sick. I can't keep anything down." She said, "What's the matter with you?" I had asked the doctor what was wrong with me. My vocabulary was not so extensive. The doctor said, "I think you've got a bad case of nostalgia." So, when I called my mother up and she said, "What's the matter with you?" I said, "Well, doc says I've got a real bad case of nostalgia. Can I come home?"
>
> Luckily, "nostalgia" was in my mother's vocabulary. She said, "Yeah, under one condition." I said, "What's that?" She said, "If it's in a box." So I was crushed. I expected her to say, "Poor baby, come on home." So, I figured that nobody wanted me at home. I might as well stay and make the most out of it.

Academics

Academic pressures contributed to the difficulty many students had adjusting to life at their prep schools. Many had been warned during the summer transitional programs that they might not yet be ready to compete successfully at the prep schools they would attend. And for many, this turned out to be true. Cecily Robbins remembers her shock and disappointment when she received her first grades in Latin: "I had gone to parochial schools and I had gone to a school where Latin was taught. We had numerical grades and none of my grades in Latin were lower than 90. Usually I got 90, 95, right? My first grade in Latin at Walnut Hill was an F. My first F in my life, my first failure, and it was horrible." Harold Cushenberry recalls that he was "almost crushed that first semester" when he got his grades: "I mean, I didn't come anywhere near flunking. Doing poorly to me was Cs. I got Cs on my compositions and I had always had 100s basically, or 99.9, and to have someone say this is worth a C was crushing to me, and not to be able to confide that sense of personal failure to anyone, not to have any support, was doubly difficult."

Some discovered rather quickly that they could handle the academic work. When, for example, LaPearl Winfrey, now a psychologist, was the only person on her dormitory floor at the Masters School to make the honor roll, she was able to relax. "I didn't go to Switzerland for Christmas," she recalls, but "I had a good sense of myself."

For others, it took a year or two to catch up. Ken Pettis's experience at the Taft School was not unusual: "On the academic side, I faltered a bit at first. . . . The level of the academics started higher than I was used to and moved a lot faster than I was used to. Once I got used to the pace, I did better. I was not a star. I was never honor roll the entire time I was there. I was an average student in that environment. . . . And it really didn't bother me, not being at the top, because there were some very smart people there. Some very, very smart people—people who had been exposed to a lot more than I had during their early years."

Some of those we spoke with were at or near the top of their classes by the time they graduated. As we shall see in the next chapter, many ABC graduates (including Ken Pettis, with his average grades at Taft) were strong enough students to be accepted by the most selective colleges in the country. In addition to the substantial evidence we gathered in our interviews concerning academic success, a study of all ABC students from 1964 through 1972 demonstrates that they had caught up with their white classmates by the time they graduated. Based on their twelfth-grade rank in class as a measure of academic performance, the ABC students were nearly evenly distributed in class rank, with a median rank just below the middle (at the forty-seventh percentile). Thus, the study concludes, their standing was "approximately the same as that of their non-ABC classmates."[15]

To our surprise, and thus of potential theoretical interest to us, the primary memory some ABC graduates have of academic life at prep school is what might be called "academic liberation." Some of these students came from tough inner city schools where they felt strong pressures not to do or be interested in academic work, suggesting the kind of orientation cultural anthropologists call an oppositional identity. Such a social identity can develop as a way of coping with the painful experience of exclusion and stigmatization. Monique Burns, who left Brooklyn to attend the Concord Academy, expressed such feelings: "I had an image of being such an academic person at my other school, and I was sort of an outcast. . . . This was part of the reason why Concord was such a good experience for me. For once I wasn't just the smartest kid. I was always threatened with physical violence and all for being so smart. So when I went to Concord, here were some people who were more like me. In terms of intellectual interests and ideals, they were very much like me."

Bobette Reed Kahn has similarly harsh memories of her high school back in Cleveland. In junior high school, she had been fortunate to have a wonderful English teacher, and she had developed a close relationship with the assistant principal. But her high school was a different story:

> There were very few days I could go through the hall and not be felt up or in other ways molested. And there were always codeine bottles in the bathroom, people shooting up, gunshot fights in the halls and things like that. The only reason why I didn't come out, I guess, scarred more than I was, was because my sister, my older sister, was hot stuff. And her friends, her street friends, protected me, and literally, at times, beat people up for messing with me. And I was just having problems coping in this school socially. I was very quiet, very shy, and it was not a good thing to be smart.

Byron Haskins, who went to the summer program at Williams in 1969 and then attended Choate, told us that his experiences had been so bad in his hometown of Detroit that he too felt liberated both academically and physically. As he explained in an email he sent to us in August 2002: "I hated the streets of Detroit. I liked to read and explore the skies at night with my telescope. My neighborhood was burnt to the ground in 1967 (my paper route was decimated). I had been the victim of robbery, attempted sodomizing, and the typical cruelty of my peers. . . . The summer at Williams in 1969 was like having the gates from a world from which I had been expelled reopened. I had found home. I spent most of the following summers trying to figure out how NOT to go home." Therefore, for some students, like Bobette Reed Kahn, Monique Burns, and Byron Haskins, a central component of their academic experience in prep school was the freedom to develop academically to their fullest potential, and this helped to balance their negative experiences there.

Their experiences are not at all atypical in predominantly black high schools around the country. There is other evidence that many academically talented black students are jeered at or attacked by their peers for "acting white," and several studies have suggested that this peer pressure has an adverse effect on school performance by setting up a conflict between the values students internalize about achieving in school and their desire to be part of the in-group. Some black students develop coping strategies, such as excelling in sports or playing the role of clown or publicly defying teachers, so that they can continue to achieve and still be accepted by their friends.

As part of his work for a master's degree, William Foster, one of the ABC graduates we interviewed, wrote about his journey from the inner city of Philadelphia to the ABC program. Though he had sufficient academic promise to be selected to participate in the ABC program, this promise was hidden below the surface of "class clown." He writes, "I had given up on education, and was wasting my tenth-grade year at Overbrook [High School]. I don't think I cracked open a book all year. I never studied for tests and was fast on my way to becoming the top banana in the annals of Class Clowndom. My grades were a disaster. I had decided to quit school within a year's time anyway. What difference did it make? If the white man didn't want me to succeed in school, I'd succeed some place else."

Given the importance of the prohibition against "acting white," perhaps it is not surprising that ABC graduate Greg Pennington, who attended the Western Reserve Academy, Harvard, and then earned his Ph.D. in clinical psychology from the University of North Carolina at Chapel Hill, would recall that he suffered "culture shock" when he went off to prep school for the first time. By that he meant figuring out how to shift from "Getting good grades without letting my classmates know that I was studying, to a school in which the group norms were far more supportive of achievement goals, and even meal times were supposed to be academic exercises."

The pervasiveness of the problem can also be seen by the fact that even the great basketball star Kareem Abdul Jabbar encountered this attitude in Philadelphia at the same time Bobette Reed Kahn and Monique Burns were under siege in Cleveland and Brooklyn. He writes in his autobiography:

> I got there [Holy Providence School in Cornwall Heights, right outside of Philadelphia] and immediately found I could read better than anyone in the school. My father's example and my mother's training had made that come easy; I could pick up a book, read it out loud, pronounce the words with proper inflections and actually know what they meant. When the nuns found this out they paid me a lot of attention, once even asking me, a fourth grader, to read to the seventh grade. When the kids found this out I became a target. . . .
>
> It was my first time away from home, my first experience in an all-black situation, and I found myself being punished for doing everything I'd ever been taught was right. I got all A's and was hated for it; I spoke correctly and was called a punk. I had to learn a new language simply to be able to deal with the threats. I had good manners and was a good little boy and paid for it with my hide.[16]

Given this tension between understandable oppositional tendencies within the black community and the demands of the school system, it makes sense that many ABC students liked prep school, contrary to our initial expectations.

Friendships between Blacks and Whites

Though most of those interviewed could recall racist comments or racist incidents while they were in prep school, almost all claimed that these were rare, and that without too much difficulty they were able to avoid those students who were openly prejudiced. Moreover, almost all of those interviewed indicate that they became close friends with white students, and in many cases they remain important lifetime friendships.

Cher Lewis recalls encountering people with racist views for the first time. Prior to attending the Abbott Academy, she had lived in a black community in Richmond, and she had never before met people who seemed to hate her only because of the color of her skin. Still, she learned to deal with these people, and she became close friends with some white students at Abbott. She has remained in regular contact with her four closest Abbott friends, all of whom are white. In fact, the five of them get together almost every year. In addition, she calls and sees them individually, or in various combinations, periodically. A few weeks after our November 2001 interview, she mentioned in an email that she and one of these friends had attended the funeral of the father of another of these friends ("I just returned from Washington," she told us, "where Paula and I went to Nancy's dad's funeral").

Harold Cushenberry experienced no overt discrimination as a student at the Taft School. "I was more of a curiosity than anything else," he recalls. He does remember feeling animosity from some of the Southern students: "I sensed a hostility there, but likewise, I don't recall anything said to me directly. I think maybe my second or third year there may have been some off-color comments every once in a while, but certainly nothing that was so troubling that they got me all bent out of shape. Confederate flags, things like that, but those were the southerners who were at the school."

A few recall more overt racial incidents, but often these memories are vague, unlike many of the other memories people have of life at prep school. For example, Greg Googer, a graduate of Andover and Vanderbilt, responded to a question asking if he recalled any racial incidents while he was at Andover in the following way:

> The only racial incident that springs to mind is the night—I don't know exactly what happened, and I've always wondered, and I always wondered if I dreamed this or if the person who told me this dreamed this. There was one friend of mine, he mentioned once walking across campus late one Saturday night. He mentioned there were some guys who were walking around in sheets. I said, "No, you gotta be kidding," but he insisted that they were, and that he knew who they were. But nothing ever came of it. Nothing ever came of it one way or another. Those guys who supposedly were wearing sheets, and like I said I'm not sure if the guy who told me this was dreaming or if I was dreaming, they never did anything to instigate anything, and no one ever delved any deeper to find out whether anything was actually happening. That was the only truly racial incident that I remember ever coming across while I was at Andover.

Many students clearly recall being offended by the naïveté of questions they were asked, and some of the women recall being offended by white students who wanted to touch their hair. Jennifer Casey Pierre responded to a question about whether she had made friends with white students when she was at the Baldwin School by saying: "Yes, I did. Over time. The major problem I had was because of the advent of the Afro a lot of my Caucasian counterparts wanted to touch my hair but what they didn't realize is that I had a lot of hair and that if they did this they messed it up, and that it was part of my pride, my symbol, and so I resented that. . . . But over time I did develop some very good friendships and things worked out well."

In 1983, while he was completing his doctoral dissertation, Greg Pennington received a grant from the Whitney Young Foundation to do a study for ABC. His final report, "The Minority Student Experience in Predominantly White High Schools," noted that there were "remarkable similarities" between what he had experienced as an ABC student in the late 1960s and what he heard from black ABC prep school students he interviewed in the early 1980s. Some of the ABC students he spoke with in the early 1980s experienced racism while at school, and some depicted ugly incidents. Still, he concluded: "The instances of actual physical assault or abuse of a racial nature are few and far between. Ignorance is far more frequent, though experienced just as painfully."[17]

As the schools increased the number of black students, and as race relations in the country changed in the late 1960s, some black ABC students chose to spend time primarily, or exclusively, with other blacks, often because they experienced pressure from other black students not to be friends with whites. Thus, the era when an ABC graduate attended prep school affected the extent to which he or she was likely to become close friends with white students. The experiences of Harold Cushenberry and Eric Coleman (the state legislator in Connecticut) underscore the changing situation.

After participating in the first summer program at Dartmouth in 1965, Cushenberry attended the Taft School. When he arrived there were five other blacks at Taft, but the closest friendships he made were with white students. "It's really strange," he muses, "the other black students I'm not in touch with, but I'm in touch with a lot of the white students I went to school with." Upon graduating from Taft in 1968, Cushenberry went to Harvard, where, as he recalls, "I had no white friends at all." Martin Luther King, Jr., had been assassinated, there had been serious racial unrest in many cities, and like many blacks at Harvard, Cushenberry chose to interact primarily with other blacks.[18] Despite his experience at Harvard, some of which he regrets ("I think I missed a great deal of what Harvard had to offer"), Cushenberry remained true to his prep school friends, many of whom he still sees regularly.

"We were all kids together," he told us, "and no matter how old you get you always see each other, not as a successful whomever, but as a skinny twelve- or thirteen-year-old, so that common bond keeps those friendships intact a lot more than later in college or law school."

Cushenberry's insights are consonant with well-known social psychology principles about the way in which common bonds, particularly the adversity faced in initiatory situations, create close social ties. His comments also demonstrate how strong and long lasting the effects of positive racial interactions can be, even starting as late as ages twelve to fifteen, given the right kind of setting.

Eric Coleman, a few years younger than Cushenberry, had a different experience at Pomfret, another Connecticut prep school. Coleman was at Pomfret when Cushenberry was at Harvard, and though he was friendly with some white students, he mostly hung out with his black friends. By that time there were about twenty black students at Pomfret, and most, like Eric, were good athletes. "We were either in classes or at basketball or football practice or track or we were in the bus going somewhere to compete at sports. After meals we would end up together."

The evaluation study of all ABC students between 1964 and 1972 includes some data that support the idea that blacks were more likely to become close friends with whites during the early years of the program than during the late 1960s and early 1970s. As one part of the study, a 127-item attitude questionnaire was administered to 125 black ABC seniors and 134 entering black ABC tenth graders in the spring of 1970 and again in the fall of 1971. One of the questions asked was: "Thinking of your five best friends, how many of them are white?" Most respondents included at least one white among their best friends, but there was a revealing difference between the responses of the seniors and those of the sophomores. Only slightly more than half (54 percent) of the sophomores stated that at least one white was among their five best friends, but nearly two-thirds (66 percent) of the seniors' responses revealed at least one white best friend. This difference may indicate that the longer blacks were in prep school, the more likely they were to become friends with whites. It may, however, reflect the development of black pride and separatism occurring at that time or the greater number of black students at the schools. Most of the seniors entered prep school in 1967 (and some in 1966); the sophomores entered in the fall of 1971. Thus, the differences between these two groups may reflect the changing times more than the impact of the schools between a student's sophomore and senior years.[19]

For the most part, however, the evaluation study shows that during the early 1970s, the interracial experiences at the prep schools were perceived by black tenth and twelfth graders, and by a "control" group of white prep school students, in more positive than negative terms. Of the eleven items dealing with racial relationships, the following three were most frequently chosen by both the black ABC students and comparison groups of white prep school students as characterizing race relations at their schools: "They learn from each other" (80 percent of the black students agreed, and 72 percent of the whites); "They tolerate each other" (80 percent and 79 percent respectively); and "They treat each other fairly" (64 percent and 82 percent respectively). In contrast, the following three items were the ones least likely to be chosen by both black and white students as characterizing race relations: "They try to put each other down" (20 percent of the black students, 7 percent of the white students); "They avoid each other" (16 percent and 15 percent respectively); and "They fight each other" (9 percent and 2 percent respectively).[20]

Those ABC graduates who recalled feeling pressure from other black students not to be friendly with white students indicated that, for the most part, this bothered them but they did not reject their white friends. Ken Pettis remembers that most of his friends at the Taft School were white, and he "picked up a lot of grief for that from the other black students." Monique Burns recalls that she was the only black freshman when she started at the Concord Academy, and though she was friendly with some of the other black students who were older than she, most of her friends were other freshmen and therefore they were white. "It was very important to me not to be exclusive," she recalls. "I didn't believe in that. I still don't as a human being. I never did. Part of it had to do with me genetically and the fact that I was so fair, that I always felt I had one foot in one race and one foot in the other. I actually had some amateur historians in my family—I knew what my family tree was." Monique Burns entered Concord Academy in 1969. Though her views did not change, the amount of pressure she felt as a student at Harvard four years later did. Thus, though this was not a serious issue for her at Concord, it became one when she was in college.

The issue persisted for blacks at prep schools at least into the mid-1970s. In "A Journey from Anacostia to the Elite White World," Gregory Witcher, a black student at Exeter in the mid-1970s, described the following event: "One of my first friends at Exeter was another sophomore named Sterling. He was white. After a Sunday brunch at the Elm Street dining hall, we were walking back to my room in Soule. We were planning a hike along the river through nearby woods to admire the parade of autumn colors. Walking toward us in the opposite direction was a group of black male students. When I waved and said hello I heard one of the fellows say loudly, 'Hey, man, what the hell are you doing with that white boy?'"[21]

Black ABC students who became friends with white prep school classmates were not only stepping across racial boundaries, but in almost every case class boundaries as well. Most of the white students were from upper-middle- or upper-class families, and some were from the wealthiest and best-known families in America. Many of those we interviewed had specific memories of their interactions with these especially wealthy students. As we've already seen, one ABC student remembered a "department store heiress" telling her that her family was paying for half the ABC student's scholarship. The following four recollections indicate that interactions with the extremely rich led to a variety of responses.

After noting that most of his best friends at Hotchkiss were "middle class whites," Alan Glenn (at the time of our 1986 interview a banker with Manufacturers Hanover Trust) described his friendship with a student who was, as he put it, from the "upper crust":

> One of my best friends at Hotchkiss was William Clay Ford III, of the Ford family, and in spite of all his money and his background, he treated me as well as anyone at Hotchkiss. We were friends. I can't say that I went out to his house in Michigan or this or that or the next thing. Because of the geographics of it that never happened, but we started out in the ninth grade in the same Latin class and we used to goof around because we had this really old teacher and she just had some strange nuances about her. She got really upset if you said "shut up" in class, stuff like that. She would send you up to the dean's office for saying "shut up" and, you know, a ninth grader is definitely going to make fun of stuff like that. And then we would always pull pranks that would get her somewhat upset, all because we wanted to disrupt class because we didn't want to be studying Latin.

Sylvester Monroe remembers being confused by what seemed to be contradictory behavior on the part of his wealthy classmates at St. George's. He remembers a particular encounter with a grandson of Averell Harriman: "He was not a good friend of mine, but I knew him. Coming from the South Side [of Chicago] I was into dressing in a certain way and I get there with all these kids with money who didn't give a shit what they look like. One of the things that threw me, I had never ever liked penny loafers. Something that I just never liked. David and these guys would wear them and the soles would wear out and they would put tape on them. I went to David once and I remember saying, 'David, why won't you buy a pair of shoes?' and he said, 'I don't need a pair of shoes.' Very hard for me to understand things like that. The same guy was bragging at that time about having bought a $600 stereo." (Some were less confused by, and more directly critical of, their wealthier classmates' spending habits. As one woman scornfully recalls, "I watched kids spend as much money in a week on junk food as my mother would spend to feed six people.")

Ken Pettis, who, like Sylvester Monroe, was from Chicago, had become a hall monitor by his senior year at Taft, and one of his younger charges was a grandson of Chicago department store magnate Marshall Field. "He was a freshman and the other kids used to really take advantage of this guy. I mean, they would borrow things and never return them, and they would give him endless shit. I didn't like seeing this, and I was just being nice to him. He invited me down to their plantation down in North Carolina. They apparently own a lot of land in North Carolina. . . . I didn't go because I thought I'd feel uncomfortable, even though I'd kind of taken care of him throughout the year."

And in some cases, ABC students established lifelong friendships with wealthy white friends from prominent families. When we asked Michael Shivers, a graduate of St. Paul's and the University of Pennsylvania, who was living and working in Winston-Salem at the time of our 1988 interview, if he stayed in touch with his St. Paul friends, he responded: "I just talked on Sunday to Blair Scribner [of the Scribner publishing family]. Blair and I went to St. Paul's together, and we ended up going to Penn together and living across from each other our freshman year, so we've known each other now for twenty years. We keep in touch. We visit one another, we call one another."

Our findings on friendship point up the complexity of race relations in America. Many genuine friendships developed that have persisted through the years. Yet the extent of these friendships depends on the number of black students at the school and the temper of the times. When there were more than a few blacks, there were fewer black-white friendships. Moreover, as Beverly Daniel Tatum, a psychologist who is now the president of Spelman College, has pointed out in her book *"Why Are All the Black Kids Sitting Together in the Cafeteria?" and Other Conversations About Race*, adolescent blacks may need and benefit from the kind of support that only other black adolescents can provide as part of the development of their racial identity. But, as Tatum also says, "racial identity development unfolds in idiosyncratic ways," and young blacks arrive at the need for such "immersion" among blacks at different times. Tatum notes that in her own case, as a black student at a predominantly white high school, she did not sit at "the Black table in the cafeteria because there were not enough Black kids in my high school to fill one." In college, however, "I was ready to explore my racial identity and I did it wholeheartedly." Therefore, whether ABC students became close friends with their white classmates probably was affected in part by the number of other blacks at the school at the time, in part by the temper of the times, and in part by where they were in their own racial identity development.[22]

Sports

In his classic book, *The Nature of Prejudice*, Gordon Allport asserted that prejudice could be reduced when there was "equal status contact between majority and minority groups in the pursuit of common goals."[23] For many newly arriving ABC students, self-conscious about their clothes and unsure about their academic preparation, the nature of much of their early contact with the "majority group" was not "equal status." Furthermore, the intensely demanding and competitive atmosphere at many prep schools made the cooperative "pursuit of common goals" unlikely (in John Knowles's *A Separate Peace*, set at a fictional boarding school called Devon but clearly based on Knowles's alma mater, Exeter, the narrator asserts, "There were few relationships among us at Devon not based on rivalry").[24]

For many of the male ABC students, participation in athletics became the great leveler. How much money your parents had meant nothing when you stepped into the batter's box or took a jump shot from the top of the key. Not surprisingly, therefore, many of the men recall that they first began to feel they belonged at their schools as a result of their participation in athletics and that ultimately through this participation they developed important friendships.

As those who planned the summer transitional program realized, ABC students encountered sports in prep school they had never played or even heard of before. For some, especially those who were good athletes, this allowed them the enjoyable opportunity to learn new sports. Bill Lewis, at the time of our 1987 interview a vice president at Morgan Stanley, and now a managing director there, became so adept at lacrosse at Andover that by his senior year he was captain of the varsity team; he went on to play lacrosse at Harvard for four years. When we interviewed him in 1987, at which time his office was on the twentieth floor of a midtown Manhattan skyscraper, his lacrosse stick leaned against a wall near a photograph of his Harvard lacrosse team, a symbolic reminder of his continuing tie to the sports culture of private schools; by the time of our October 2001 interview, at a different midtown Manhattan office, this one on the thirty-second floor, the lacrosse stick was not in sight, though there was still a photograph as a reminder of his years as a lacrosse player. Ed McPherson, a track star at Andover and a banker with Swissbank in New York at the time of our first interview with him, recalls that a boarding school friend of his from Maine had taught him to play hockey, and he, in turn, taught his friend to shoot pool.

Some ABC students were exceptional athletes who would have participated in varsity sports at any secondary school in the country. Many, like lacrosse player Bill Lewis, track star Ed McPherson, or Rhodes Scholar Jesse

Spikes, went on to participate in varsity sports at the college level. Some ABC graduates have become professional athletes. One of these is Freddie Scott, a graduate of the public school program in Amherst, Massachusetts, and Amherst College, who was a wide receiver in the NFL for the Baltimore Colts and Detroit Lions for ten years (in April 2001 he was elected to the College Football Hall of Fame). Another, Hayden Knight, born in Trinidad but raised in Brooklyn, a graduate of the public school program in faraway Appleton, Wisconsin, was the all-time leading goal scorer at Marquette University, and then played professional soccer throughout most of the 1980s in Dallas, Milwaukee, Chicago, and Edmonton before he returned to coach at a high school in Cedarburg, Wisconsin, an essentially all-white town. Patricia Melton was a star track and field athlete as an ABC student at Middlesex, and then at Yale; after she graduated from Yale, she became a professional track athlete and was a finalist for the 1988 U.S. Olympic team.

Other ABC graduates, less gifted as athletes, acknowledged that because the competition was not as stiff as it would have been at their public high schools and because their prep schools have teams below the varsity level, they were given an otherwise unavailable chance to participate. Harold Cushenberry's comments are instructive:

> Sports was the way for me to initially show . . . that I belonged. I wasn't and would not have been a great athlete in other places, but I was pretty good at Taft. . . . In the fall I played football and that's when I first began to demonstrate some of my athletic ability. I was pretty good in football. Because of that, it helped break down the social barriers, and I began to be buddies with some of the folks and became co-captain of the lower-mid team and eventually went up to varsity as captain of the varsity football team. And, likewise, in the wintertime, I played basketball and eventually became captain of the basketball team. And I played baseball—I disappointed so many of the people there who [assumed] that because I was black I'd be a great baseball player. And I was not. I was a horrible baseball player. I could never hit a curve ball. But I found another sport which I ended up being fairly good at, which was lacrosse. I ended up playing lacrosse after failing in baseball miserably as a lower-mid. So I played lacrosse the rest of the time.

The well-known black historian C. L. R. James writes in *Beyond a Boundary* that playing cricket at prep school during the First World War—and coming to understand what "wasn't cricket"—taught him what "fairness" was about. He did not, he asserts, learn moral discipline from the Oxford and Cambridge masters at the secondary school he attended in his native Trinidad, Queens Royal College. "Inside the classrooms," he admits, "we lied and cheated without any sense of shame." But on the playing fields things were different. There he learned basic concepts of fairness, of sportsmanship, of generosity, and of subordinating one's personal inclinations for the good of the team. "This code," he claims, "became the moral framework of my existence."[25]

Though their participation in sports may not have provided the ABC students with the moral framework of their existence, it did provide valuable information about their fellow students. Did they play fair? Were they willing to subordinate their inclinations for the good of the team? Were they gracious in defeat? Did they earn respect—as opponents and as teammates? Those who participate in sports, whether at the professional, the varsity, or the "lower-mid" level, often assess such qualities in those with whom they participate. So, in the equal-status context of athletics, black ABC students had the opportunity to gain some particularly valuable insight into their classmates. Some they liked and admired, some they didn't. Some they became friends with, some they did not.

Fred Williams, a 1969 graduate of the Berkshire School, now a law professor at North Carolina Central University, explained to us how a shared interest in athletics led to a lifelong friendship with a white classmate from a wealthy Connecticut family. In our 1987 interview with Williams, he told us: "[I am in touch with] Bill Keeney, who happens to be a carbon copy of me in terms of our interest in sports. He was the other end on the football team. He was the other forward on the basketball team. He was my high jump partner. He was my pole vault partner. He was my friend. He was the only person that I pretty much did everything with, and we had similar interests. We were devilish in the same ways. We had the same kind of let's-get-back-at-the-establishment kind of ideas. I was always invited home with somebody over long weekends, and I started wondering whether anybody would ever come to my home in Durham. . . . He came to stay with me during spring break . . . and he got to feeling comfortable around my friends at my old high school. I see him to this day." Fourteen years later, when we interviewed Williams in June 2001, he told us that in 1999 he and Keeney had gone to their thirtieth reunion at the Berkshire School, and that he had recently gone to Denver to buy a truck from Keeney ("He sold it to me cheap").

For the women, athletics was less central to their prep school experience, and they were less likely to refer to participation in sports as important to becoming accepted by their peers (given the tremendous changes that have taken place in terms of women's participation in sports, this may be less true now than it was then). The women ABC graduates were more likely to express surprise and satisfaction that they had become proficient in sports they had never heard of before enrolling in prep school. The following comment by Monique Burns was not atypical: "I had not even, until Mt. Holyoke and

Concord, really done any sports. I found actually that I was talented and I did very well. I learned to play all these preppy sports, like lacrosse. By the time I was a senior I was captain of that team. Soccer, basketball and all, I was pretty good at that stuff."

Popularity and Student Politics

The evaluation study of early ABC students found that they believed they were popular with their classmates. In fact, in response to an item asking, "How popular do you think you are in school this year in comparison with all the other students in your grade," black ABC students indicated they felt more popular than did a control group of white students at their schools. (More than one-third of the black respondents felt themselves to be among "the most popular," and less than one-tenth thought themselves to be among "the least popular.")[26]

Not only were black ABC students popular, they were also valued as leaders in dealing with teachers and administrators. In the charged atmosphere of the late 1960s, with its demands for all kinds of freedoms, they could become the central figures in negotiations with a frequently divided faculty and a seemingly intransigent administration. Just such a situation arose at Andover, where an intriguing series of events revealed how black ABC students could be both popular among their peers and useful in bringing about institutional change. Ironically, the person they had to confront and defeat was one of the headmasters who helped create the ABC program.

As was true at many schools in the late 1960s, the Andover student body challenged the administration to abolish various long-standing rules concerning such things as compulsory chapel and the wearing of coats and ties to dinner. Simultaneously, some faculty were increasingly upset by the length of some students' hair and began calling for restrictions on hair length. According to the Andover historian, hair length was a "highly emotional issue that exercised the School community . . . and polarized the Phillips Academy Faculty." After one particularly heated faculty debate on the topic of hair length, the headmaster declared that he would be "czar" on this matter. Under his policy, if a faculty member thought a student's hair or sideburns were too long, he would send the student to the headmaster who would make the final decision to trim or not to trim.[27]

The history of Andover presents this episode in a jocular tone, as if to recall how silly things got in the late 1960s. It points out, for example, that one boy with an "impeccable" "page boy hair-cut" was forced to cut his hair and "emerged looking much worse than before."[28] But in actuality, the disputes over hair length, the dress code, and required attendance at chapel reflected a serious challenge to institutional authority. These conflicts revealed a breakdown in confidence and communication between Andover students and the headmaster who had provided leadership at the school for more than two decades.

It was in this atmosphere that the student body of 840 students (40 of whom were black) surprised many people (including the faculty, the administration, the *New York Times*, and, most likely, themselves) by electing blacks as presidents of the sophomore, junior, and senior classes for the 1969–70 academic year. As the *New York Times* breathlessly and historically informed its readers, Andover, "the alma mater of the Lees and Washingtons of Virginia and the Quincys and Lowells of New England, has elected three Negro students from the ghettos of Chicago and Oakland as class presidents for 1969–70."[29]

By electing blacks as class presidents, Andover students had managed to make things much more difficult for the Andover administrators, who were forced to move cautiously to ensure that student–administration differences didn't take on racial overtones. Newly elected senior class president Freddie McClendon preferred wearing a dashiki to a coat and tie, but could wear it only to those classes whose teachers had given special permission. When he asserted that "the administration doesn't understand the white social values imposed by the coat-and-tie regulation," Andover's administration suddenly had a tougher issue on its hands (the accusation of institutional racism) than a simple challenge to the dress code. One student, referred to in the *Times* as an "upper middler" (an eleventh grader), provided the following political analysis after the election: "There's no doubt in my mind that they elected guys who were going to be militant and get something done about the rules." Another referred to Freddie McClendon (who had a beard) as "the only guy on this campus strong enough to stand up to the headmaster." More sardonically, one of the black students commented, "It's ironic that a rich little white boys' school elects three blacks to defend them from a white administration."[30]

Ed McPherson was one of the three Andover students elected class president in 1969. He thinks the *New York Times* account overemphasized the differences between the students and the administration in order to highlight what he called "the us-them conflict" in the country at the time. Each of the three class presidents, he believes, won for different reasons. Still, he acknowledges the element of truth in the claim that students had chosen leadership capable of confronting an established headmaster. McPherson remembers the campaign in sharp detail:

There may have been some cynical students who were voting for Freddie McClendon out of a sense of what Freddie was saying as being anti-administration, and I think, yes, Freddie articulated a point of view that was very true for his class. . . . Freddie was a true radical. . . . The seniors had a real intense us-them attitude, and Freddie's hard-line stance was what the seniors were voting for. . . . Freddie was a musician, straddled five or six different constituencies if you will. The other people who ran against him only had one constituency. It was no surprise he won; he voiced their concerns best.

Tim Black was the eleventh-grade class president. Tim was a musician, a singer; he's a professional musician in California today, very soft-spoken. . . . Freddie and Tim are complete opposites, so certainly the eleventh-grade students weren't voting for Timmie for the same reasons the twelfth-graders were voting for Freddie.

And there I was, also very different from both of them. . . . I didn't even campaign. My class presidency was really a popularity contest, with a lot of guys wanting to show up [my opponent] because [he] was an honor roll student and a very bright guy and a very serious guy. By contrast, I was a much more relaxed guy.

Whether they were voting for McClendon's "hard-line stance," Tim Black's "soft-spoken" qualities, or McPherson's "relaxed" personality, the Andover students revealed their admiration for and confidence in their black classmates, and, in doing so, they helped bring about some changes that were already in motion. Although the headmaster "had always insisted that compulsory chapel would never be abolished while he was Headmaster,"[31] within a year of the election, compulsory chapel had been eliminated; so had rules on hair length, facial hair, and the wearing of jackets and ties to class. As McPherson indicated, "soft-spoken" Tim Black became a professional musician. Freddie McClendon may have been a "true radical," as McPherson claimed, but he was also an excellent student—he became an anesthesiologist.

The Importance of the Headmaster

"As the high priest of the status seminary," write two sociologists who studied private schools in depth in the 1980s, "the head presides over the prep rite of passage, ensuring that the school's program and personnel are committed to the goal of producing an elite cadre of patricians and parvenus."[32] More specific to the focus here, the interviews with ABC graduates demonstrate that who the headmaster or headmistress is, and what kind of leadership he or she provides, can make a major difference in the experience of a young black student trying to survive the prep rite of passage. Frank Borges provided perhaps the most graphic evidence of the importance of the head. Described by one journalist as "a nattily tailored corporate lawyer who often employs a street fighter's jive-talking demeanor,"[33] Borges has very vivid memories of two different headmasters when he was a student at the Millbrook School. The first he does not recall fondly:

One day the son of a bitch was standing in front of a tree, and he pulled me over and he said, "You know, Frank, you'll never make it in this place." I was, like, maybe I'd just turned fifteen. I was a kid. And this grown man—I was struggling, let me tell you, I was struggling academically. And I was scared shitless because I knew my father. If I flunked out—other kids, if they flunked out, it meant they'd take a yacht trip around the world that summer—I was into an ass whupping if I flunked out. This guy said to me, "Frank, you'll never graduate."

When this headmaster was forced to retire because of physical problems,

> they had to find another guy, so they brought in Hank Howard, who had retired years before. He was a peach of a guy. It was my junior year. He was very understanding. . . . This guy, Hank Howard, used to put me in his little fucking Volkswagen bug—he and I and his wife—and he would take Mike Goodwein [another ABC student]—he took the black kids, it was just us because we didn't have parents to come visit us on weekends and take us to go visit colleges. Then Hank used to drive us, personally, and this guy was in his seventies . . . he would drive us around. He liked Trinity. He thought that that was the place I wanted to be. It's a smaller school, pretty good academically, competitive. He thought I could really excel here. And he came down, he visited with me, we visited the admissions folks. He worked with them on financial aid because, I couldn't afford to go to school. And that's how I ended up at Trinity.
>
> If you ever talk to anybody who has had anything to do with Millbrook, they'll say Hank Howard was a peach.

Though the headmaster or headmistress often sets the tone for what is accepted, and expected, at a prep school, other administrators and individual teachers can have an enormous impact on students. Doris McMillon, a television newscaster, recalls that if the dean of students at the Cushing Academy had not intervened, she would not have been able to attend college. Her mother wanted her to come home and refused to fill out some financial aid forms. She relented only after the dean of students called her long distance and persuaded her to complete and send in the forms. Similarly, other ABC graduates recall particular interventions, or the more general impact, of various prep school administrators, faculty members, or advisors (Jay Farrow said of his advisor at Westtown: "My advisor was like a father to me. I wouldn't have made it through the school without him").

Social Life

For almost all the ABC graduates we interviewed, their social life was either limited or nonexistent while they were in prep school. One former ABC student summed up the views of many: "Socially I thought it was a retarding experience." Most, especially the older graduates, were at single-sex schools, and one of the few opportunities for contact with the opposite sex was to attend "mixers" with students from other schools. In some cases these were voluntary, and a student who wished to participate would indicate his or her interest by signing a sheet on a bulletin board. In other cases, participation was mandatory. In some instances, the students were matched with dates of the same race; more often they were not. Always, it seems, they were matched by height. At a designated time and place, students would meet their preassigned dates. The pair was supposed to remain together for a meal and a dance (and sometimes for additional activities like a glee club concert or a football game). They were not supposed to ditch their dates, though many did. Their memories of these mixers ranged from Eric Coleman's laconic "I don't remember any pleasant experiences" to Frank Borges's description of them as "torture."

Most ABC students went to at least a few mixers but found them to be anything but relaxing or fun. When possible, they socialized with other black students at other prep schools, especially by attending conferences on issues related to race and ethnicity. Alan Glenn recalled that during his first three years at Hotchkiss, before it became coeducational, the mixers were not much fun but the conferences were: "These were basically black parties. They called them conferences because there was the guise of, 'Well, we're having these meetings to discuss minority problems at prep schools,' which we did, but that was the small part. After that came the party, which is why everyone really came."

For other students, the network established during the summer program provided contacts and friends. Bobette Reed Kahn recalled that her boyfriend attended another prep school ten miles down the road; he was a middle-class black student she met because he roomed with a male ABC student she became friends with during the transitional summer program. Some students relied on their summers and their rare visits back home for any real social life. This, however, was problematic in itself, because for many, the longer they were in prep school, the more difficult it was for them to spend time at home. Their new class and style were beginning to drive a wedge between them and their friends and family.

GOING HOME

As the ABC students adapted to the regimentation and academic expectations of prep school life, they began to change. How much they were changing became apparent to them when they went home. More than one recounted painful experiences that demonstrate the gap between the two worlds in which they found themselves. Sylvester Monroe, the oldest of seven children, remembers trying to get his entire family to sit down and have a formal meal, with all the silverware in the right places, just as he had learned to dine at St. George's, and being told by one of his sisters, "Why don't you leave that St. George's bullshit at St. George's?"

Monroe learned a lesson from that experience. And he became much more cautious about instructing his family and friends to change their behavior. Instead, like many other ABC students, he tried to lead two separate existences. As he puts it, "I dressed, acted one way in Newport, Rhode Island, and when I went home on vacations, I left all of that in Newport." This seemed to work, and his Chicago buddies, most of whom were members of street gangs, accepted him: "These guys knew me and they sort of looked upon me as a nice guy, kind of a bookworm, a smart guy, nice to have around. They sort of gave me a nickname—'Big Time Vest.' I don't know if they understood that I was saying Newport and not New York or whatever, but they would say, 'Vest. Back from the big time!'"

But even for Big Time Vest, accepted by his old street buddies, there wasn't much left in those Chicago friendships after a few years. He still enjoyed returning to Chicago to see his family, and he felt no animosity toward his old friends, but more and more he found that "we'd talk and sort of reminisce about old times, but when we stopped with the old times there was nothing to talk about."

Some did experience hostility from their friends back home. Alan Glenn clearly remembers that going back to Harlem from Hotchkiss was not easy: "There were definitely animosities from people in my community. A lot of my friends looked at it as [though] I thought I was better than they were and I thought I was trying to be white. They wondered why I had to go away to this fancy school. Harlem was good enough for me before—why isn't it good enough for me now?"

Whether or not they encountered hostility on the streets back home, as time passed they had fewer and fewer things in common with their old friends, and they found themselves feeling lonely when they did go home. Eric Coleman's comments about returning to his hometown of New Haven while he was a student at Pomfret were not atypical:

I still identified with my neighborhood in New Haven. The biggest problem for me, I guess, was because there had been so much distance and time placed between me and the friends that I had when I went off to Pomfret. By the time that I would come home for a vacation, they were into different things. Some of them had new girlfriends they would spend most of their time with, so I lost contact with them in that way. Guys that I would consider hanging partners had gotten into trouble and maybe were in correctional institutions. Others of them were working full time, maybe having dropped out of school. Others were just in a different circle. I had lost contact with many of them so that when I came home for vacation it was usually really a kind of lonely time for me.

As he described these lonely feelings, Coleman focused on the loss of one particularly close friendship. One of his best friends had decided against participating in the ABC program. When Coleman came back, the relationship had changed: "There was a little bit of envy, I think, and a little bit of tension." They remained friends and years later, they attended each other's weddings. But the closeness of the friendship, lost when Coleman went to Pomfret, has never been regained.

The way in which speech can drive a wedge between ABC students and their families and friends emerged in a 1974 interview with an ABC student from Richmond, Virginia, who had graduated from Groton and at the time was an undergraduate at Stanford. In response to the questions, "Did you notice a difference in language? Did they [students at the prep school] pronounce any words differently?" he reported on the effect of his newly acquired "British accent" when he went home:

Yeah, definitely. The first time I came home I was really, people laughed at me. It wasn't like just the people up North would have a northern accent. It was like a British accent from going where I went to school. That was kind of funny coming home, and my brother and a lot of people would just look at me and say, "What's wrong with you," you know, "Where you been?" The language pronunciation was a little bit different I thought. It was northern Massachusetts and yet it was distinct from a northern accent. I think it was close to a British accent. Well, Groton was designed on a British school called Eton anyway. Some of the professors had gone to England. It was more like a proper form of English.[34]

As is true for many teenagers during their high school years, and especially during the stressful first few months away from home, these ABC students had ambivalent feelings toward their parents. Though many had talked their parents into letting them participate in the ABC program, others had been encouraged or even pressured by their parents (Jesse Spikes referred to his involvement in the program as a "conspiracy" between his mother and his homeroom teacher). Many asked themselves why their parents had sent them away. Harold Cushenberry recalls "wondering why my parents could possibly do this to me."

In a painfully honest acknowledgment of her feelings at the time, one woman described her difficulty in adjusting to the world back home while she was in prep school:

I had trouble adjusting to my former home. . . . I went through a period when I absolutely hated it, and I was ashamed of my parents. That feeling lasted probably until I graduated, until I went to college.

It was painful. All around me, I saw—we lived in a house, a nice house—but all around me I saw burned-out buildings and people sitting along the streets not doing anything, and graffiti. Physically, it was ugly and it was a hopeless situation and I didn't want to be a part of it. I didn't want to acknowledge that I had been a part of it. On some levels I was angry with my parents for not having— it makes no sense and I knew it made no sense at the time—I was angry at them for not having been like the parents of my classmates at prep school who were well educated and moneyed and always went off on great vacations.

[My parents] were pretty easygoing about it. I think they were hurt, but they took it in stride. I suppose my father was more understanding about it and he would talk to my mother and I would hear them talking. He would say, "You know, this must be a shock to her system. Give her time and she will come out of it." And eventually I would. The adjustment—I would go through adjustment periods. In the summer I would go through a four-week adjustment period. It was kind of like divers coming up from below or something—if you come up too quickly you get the bends. I felt weak and depressed and upset for about a month, and then it sort of passed.[35]

The problem of managing the dual identity of prep school graduate and lower-class black is a difficult one. Those we spoke with had to wear masks, and it is not likely that we captured the full depth of their feelings in one interview. We will be returning to this issue at several points in our account. For now, though, it is enough to say that most of those we interviewed seem to have dealt with this problem reasonably well.

Still, for some ABC students it was too difficult to try to live in two worlds. They left school, either because they chose to drop out or because they were asked to leave.

DROPPING OUT

Homesickness, being needed by the family back home, not feeling accepted at their new prep schools, or a combination of those factors led some students to pack their bags and go home. Many students who left prep school of their own volition returned home, attended their local public high schools, graduated, and went on to college. Some of the ABC students we interviewed referred to friends who had dropped out of prep school and later gone on to attend selective colleges and earn higher degrees. For example, Bill Lewis mentioned an Andover friend who had decided to quit Andover and go back home to St. Louis. When he finished high school in St. Louis, he went on to Dartmouth. Similarly, Alan Glenn mentioned a friend who didn't like Hotchkiss, so he went back to Brooklyn, finished high school there, and then went on to the University of Pennsylvania and New York University Law School; he's now a successful New York lawyer. Clearly, for some of those who dropped out of prep school (and the ABC program), leaving did not halt their academic achievement or their upward mobility.

Other ABC students did not choose to leave their prep schools but were asked to leave, generally for one of two reasons: either their grades were unacceptably low, or they got into trouble of some sort. In the early years of the program, not many students were asked to leave because of poor academic performance. The schools and the program appear to have been committed to helping the ABC students catch up, and when necessary they were willing to give the students time and special assistance to enable them to reach an acceptable level of performance. In some cases, however, students did flunk out of prep school. When this occurred, the students were sometimes given a second chance at another ABC school. In *Mixed Blessings*, an autobiographical account of her search for her biological mother, television newscaster Doris McMillon describes a meeting at the end of her first year at the Concord Academy with the school's headmaster. "He was sitting at his desk in his office looking at me kindly, trying to find excuses for my disappointing first-year grades," she writes, and then goes on:

> I looked at him dully. In my heart, I'd already heard the slamming of all the windows and doors. I'd screwed up the biggest break of my entire life. I'd justified Mom's worst estimate of my value. I was desperate, miserable, and furious with myself.
>
> "I feel you may do better in another environment—not a lesser environment," he hastened to add, "simply a different environment. One less rigid," he eyed me speculatively, "and old-world. One with a little more give and take. I think you'll flourish with a bit more of the human touch and with your feet flat to the earth.
>
> "Let me tell you something about Cushing Academy," he settled into a gentle propaganda pose. "Cushing's here in Massachusetts, an excellent school, high honors, select enrollment. Unlike Concord, a coed school. Bette Davis matriculated at Cushing." He grinned slightly, then ran through a roll call of names I knew from the headlines, from the movie page, from the arts as well.
>
> He was offering me an honorable second chance, one I was well aware I hadn't proved I deserved. I snatched it, of course.[36]

Two years later she graduated from Cushing. She is now a broadcast journalist who has worked with NBC News, WABC-TV, Fox Television, Black Entertainment Television, and the United States Information Agency's WORLDNET news program. She has also served on the boards of both the Cushing Academy and A Better Chance.

Other students were asked to leave because they could not, or would not, adjust to the many rules, restrictions, and expectations at their prep schools.

They were thrown out, often following a lengthy period of rebellion that culminated in a decisive event. Eric Coleman remembers one friend who was asked to leave Pomfret: He "had a bit of temper and I guess he had gotten into a couple of run-ins with some of the students there. He was finally expelled from school because one weekend after he had come back from vacation, I guess he had brought a pint of vodka with him, and he stayed in his room and he drank it and ended up intoxicated and was wandering around doing all sorts of foolish things. I guess as far as the headmaster was concerned, that was the last straw for him."

Some of the stories about friends being thrown out had tragic endings. Alan Glenn spoke of a youngster who entered Hotchkiss with him: "He left Hotchkiss halfway through his tenth-grade year. His life just went downhill after that. He was one of those that they say you can't get the street out of him. He didn't want the street out of him, so even at Hotchkiss he was like a somewhat streety person, always getting into the wrong things. You can't run around at Hotchkiss the way you would at a public school here in New York. There are just too many monitors and too many people who care who aren't going to let you do that. Because of that he left Hotchkiss. . . . Later I found out he was in New York selling drugs, next thing I heard he was in jail for having murdered somebody."

Some former ABC students indicated that those of their friends who were more confrontational in their approach to people and issues were more likely to leave or to be asked to leave. Harold Cushenberry reflected on why some friends left Taft and why he stayed: "Some people's personalities were just very different. They were combative. They weren't as willing as I—I have to be honest with myself—to overlook things that I care about. Look, you can be racist and mumble things under your breath and I'm not going to go out and slug you. Some of those type people just had very difficult, very different experiences. They weren't willing to internalize a lot of the stuff that I internalized and sort of use to motivate myself in other ways. And they fell by the wayside." We suspect that many of the students who fell by the wayside had developed the kind of "oppositional identity" discussed by anthropologists who study the attitudes of subjugated minorities.

However, two studies of the ABC program indicate that in the early years ABC students were no more—and perhaps less—likely to leave prep school than their non-ABC contemporaries. In a 1969 follow-up study of the eighty-two boys who had participated in the summer transitional program at Dartmouth in 1965 reveals that during the four-year period, only eight students (about 10 percent) had dropped out, and another seven had either chosen to leave or been asked to leave by the end of the summer transitional program.[37] The second study, the evaluation study that examined the performance of all ABC students from 1964 through 1972, shows that the attrition rate for 1,640 ABC students was about 20 percent, which compares very favorably with the estimated 30 percent attrition rate for non-ABC students in the same schools during that time. Even if the estimate of 30 percent is a little high, the ABC students clearly did at least as well as their white counterparts when it came to graduation rates.[38]

Just after the time the evaluation report was written, the attrition figures were on the rise for ABC students. By 1972, the figure reached 28 percent. Differences within subgroups of ABC students also began to emerge: females were less likely to drop out than were males; Southern students were less likely to drop out than were students from other parts of the country; white and Native American ABC students were more likely to drop out than were black or Puerto Rican students; and students whose parents were together and employed were less likely to drop out than were students who were from broken homes or whose parents were on welfare.[39]

THE BLACK ABC PREP SCHOOL GRADUATE

Those black ABC students who survived the prep school crucible were not the same people when they graduated that they had been when they arrived. They were not only two, three, or sometimes four years older, and the recipients of excellent secondary school educations. Most had adopted the styles that prevailed in their schools; they dressed like prep school students, they liked the music prep school students liked, and they spoke like prep school students. They bear witness to how rapidly the much-vaunted upper-class style can be acquired. The pressure some felt to change their style when they moved from the prep school world to their world at home caused anxiety; for others, this shift simply resulted in lonely times at home.

The follow-up study of the males who participated in the 1965 Dartmouth summer program is helpful in considering some of the changes experienced while in prep school. Its authors interviewed and administered a battery of tests to almost all of the eighty-two boys who began the 1965 transitional program. In addition, they analyzed data for a subsample of twenty-three ABC students and twenty-three students in a control group consisting of students who stayed at their local high schools, but were matched with the twenty-three ABC students by race, age, and IQ. It reports that about half of the ABC students interviewed said they had "changed a great deal," mostly in positive ways. The students said they felt more academically competent, more socially aware, more at ease socially, more self-aware, more politically aware, more tolerant, and more articulate.

About one-fourth of the ABC students interviewed also reported feeling greater "tension and anxiety" than when they had arrived. This finding was supported by the data from one of the tests, the Cattell High School Personality Questionnaire (HSPQ). On the HSPQ, students in the ABC subgroup showed increases on all the measures related to anxiety, including measures of "emotionality," "reactivity to threat," "apprehensiveness and worry," and "tension and drive." The students in the control group did not show increases on any of these measures. Interestingly and revealingly, the same ABC students who showed themselves to be more anxious also demonstrated a significant increase on a ten-item scale measuring "casualness"—a testimony perhaps to the pressures at prep school to be, or appear to be, casual.

The report's authors also administered the California Personality Inventory (CPI) to all of the ABC students (but not to the control group) and found that their scores had increased significantly on a number of scales. They scored higher on capacity for status (a scale assessing the personality attributes that underlie and contribute to status), social presence, self-acceptance, tolerance, achievement via independence, and flexibility. (They also scored lower on the socialization, self-control, and achievement via conformance scales; lower scores on these scales might be expected of adolescents during the rebellious atmosphere of the late 1960s.)[40]

When we asked ABC graduates how they had changed as a result of attending prep schools, two responses were prominent. Many said they had become more independent. And many became more aware of the possibilities open to them. Alan Glenn put it directly: "I got to see the other side of the fence. I got to see the jet set, the high flyers, the people that make this country run. I was exposed to a lot of different things. I was exposed to a part of society that, if I had not gone to Hotchkiss, I may have never been exposed to."

Although our interviewees revealed many painful examples of the racism they endured, and admitted to much tension or loneliness when they returned home, these negative feelings were far less extensive than we expected. By contrast, we were surprised by the degree to which the graduates looked back on their prep school days with fondness. We recognize that they may have felt differently while they were going through the experience itself, but the crucial point in terms of their current lives is that for the most part their memories of their initiation into the elite world of private education form a very positive part of their present outlooks and personalities. The question naturally arises whether they really benefited from their experiences in prep school, but all available indications suggest that they did, contrary to what many skeptics might assume. The follow-up study of those who attended the 1965 Dartmouth summer program shows they gained in self-confidence and felt more at ease socially and more socially and politically aware, which corresponds to their responses to our questions and to our impressions of them as well.

For a time we worried that we were not being sensitive enough to the difficulties these young people faced. Then we decided we were being overly sensitive. We do not overlook those who dropped out or were hurt by the experience, but these individuals were no more numerous among ABC students than among the privileged white students. Prep school, after all, is a crucible for power for all the students. We came to realize that the ABC students seized a great opportunity, made the best of it, and showed resiliency in negotiating between home and prep school identities.[41]

As they headed off to college, then, the world was opening up for these black prep school graduates and offering them new choices: where to go to college, what subjects to study, what careers to pursue, and what travels to undertake. Leaving prep school and entering college in the late 1960s or early 1970s, they could not have had better timing.

NOTES

1. R. Gaines. *The Finest Education Money Can Buy* (New York: Simon and Schuster, 1972), 10.

2. Peter W. Cookson, Jr., and Caroline Hodges Persell, *Preparing for Power: America's Elite Boarding Schools* (New York: Basic Books, 1985), 46–47.

3. Ibid., 20.

4. Ibid., chap. 7, "The Prep Crucible," esp. 124.

5. Ronald Raymond, "On Becoming Uprooted: The Beinecke Symposium," *WoosterNews* (Spring 1985): 20–21. See also Ronald Raymond, *Grow Your Roots Anywhere, Anytime* (Ridgefield, Conn.: Wyden, 1980).

6. Frederick S. Allis, Jr., *Youth from Every Quarter: A Bicentennial History of Phillips Academy, Andover* (Hanover, N.H.: Phillips Academy, Andover, 1979), 616, 626. For a detailed historical analysis suggesting that Western racism developed out of the anti-Semitism that emerged in fifteenth century Spain and that the two have been intertwined ever since, see George M. Fredrickson, *Racism: A Short History* (Princeton, N.J.: Princeton University Press, 2002).

7. Paul Cowan, *The Making of an Un-American* (New York: Viking, 1967), 4.

8. John Neary, *Julian Bond: Black Rebel* (New York: William Morrow, 1971), 43.

9. Ibid., 44–45. Neary reports that after this story appeared in a magazine article about Bond people at the George School claimed it was false. The Reverend James H. Robinson, the founder of Operation Crossroads Africa, wrote in his autobiography, *Road Without Turning: The Story of Rev. James H. Robinson* (New York: Farrar, Straus, 1950) that in the early 1940s he was invited by the graduating class of the George School to be their commencement speaker, but "the board of directors forced the president to withdraw the invitation" (253–254).

10. Francis X. Clines, "Caseworkers Pool Funds to Aid Groton-Bound Harlem Student," *New York Times*, August 2, 1969, 17.

11. Peter S. Prescott, *A World of Our Own: Notes on Life and Learning in a Boys' Preparatory School* (New York: Coward-McCann, 1970), 40.

12. John Sedgwick, "World without End," *New England Monthly* 5, no. 9 (1988): 54.

13. Gail Lumet Buckley, Lena Horne's daughter, in her book about the Horne family (*The Hornes: An American Family* [New York: Knopf, 1986]), tells the following story about her mother visiting a Hollywood set in the early 1940s: "Tallulah Bankhead, the star of the picture, greeted Lena with open arms—and with the words 'My daddy had a beautiful little pickaninny just like you.' Lena was so bowled over by the sheer audacity of Tallulah, who had been one of the great theatrical stars of the 1920s (as well as a famous 'free spirit'), that all she could do was laugh. And she laughed the rest of the afternoon. Tallulah was no bigot—she was, in fact, one of show biz's great liberals" (184–185).

14. Robert Sam Anson, *Best Intentions: The Education and Killing of Edmund Perry* (New York: Random House, 1987), 91.

15. George Perry, "A Better Chance: Evaluation of Student Attitudes and Academic Performance, 1964–1972," study funded by the Alfred P. Sloan Foundation, the Henry Luce Foundation, and the New York Community Trust (March 1973), ERIC Document 075556, pp. 38, 42.

16. Kareem Abdul-Jabbar and Peter Knobler, *Giant Steps: The Autobiography of Kareem Abdul-Jabbar* (New York: Bantam Books, 1983), 16. Cited in Signithia Fordham and John U. Ogbu, "Black Students' School Success: Coping with the Burden of 'Acting White,'" *Urban Review* 18, no. 3 (1986): 177. See also Roslyn A. Mickelson, "The Attitude-Achievement Paradox among Black Adolescents," *Sociology of Education* 63 (1990): 44–61. In a study of forty-two African American students who attended white elite independent schools through the Baltimore Educational Scholarship Trust (BEST), Amanda Datnow and Robert Cooper found evidence that their fellow African American prep school friends provided similar support for their academic efforts. They concluded: "The most striking feature of these networks was the social value their members placed upon high academic achievement and hard work in school. They allowed students to be 'smart' without feeling as though they were 'selling out' or 'acting White.'" See Amanda Datnow and Robert Cooper, "Peer Networks of African American Students in Independent Schools: Affirming Academic Success and Racial Identity," *Journal of Negro Education* 66, no. 1 (1997): 56–72 (cited passage from p. 4 of the downloaded version). For the most recent data on oppositional attitudes in black and white students, see Roslyn A. Mickelson, "The Contributions of Abstract, Concrete, and Oppositional Attitudes to Understanding Race and Class Differences in Adolescents' Achievement," paper presented at the annual meetings of the American Sociological Association, Chicago, August 19, 2002.

17. Gregory Pennington, "The Minority Student Experience in Predominantly White High Schools," report for the Whitney M. Young Foundation and A Better Chance, December 1983, pp. 1, 15.

18. ABC graduate Sylvester Monroe, who was attending Harvard at this time, wrote an article that appeared in the *Saturday Review of Education* ("Guest in a

Strange House: A Black at Harvard" [February 1973]: 45–48) in which he criticized himself, and fellow blacks, for this stance. See chapter 4.

19. Perry, "A Better Chance," 23. Perry was not unaware of the difficulties inherent in interpreting these findings. He wrote: "It might have been better to test the same group of students twice. At this point, however, it is necessary to base tentative conclusions on the comparison between sophomores and seniors, acknowledging that there are several problems with this methodology."

20. Ibid.

21. Gregory B. Witcher, "A Journey from Anacostia to the Elite White World," *Washington Post*, January 13, 1980. The article was reprinted in the May 1980 issue of *Independent School*, 31–33.

22. Beverly Daniel Tatum, "*Why Are All the Black Kids Sitting Together in the Cafeteria?*" *and Other Conversations About Race*, rev. ed. (New York: Basic Books, 1999), 67, 75–76. See also Janet E. Helms, ed., *Black and White Racial Identity: Theory, Research and Practice* (Westport, Conn.: Greenwood, 1990). Tatum and Helms are not without their critics. See Elisabeth Lasch-Quinn, *Race Experts: How Racial Etiquette, Sensitivity Training and New Age Therapy Hijacked the Civil Rights Movement* (New York: Norton, 2001, chap. 4, 110–134).

23. Gordon W. Allport, *The Nature of Prejudice* (Garden City, N.Y.: Doubleday, 1958), 254.

24. John Knowles, *A Separate Peace* (New York: Macmillan, 1959), 36.

25. C. L. R. James, *Beyond a Boundary* (1963; reprint New York: Pantheon, 1983), 35.

26. Perry, "A Better Chance," 133.

27. Allis, *Youth from Every Quarter*, 655.

28. Ibid.

29. John Leo, "Negroes Elected President of Three Classes at Andover," *New York Times*, June 11, 1969, 33.

30. Ibid. The headmaster was not happy with this analysis. In a letter to the editor ("Events at Andover," *New York Times*, July 3, 1969, 30) in response to the article, he wrote: "It was no kindness to the three newly elected presidents to put them on the spot of attempting to measure up to the statement that 'some observers think they will speak of demands and confrontations . . . when their numbers are large enough.'"

31. Allis, *Youth from Every Quarter*, 660.

32. Cookson and Persell, *Preparing for Power*, 123.

33. Daniel J. Shea, "The Rebuilding of Frank Borges," *Bond-Buyer*, June 1, 1987, 1.

34. Interview with John King conducted for G. William Domhoff by research assistant Deborah Samuels, September 1974.

35. In his follow-up study of those who had participated in the summer program at Dartmouth, Alden E. Wessman found that many students became critical of their home neighborhoods during their first few years in the ABC program. In response to a question concerning their feelings about their home neighborhoods, 19 percent gave "moderately critical" responses and 22 percent "extremely critical" responses ("Evaluation of Project ABC [A Better Chance]: An Evaluation of Dartmouth College- Independent Schools Scholarship Program for Disadvantaged High School Students,"

final report, Office of Education, Bureau of Research [April 1969], ERIC Document 031549, p. 181).

36. Doris McMillon with Michele Sherman, *Mixed Blessings: The Dramatic True Story of a Woman's Search for Her Real Mother* (New York: St. Martin's Press, 1985), 81–82.

37. Alden E. Wessman, "Scholastic and Psychological Effects of a Compensatory Education Program for Disadvantaged High School Students: Project ABC," in *Educating the Disadvantaged*, edited by Edwin Flaxman (New York: AMS Press, 1971–1972), 272–273.

38. Perry, "A Better Chance," 46.

39. Perry, "A Better Chance," 72.

40. Wessman, "Scholastic and Psychological Effects," 276.

41. Various authors have noted that this is an issue for other groups experiencing class mobility. See, for example, Richard Sennett and Jonathan Cobb, *The Hidden Injuries of Class* (New York: Random House, 1972), 20–23; and Richard Rodriguez, *Hunger of Memory: The Education of Richard Rodriguez: An Autobiography* (Boston: D. R. Godine, 1982).

4

ABC Students in College

Once upon a time, the graduates of the country's most prestigious prep schools had a virtual guarantee that they would be accepted to the Ivy League college of their choice. But all that began to change after World War II, and by the 1980s, "only" 34 percent of the incoming freshmen at Harvard and 40 percent at Yale and Princeton were from prep schools.[1] As of 2001, the percentage of incoming students who had gone to private school was about the same at Harvard (35 percent), though it had increased to 47 percent at Yale.[2]

It remains, however, a distinct advantage for an applicant to an Ivy League school to attend an elite prep school. One study found that the Harvard admission staff placed applications from certain boarding schools in special colored folders to set them apart from other applications. Applicants from these schools are more likely to be accepted, even when parental background, grades, and SAT scores are comparable with those for students from public schools.[3] Looking at the rates of admissions to Ivy League schools for a wide range of applicants, another study found the acceptance rate at each of them was highest for students from a list of the sixteen highest-status prep schools.[4] Since there's extensive evidence that attending a prestigious college is related to subsequent occupational success, there's no doubt that attending an elite prep school is a "booster shot" into the elite.[5]

GETTING IN

Early in their senior year, ABC students, like other seniors at their schools, begin to prepare to apply to colleges. All the seniors at elite prep schools have the advantage of highly professionalized college advisory programs.[6] Due to the intense competition to get into the top colleges, the schools have elaborate systems of instructing students how to write effective applications, and they train their staffs how to recommend students in the best possible terms. Since it was a foregone conclusion that almost all the graduates would go to college, the real goal was to get them into the best colleges.

The question that faced ABC students graduating in the late 1960s and early 1970s, therefore, was not whether to go to college, but where to go. Indeed, one of the more remarkable statistics describing the progress of ABC students is that 99 percent of the 1,011 students who had graduated from independent schools by June 1971 had entered college by 1972. These figures compare quite favorably with the attendance rates for various comparison groups. At that time, for example, between 55 and 60 percent of all high school graduates entered college, as did slightly fewer than half the students who enrolled in the Upward Bound program. The most revealing comparison, however, is with a "control" group of students who had applied for admission to the ABC program in 1967, but could not be placed because of the cutback in federal funding ABC experienced that year. As part of the extensive evaluation of the ABC program performed in 1972, the investigators matched forty-seven ABC applicants for whom there had not been sufficient funds with forty-seven students who participated in the program on such factors as academic ability and family background. Of the forty-seven students who returned to their local high schools, twenty-nine (62 percent) entered college. In contrast, of the forty-seven ABC students, eight dropped out of the program and returned to their high schools, and five of these eight entered college. But all thirty-nine who graduated from ABC schools went to college. These differences provide clear evidence that the program benefited its students; far too many talented students at public high schools did not continue on to college.[7]

ABC graduates not only benefited from their prep school credentials, they had another thing going for them as well. By the late 1960s, prestigious colleges and universities were actively seeking black students, especially in the face of a recent report showing that only .69 percent of the students at New England colleges were black. "It is rather clear," the report admonished, "that as far as the main body of American Negroes is concerned, it would not matter at all if New England colleges and universities closed their doors tomorrow."[8] Faced with that embarrassing conclusion and the broader pressures stemming from the civil rights era, the battle for black enrollment began just as the first ABC students were applying to college. As a dean for special academic affairs at Wesleyan University wrote in a widely read magazine of the day, "The question 'How many blacks will you have in September?' replaced earlier queries concerning athletes, National Merit Scholars, and Scholastic Aptitude Test medians." He predicted that the search for black students would be "the fiercest competition for any group of students in the history of American higher education."[9]

But, he continued, "the simple fact is that students who even come close to former levels of academic expectations are few." This, then, was the dilemma faced by admissions officers in the late 1960s: how to find black students who could meet the academic expectations of the institution. Not surprisingly, ABC students were much sought after. If they could handle the work at the elite prep schools, which were known to be academically demanding, and if they could withstand the social pressures of the prep school environments (environments not unlike those at many of these colleges), then they were particularly good bets to succeed in college.

Not surprisingly, then, the early graduates of the ABC program went to very good colleges and universities. Table 4.1 lists the fifteen schools most frequently attended by ABC graduates cumulatively through 1972 and through 1981, and the top ten through 2000. The list includes many elite colleges and universities, including all eight of the top Ivy League schools (Princeton was not on the 1972 list, but by 1981, it was among the top fifteen; Columbia was on the list in 1972 but had dropped off by 1981). As of the spring of 2000, the top ten colleges and universities attended by ABC alumni remained virtually the same, though the ordering had changed.[10]

The value of attending elite secondary schools is perhaps most dramatically reflected in the patterns of college attendance between the forty-seven

Table 4.1. Colleges Most Frequently Attended by ABC Graduates

Through 1972	Through 1981	Through 2000
#1 Harvard	#1 Harvard	#1 Univ. of Penn.
#2 Dartmouth	#2 Dartmouth	#2 Harvard
#3 Univ. of Penn.	#3 Tufts	#3 Columbia
#4 Tufts	#4 Univ. of Penn.	#4 Brown
#5 Carleton	#5 Brown	#5 Wesleyan
#6 Williams	#6 Wesleyan	#6 Yale
#7 Yale	#7 Carleton	#7 Tufts
#8 Brown	#8 Williams	#8 Cornell
#9 Stanford	#9 Northeastern	#9 Dartmouth
#10 Columbia	#10 Yale	#10 Stanford
#11 Wesleyan	#11 Stanford	
#12 Oberlin	#12 Boston Univ.	
#13 Northeastern	#13 Princeton	
#14 Cornell	#14 Oberlin	
#15 Trinity	#15 Cornell	

ABC students and the forty-seven students who would have participated in the program if funding had been adequate. Whereas ten of the ABC students attended Ivy League schools (with five going to Harvard), and many others attended such highly selective schools as Carleton, Middlebury, Oberlin, Tufts, and Wesleyan, many in the control group went to good state universities but only one went to an Ivy League school (Cornell).[11]

Many of the ABC graduates interviewed for this book attended the most prestigious colleges and universities. Given the competition for black students at the time, many had been accepted by four or five Ivy League schools. How did they decide which school to attend? Some simply chose the school they thought was the most prestigious. As Monique Burns said in explaining why she decided to attend Harvard rather than Yale or Brown, where she had also been accepted: "I liked Cambridge—also, it's hard to say no to them." Bill Lewis, who was planning to attend the University of Pennsylvania, explained how he came to conclude that he could not choose Penn when he had also been accepted at Harvard:

> When it was time to apply to college, I was going to go to University of Penn because I played lacrosse and the lacrosse coach recruited me. I also wanted to be a civil engineer and Penn had a school of civil engineering. And then two things happened. I saw a graph that showed lifetime earnings of an engineer versus lifetime earnings of a liberal arts major. And what you saw—I imagine it's still true today—is that an engineer started out at a much higher salary, say $25,000, but the slope of that line was pretty flat, so that over the course of a career, you weren't making a lot more than $25,000. Liberal arts majors on the other hand started out a lot lower than $25,000, but for any number of reasons, they made a lot more money over the course of a lifetime.
>
> The second thing was that my football coach made a comment to somebody else, which got back to me. It was a very simple comment and, quite frankly, it's the kind of simple thinking that I typically use to guide myself and most of the decisions I have to make. The guy said, "Bill Lewis has a full scholarship to go to Harvard. What's there to contemplate? Harvard is Harvard."[12]

Others chose a particular school because friends had gone there and recommended it, or because they believed it to be particularly strong in a field in which they were interested. Ken Pettis, for example, explains why he chose Brown over a host of other schools that accepted him:

> At the time I was going into the college application process, based on the previous experiences I had had at Taft, I thought I might want to be an engineer, and one of the other black students who had left Taft a couple of years before me had gone to Brown. . . . He would come back from time to time and he had nothing but good things to say about Brown. I through research found out that

Brown had a very good engineering department. . . . It was an Ivy League school, and I decided Brown was going to be my first choice. I also applied to every other Ivy League school except for Columbia and one of the other ones, maybe Cornell. Then I also applied to the University of Illinois as a fallback—everybody had to have a fallback. And I also applied to Wesleyan because this woman I knew had applied there. I got into every school I applied to except the University of Pennsylvania.

For some, geographic location was a key factor. Eric Coleman explained his decision to attend Columbia in the following way:

When I was coming out of Pomfret, I had gotten accepted to every school I had applied to—Yale, Dartmouth, NYU, Columbia, Brown, Boston University, Northeastern, University of Connecticut—and my choices came down to Yale and Columbia. I chose Columbia because I didn't really want to go back to New Haven to go to college. I had heard so much about New York City in terms of it being an exciting place to be that I thought it would be a good opportunity to experience New York City. Columbia's reputation as a school was fairly good at that time, and it was an Ivy League school, so I didn't think I would be losing much by going there rather than going to Yale, so I went to Columbia.

Cher Lewis also chose to attend college in New York City, though she made her decision later than most applicants, much more spontaneously, and against the advice of both her parents and her prep school guidance counselor:

I applied to Skidmore, Goucher, Smith (even though I was told I wouldn't get in) and I got into all of the schools I applied to, mainly because my timing was wonderful, I mean with the civil rights movement and all. . . . I was applying in 1968. In every place I got scholarships. Then, in April, I came to New York with a friend. We were allowed to sign out for a weekend if someone's parents promised that they would watch over us. I was just totally fascinated and said that this is where I want to come. I had never been to New York. We were down in the Village. I went into NYU, I applied—they accepted me on the spot and gave me a full scholarship. And everyone tried to talk me out of it (at that time, no one from Abbott went to NYU), but I was so excited about being in New York. My parents were heartbroken and thought I was going to be killed.

Some of the Southern students returned to the South. Greg Googer, who was from Atlanta, decided to attend Vanderbilt. In addition to his wish to be able to see his family more frequently, his decision was directly tied to his eventual plan to live and work in Atlanta: "I knew that if I wanted to work in Atlanta, there was a cultural tie that I had to make. Atlanta's not one of those types that accepts you readily if you're from the North or have those northern tendencies about you." When he graduated from the Berkshire School in Massachusetts, Fred Williams decided to return to his hometown of Durham, North Carolina. Whereas some of his relatives had attended North Carolina Central, Williams applied to and was accepted at Duke. He wanted to be back home, and, as he put it, "I wanted to see what it was like over at the white school." Gail Warren, who had been so homesick at Andover that she racked up huge phone bills calling home, applied to only two schools, both in the South, and chose to attend Agnes Scott, which is in her hometown of Atlanta.

But going back home seemed risky to other ABC students from the South. During his senior year at the Taft School, Harold Cushenberry, a native of Henderson, North Carolina, was the first black to win a Morehead Scholarship to the University of North Carolina. The much sought-after Morehead pays for all of a student's expenses, so Cushenberry was tempted. He visited the University of North Carolina for a weekend, along with all the other Morehead recipients. "My parents," he recalls, "were tickled to death." One of the events of the weekend was a group sing-along. Cushenberry laughed at the memory of the sing-along: "They sang 'Old Black Joe.' Just blatant insensitivity. 'Old Black Joe.' And I'm sitting there, and I said to myself, 'No, it's not time yet. Maybe later.'" So Cushenberry decided not to return to the South. Instead he settled for Harvard, where he had also been accepted with a scholarship, though it was "nowhere near the type of ride the Morehead is."

Not all the students who were accepted ended up going to college. The experiences of one of those who didn't, Christine Dozier, reveals the problems that can arise for ABC students.

CHRISTINE DOZIER

Christine Dozier—then Christine Harley—grew up in a housing project in Washington, D.C. When she was in the ninth grade, she was recruited to participate in the ABC program. With her parents' encouragement, she decided to leave her close-knit family and familiar neighborhood to spend her high school years at the Abbott School in Andover, Massachusetts. In our 1987 interview in downtown Washington, she remembered the struggle she experienced as one of four black students at Abbott. The struggle was not academic; she did quite well as a student. Rather, she found living at Abbott to be a frustrating and at times an infuriating experience. Looking back, she attributed some of her frustration and anger to her own personality and temperament. As she put it: "I've always been somewhat of a rebel, and that rebellious spirit that I showed there got me into a lot of trouble. I was considered a person who was not willing to conform to get along. I said what needed to be said and I did what needed to be done." In short, she had the cultural pride that is an important facet of the oppositional tendencies that may develop to cope with racial insults and slights.

In her view, ABC did nothing to prepare the prep schools for the arrival of black students. Though the program provided an orientation for students, there was no orientation to prepare the schools for black students. As far as she was concerned, the schools very much needed better preparation for the arrival of young blacks from economically underprivileged environments. As a result, she believes "they left a lot of scars on these students." She herself emerged from her experience at Abbott "with a lot of resentment" and so unhappy with that academic environment that she never earned a college degree, a decision that "has haunted me in later life."

What upset her most was the assumption on the part of the people at Abbott that culturally she came with nothing of value and that, therefore, the purpose of the experience was to teach her to be like other Abbott girls. "I realized once I got there that was the basic factor that separated me from them: they had and I was perceived to have not. And it was like they were doing me a favor by allowing me to participate in this cultural awakening. They were opening doors to me that I may never have had opened to me had I not gone there. I had gone to museums before I went to Abbott. I had gone to concerts before. I had read books before. . . . The door that you opened to me was the credibility that on my academic record it was going to say that I attended this school, and that gave me some credence. I couldn't get them to understand that the person who came to Abbott was not a person who was there to be molded, but was a person who was there to learn, and to teach, because I thought I had a lot they could learn from me." From her point of view, the institutional racism she describes is perhaps so encompassing as to be called "cultural racism." The experiences and cultures of those not in the dominant majority are seen as irrelevant.[13] This is the recipe for creating oppositional identities.

Christine Dozier might have had similar experiences at most prep schools in the late 1960s. By the 1980s and 1990s, however, with at least two decades of trying to figure out how to diversify their student bodies, prep schools varied considerably, both in the number of black students (and other students of color) and in the ways that the school cultures had changed. Some schools seem to have been much better than others at welcoming and even embracing their more diverse student populations. In an article comparing the experiences of two Quaker boarding schools, Westtown and Germantown Friends School (GFS), the authors demonstrate how the creation of a "community scholarships program" in 1965 at Germantown Friends led to significant changes in that school's culture. The scholarship fund was designed to attract black students with financial need from the local area, and many faculty, administrators, staff, and alumni invested in the program both financially and emotionally (for example, by the early 1980s over half the faculty contributed to the program through payroll deductions). In addition, the parents of the students who lived nearby became involved in the program and the school. As a result, there was both sensitivity to the needs of these students of color, and pressure on their behalf, thereby "challenging and changing GFS from within." The authors conclude that GFS benefited from "student-adult activism around student-of-color issues" in a way that Westtown did not.[14] The community scholarship program at GFS also reveals how some schools became less reliant on the ABC program by developing their own scholarship programs to attract students of color.

Though highly critical of Abbott Academy, Christine Dozier stayed and she did well. (Why? "Fear of the behind-whipping I'd get from my parents.") When it came time to apply to college, she was ready to be closer to home, so she applied to American University and Goucher. She was accepted with full scholarships at both, and decided to attend American University so that she could be in Washington, D.C. But during the summer between her senior year of prep school and her freshman year of college, she decided she needed a break. She had a job with American Airlines that she liked, and her employers were glad to have her stay. American University assured her that her scholarship would be waiting for her a year later, but said that they could not hold it longer than that.

A year later, however, her boyfriend of many years was drafted and scheduled for duty in Vietnam. They decided to marry, had a baby within a year, and Christine never used her scholarship to American University. As of 2001, she was working as an administrator at the National Science Foundation. Over the years she has taken college courses here and there, mostly to satisfy requirements she has needed for advancement and promotion in her career, but she has never completed a college degree. Her unhappy experience at Abbott was certainly not the only factor in her not becoming a full-time college student, but in her view, it was a significant contributing factor.

Christine Dozier was strong academically and self-confident in her interpersonal relationships. Other ABC students were not so strong academically, and many lacked the self-confidence that helped her survive. For them the prep school crucible was often an unbearably painful experience. When senior year rolled around and they, unlike so many of their ABC friends, received rejection letters from colleges, the damage to self-esteem could be considerable. Eric Coleman mentioned a friend at Pomfret who he felt had been badly hurt by the experience of attending that prep school:

One of my good friends probably developed an inferiority complex as a result of being there. He wasn't a great student. He was a hell of an athlete, and I'm sure he got a great deal of gratification out of what he did as an athlete. . . . But most of his classmates probably looked down on him because he didn't do well academically as a student. I think around the time that it came for the members of our class to start receiving acceptances to colleges, it really began to take its toll on him. He wasn't encouraged to apply to the best schools, and even those that he did apply to were either slow in response or when they did respond the results were negative. I think that was the icing on the cake as far as damage to his self-esteem was concerned.

Even though almost all ABC graduates did attend college, some did not, and others may have done so, as Chris Dozier puts it, with "a lot of scars."

ROOMMATES AND FRIENDS

As they headed off to college, most ABC students again faced the challenge of living with unknown roommates. Most frequently the colleges matched ABC students with other incoming freshmen, some white and some black. When Jennifer Casey Pierre arrived as a freshman at Carnegie Mellon, she found that she had been assigned to room with a black woman from Pittsburgh (they remain good friends to this day). Ken Pettis's freshman-year roommate at Brown was a white Exeter graduate: "It was an assignment based, supposedly, on interests and background and things like that. Bob and I, as it turned out, had a lot in common, but there is nothing they could have told from an application. We had both gone to prep school and that was about it." The assignment worked out well; though they didn't room together the following year, they did become good friends and stayed in touch after graduating from Brown.

Although Pettis switched from his white Exeter roommate to another white roommate who had also attended Taft, the more frequent pattern was to switch from white roommates to black ones (or, when possible, to single rooms). Frank Borges's experience was not unusual. During his freshman year at Trinity, Borges was the only black in a suite of four males. During the next three years he roomed with blacks. Still, he remained good friends with those he had roomed with freshman year: "Callahan and I played football together, and so we were good friends, and Browse and I were good friends. I socialized with a whole group of folks."

Not only did most of the ABC graduates we interviewed socialize with whites, but many developed close friendships. In some cases, they have maintained these friendships. Alan Glenn described his relationship with a friend from Brown in the following way: "One of my friends is a white guy from Brown. I know him, he knows my family, I know his family. When we have functions, he comes to them; when his family has functions, I go to them. It's a friendship. His family accepts me as Alan Glenn a person, not Alan Glenn, Fred's black friend, and my family accepts him as Fred Cooper, Alan's friend, not Alan's white friend."

In a few cases, those we interviewed said that most of their college friends were white. For example, Barry Greene, at the time of our interview a vice president with F & M Bank, graduated from the Peddie School and returned to his hometown of Richmond, Virginia, to enroll at the University of Richmond. He was one of very few black students at the school. After some of his friends encouraged him to join Zeta Beta Tau, a Jewish fraternity, he did so. Many of his closest college friends were Southern white Jews. As he put it: "A black Catholic at a Southern Baptist school in a Jewish fraternity. It was kind of funny. I enjoyed it."

After graduating from Andover, Greg Googer found that most of his friends at Vanderbilt were not only white but also graduates of prep schools. He described his college friends, and the ease with which they recognized their shared prep school backgrounds, in the following way:

> The majority of my closest friends were from prep schools—day schools or boarding-school-type situations. Those were my closest friends. . . . The year I attended, there were five of us, I think, from Andover (myself the only black), a bunch of kids from Choate, Deerfield, a bunch of girls' schools out of Virginia like Madeira, schools of that nature. We all knew each other. We could identify each other from just walking around. Or we would hear that this person went to that school and go up and say 'Do you know . . . ?' and play the name game.

He remembered identifying one student as a prep school graduate and even being able to decipher which school he had attended:

> I walked up to him and said "I bet you went to a prep school." He said, "Yeah." I said, "I bet you went to Lawrenceville." He said, "How did you know that?" I said, "You look like a Lawrenceville prep." You know, he had a pink shirt on and had khakis on, and long blondish gold hair, and I don't know why, but that seemed to be the uniform of the day at Lawrenceville. He said, "Well, you're right, I did. I did go to prep school and I did go to Lawrenceville." That guy and I became very good friends after that.

However, developing and maintaining friendships with white students was not always easy. As was the case for some black students in prep school, many black students in college felt intense pressure from their black friends not to associate with white students. Cher Lewis described the dilemma she faced when she arrived at NYU in the fall of 1968:

I had a white Jewish roommate who was a real New Yorker, raised in Manhattan. To me she was Miss Savvy, a sophisticate, whom I really adored and thought was wonderful. My resident fellow, I wish I could remember her last name, but her first name was Martha, was totally black power—you know, you shouldn't even speak to white people. In our dormitory at one point a line was painted down the middle of the floor; blacks were to walk on one side. It was very difficult because I had both black and white friends.

Cher Lewis resisted the racial polarization she found at college. Some accepted or endorsed it. Following Sylvester Monroe's freshman year at Harvard, when he had roomed with a white friend from St. George's School, he roomed only with blacks, among whom were some who have become people of considerable impact and even renown. One roommate, Cornel West, became one of the most visible professors in America (West left Harvard for Princeton in a huff in early 2002 when the new president suggested he spend more time on scholarship and less time on rap CDs and political speeches). NFL and NBA fans around the country know another of his roommates, James Brown, a prominent sportscaster (formerly with CBS, now with Fox). "After freshman year," Monroe told us in our 1986 interview, "I led a completely black existence." In his senior year, as he was about to graduate, he wrote "Guest in a Strange House: A Black at Harvard," an article that was published in the *Saturday Review of Education*. In this article, he described the extent of his self-imposed isolation:

In the spring of my freshman year, during a humanities lecture, I suddenly found myself wondering what possible connection there could be between *Beowulf* (the subject of the lecture) and any solution to the problems of black people in America. Quickly I decided there was none, walked out of the lecture hall, and stopped attending the course. In the same way I canceled my participation in many other black-white activities that seemed to me of no particular value in preparing to help better the plight of all the black people I'd left back home in Chicago. I stopped eating at mixed dining-hall tables in order to avoid going through the empty motions of talking to white students. I stopped taking courses that weren't taught entirely in lectures, because I didn't want to talk with white teaching fellows.[15]

By his senior year, however, Monroe had come to suspect that some of his actions may have stemmed from insecurity and fear. In that same article, he included comments about black students at Harvard that, he recalled twenty years later, were "very unpopular" with his friends:

But the blame does not belong only to the whites. Blacks have been equally complacent about their own responsibilities as students. More and more young blacks who come here are becoming much too comfortable behind a superficial shield of black solidarity. Somehow they are blinded, it seems, by the small amount of effort it takes to isolate oneself from almost everything that isn't particularly appealing. In essence, too many blacks simply misuse the ideological strength of black solidarity as a kind of cover to dupe the white community into believing that behind their united front of blackness they are mature, self-confident, and functioning black individuals who know exactly what they want and how they will get it. But what I see and hear instead are insecure and frightened young black men and women.

He concluded the article with a painfully honest statement about his own insecurity and confusion: "Quite frankly, I feel very inadequate about my past three years at Harvard, which were lived in an almost totally isolated black vacuum. To be sure, I am thoroughly confused."[16] Part of his confusion was due to the lack of African American professors that he and his friends could turn to in times of trouble. But this is a story that Monroe himself needs to tell, and we can only encourage you to read the book that he is writing about the experiences that he and other African Americans had at Harvard as part of the class of 1973.[17]

Sylvester Monroe was not the only one of those we interviewed who sequestered himself within the black student community during his college years. Most, however, indicated that they resisted the pressure to do so. A number of those we interviewed recalled their refusal to eat all their meals at the all-black tables in the dining hall. Ken Pettis, for example, recalled: "I didn't always eat at the black table, and some people couldn't deal with that. I've always approached that as it's their problem, not mine." Some reacted angrily to the pressure. Monique Burns, who entered Harvard at about the time Sylvester Monroe was graduating, said she too felt the pressure to associate only with blacks:

I would not accept that pressure. I refused to. I actively refused to. The reason being, I had some friends from prep school who were white who had come to Harvard, and I was not going to stop speaking to them. I mean, that's absurd. As a human being, that was unacceptable to me. I was asked why I didn't come to sit at the black table and basically it was that if it were the green table or if it were the newspaper table I wouldn't have sat at it every night. I wanted to have the freedom to sit where I wanted. Sometimes I sat with other black students, sometimes I sat with white students, and sometimes I sat with mixtures of them. I hated this idea of sitting at the black table.

Also what angered me was what I saw as hypocrisy, because the students who were sitting at the black table, for the most part, and shouting "black power" and "we're not getting our rights," were actually black students who did not come through ABC but who were of upper-middle-class backgrounds, whose fathers were doctors, lawyers, and professors, and who lived in Scarsdale and other wealthy suburbs. As you know, there are black families of this type. They had not seen anything like what I had seen, so I thought to hell with this hypocrisy, I'll sit where I damn well please. That created some difficult moments as a freshman for me. As time went on I got to know other black students, but on my own terms, and because I liked something in them or in their character or they were friendly or because I dated them—but not because I "had to" or because they were black.

Jeffrey Palmer, at the time of our 1987 interview the president of a printing company in Chicago, and now a senior executive with Pep Boys in Philadelphia, was the first black to attend the Kimball Union Academy in more than sixty years (a black had graduated in 1903).[18] In our 1987 interview with him, he made it clear that he was not about to yield to pressures from either blacks or whites concerning who his friends should be when he got to Yale: "I had never succumbed to any pressures from anybody about anything, so the last thing somebody was going to do was to tell me who I could be friends with. And I have always had friends from every hue and complexion of life that there is, so nobody would even mention that to me. They would probably have had a fight on their hands if they did."

There is evidence that the tendency of most ABC graduates to reject racial separatism was not atypical for black college students attending predominantly white colleges in the early 1970s. During the 1972–73 academic year, William Boyd, then the president of ABC, oversaw a national study of blacks attending white colleges. With a grant from the Ford Foundation and assistance in the design and data analysis from Daniel Yankelovich, Inc., he hired fifty college-educated blacks to interview 785 black students at forty colleges and universities across the nation. "Separatism," he concluded, "is the balloon in which the largest amount of hot air has collected." He discovered that separatism was a "minority viewpoint among black students." Moreover, he concluded that black students at the more selective colleges were more likely to participate in all extracurricular activities and less likely to prefer all-black housing than black students attending less selective colleges.[19]

GRADES AND GRADUATION

Many of those we interviewed did exceptionally well as college students. Some were obviously academic stars. For example, Jesse Spikes graduated magna cum laude from Dartmouth, was elected to Phi Beta Kappa, and won a Rhodes Scholarship. Others did well enough to be accepted into the most competitive law schools, business schools, and other graduate programs in the country. Some we interviewed indicated that they were average students in college, and a few said they were below average. The systematic evaluation study of the performance of all ABC students from 1964 through 1972 again provides a valuable supplement to the information we derived from our interviews because the investigators were able to obtain college grades for 289 of the more than 1,000 ABC students who went to college. As college freshmen, they had a collective grade point average of 2.3 on a 4.0 scale, the same average reported for all freshmen nationally that year. Furthermore, at three "highly selective" colleges, the grade point averages for sixty-four ABC students were compared with those for a control group "matched on the basis of high school grades, SAT scores and family background." At one college, there was no significant difference between the two groups; at another, the ABC students had slightly higher grades than the control group; and at the third, the control group had slightly higher grades than the ABC group. The report concluded: "ABC students were enrolled in colleges which were more selective than those they would have attended had they not participated in the ABC Program. However, it cannot be claimed on the basis of this study that ABC students' grade point average in college was increased as a result of having attended independent school."[20]

This evaluation study also supports our interview finding that ABC students were likely to attend top graduate and professional programs after graduating from college. Among the first ABC college graduates, 40 percent entered graduate school immediately and at least half the others expressed the intention of doing so. They attended excellent graduate programs in a variety of fields. "It is apparent," the report noted, "that they were continuing in the elite channel which began with their enrollment in independent school nearly ten years ago."[21]

All evidence, then, suggests that the ABC program did a superb job of reaching its immediate goal of enrolling minority students in the best colleges and universities. The vast majority of ABC participants completed the program, almost all of the graduates went on to college, and many attended the most selective colleges, graduate schools, and professional programs in the nation. These results led an education writer for the *New York Times* to claim in 1982 that "the impact of the program is stunning when one considers the difference ABC has made in bringing minority students to the nation's most prestigious educational institutions."[22]

The evidence also suggests that most of the ABC students were integrated with white students on the campuses. Although some encountered prejudice and discrimination, isolation from whites was often of their own choosing (or due to pressure from other blacks). At least some integration was possible if they wanted it. It is now time to see if this pattern continued after college in terms of friendships, dating, and marriage. Then in later chapters we examine the extent to which these men and women achieved the goal ABC set for them of "assuming leadership roles in business, in the professions, in government and in the community."[23]

NOTES

1. Peter W. Cookson, Jr. and Caroline Hodges Persell, *Preparing for Power: America's Elite Boarding Schools* (New York: Basic Books, 1985), 171–172.

2. These data are based on the entering classes of 2001, as reported in the 2002 edition of the *Princeton Review*. The percentage of private school students in the incoming classes at other Ivy League schools in 2001 were as follows: Brown, 40 percent; Colgate, 33 percent; Dartmouth, 38 percent; Princeton, 40 percent; University of Pennsylvania, 45 percent; data were not available for Cornell.

3. David Karen, "Who Gets into Harvard? Selection and Exclusion," Ph.D. diss., Harvard University, 1985. The second study was by Robert Klitgaard, *Choosing Elites* (New York: Basic Books, 1985), Table 2.2. Both are cited in Caroline Hodges Persell and Peter W. Cookson, Jr., "Chartering and Bartering: Elite Education and Social Reproduction," *Social Problems* 33, no. 2 (1985): 116.

4. Persell and Cookson, "Chartering and Bartering," 119–121. A recent study of students at Harvard, Yale, and Princeton who graduated from high school between 1998 and 2001 demonstrated that students at elite private schools are much more likely to get into those three elite colleges than students from public schools (94 of the top 100 "feeder schools" were private). See Reshma Memon Yaqub, "Getting Inside the Ivy Gates," *Worth* (September 2002): 97–104.

5. Cookson and Persell, *Preparing for Power*, 198. The following studies demonstrate the advantages to one's career of having attended an elite prep school: George Pierson, *The Education of American Leaders* (New York: Praeger, 1969); Vincent Tinto, "College Origin and Patterns of Status Attainment," *Sociology of Work and Occupations* 7 (1980): 457–486; Michael Useem and Jerome Karabel, "Pathways to Corporate Management," *American Sociological Review* 5 (1986): 184–200.

6. Cookson and Persell, *Preparing for Power*, 177–178.

7. George Perry, "A Better Chance: Evaluation of Student Attitudes and Academic Performance, 1964–1972," study funded by the Alfred P. Sloan Foundation, the Henry Luce Foundation, and the New York Community Trust (March 1973), ERIC Document 075556, pp. 100–101.

8. Cited in John C. Hoy, "The Price of Diversity," *Saturday Review* (February 15, 1969): 96.

9. Ibid.

10. *A Better Chance News* (Spring 2000): 5.

11. Perry, "A Better Chance," 106.

12. This passage is quoted from an interview with William M. Lewis, Jr. that appears in Caroline V. Clarke, *Take a Lesson: Today's Black Achievers on How They Made It & What They Learned Along the Way* (New York: John Wiley and Sons, 2001), 125.

13. Such institutional insensitivity continues, at least at one California girls' school. See, for example, Erin M. Horvat and Anthony L. Antonio, "'Hey, Those Shoes Are Out of Uniform': African American Girls in an Elite High School and the Importance of Habitus," *Anthropology & Education Quarterly* 30, no. 3 (1999): 317–342. Although it is not at all clear that this school is typical of private schools in California, or in other parts of the country, the authors do provide some striking examples of how "ignorance and insensitivity of the wealthy families [of some students] culturally dominated the school," (p. 230).

14. Pat McPherson and Rita Goldman, "Schooled in Diversity: How Do Schools Change?" in *Schooled in Diversity: Stories of African-American Alumni*, edited by Pat McPherson (Philadelphia: Friends Council on Education, 2002), 5.

15. Sylvester Monroe, "Guest in a Strange House: A Black at Harvard," *Saturday Review of Education* (February 1973): 47.

16. Ibid., 48.

17. The working title of Monroe's book is *The Class of '73* and it will be published by Random House.

18. "Alumni Achievers' Award," *Kimball Union Alumni Magazine* (Spring 1986): 33.

19. William M. Boyd II, *Desegregating America's Colleges: A Nationwide Survey of Black Students, 1972–73* (New York: Praeger, 1974), 13, 35, 74–75. For a study of the experiences of fifty-six black women (thirty-one from the working class, twenty-five from the middle class) who were "pioneers" at predominantly white secondary schools and colleges in the late 1960s, see Elizabeth Higginbotham, *Too Much to Ask: Black Women in the Era of Integration* (Chapel Hill: University of North Carolina Press, 2001). She found that the eight working-class black women who attended "elite high schools" (private, parochial, and urban specialized high schools) did not become lifetime friends with their white high school classmates, but the nine middle-class black women who attended elite high schools "made good friends during this period of their lives . . . [and] some even indicated that they are still in touch with these friends" (139–140).

20. Perry, "A Better Chance," 111–116.

21. Ibid., 125–126.

22. Gene I. Maeroff, *Don't Blame the Kids: The Trouble with America's Public Schools* (New York: McGraw-Hill, 1982), 91.

23. "What ABC Is All About," Annual Report, 1975–76, 1.

5

Relationships: Friendships, Dating, and Marriage

When they headed off to their prep schools as young teenagers, black ABC students were worried about everything from heavier academic loads to how their old friends would treat them when they came home for holidays. It is unlikely that they spent much time worrying about whether or not they would end up marrying upper-class whites from their prep schools.

Worries about interracial dating and marriage, however, may have been very much on the minds of whites who were troubled by the integration of elite prep schools. After all, prep schools were the established meeting ground for upper-class children to find marriage partners. A Swedish observer of "the American dilemma," Gunnar Myrdal, asserted that concern about intermarriage "constitutes the center in the complex of attitudes which can be described as the 'common denominator' in the problem."[1] In this chapter, we examine the extent to which these white fears still existed, and the extent to which qualms about interracial dating and marriage affected the romantic relationships of ABC students.

FRIENDSHIPS

As already noted, many ABC students developed lifelong friendships with white classmates at their prep schools. This was especially true for those who entered the program in its early days, when they were the only, or one of very few, blacks at their schools. Many of our interviewees told us of regular phone calls to and visits with white friends they made while in prep school. Cher Lewis, for example, was one of four black women at the Abbott Academy in the late 1960s and yet, as we indicated in chapter 3, she is in closer contact with four white students than with the other three black students. They were members of each other's wedding parties. They speak regularly on the phone, even though they live in different parts of the country, and almost every year they gather as a group.

More than a few of the people we interviewed mentioned that in prep school they had become friends with Jewish students, who themselves only came to be treated somewhat more decently at private schools in the 1960s. In 1986, Greg Pennington told us: "One of my best friends is a Jewish guy who was one year ahead of me [at Western Reserve Academy]. I spend a lot of time with him now." And Alan Mitchell, a Worcester Academy graduate who at the time of our 1987 interview worked as an administrator for the Cleveland Board of Education, commented that while a student at Worcester, he had visited the homes of Jewish students. "I'd go home with Jewish guys from Chicago," he recalled, "and I'd go to bar mitzvahs and the whole bit, because I was interested. We were good friends and a lot of us still are."

Cecily Robbins, a graduate of Walnut Hill and the head of the Big Sisters program in Washington, D.C., at the time of our first interview with her, explained that it was more than her interest in people of various backgrounds that led to her friendships with Jewish girls. As she put it: "I came from an entirely working-class neighborhood [in Philadelphia]. My mother was born in the house where my family still resides. The neighborhood was not predominantly anything. . . . So when I went to WASP, blond New England, I met some Jewish girls and I formed some real tight friendships with them. I found more ethnicity. I was comfortable with myself and found more ethnicity in some of the other girls. They weren't all WASPS. I mean, there's nothing wrong with being WASP, but it's just that when you come from a black, Catholic, West Indian background and you live in an Italian neighborhood and you're thrown into WASP New England, it is a little bit of 'Where do I fit in? I don't.'"

In the previous chapter, we noted that Barry Greene had joined Zeta Beta Tau, a Jewish fraternity, while in college and that among his closest friends in Richmond were former fraternity brothers who are Jewish. Several others also noted that they had become close friends with Jewish students while in college. There were clearly close and lasting bonds established between some black ABC students and Jews. We will return to this theme when we discuss intermarriage; as we will see, when black ABC students did marry whites, they were likely to marry Jews.

DATING

In our interviews, we asked each ABC graduate if he or she had dated interracially while in prep school. Their responses varied.

As we indicated in chapter 3, many ABC graduates found social life at prep school to be somewhere between minimal and nonexistent. One responded to our question about social life by asking in return, "What social life?" Some went on to say that they paid a price when they were in college. Few had anything positive to say about the system of mixers whereby they were paired with opposite-sex students from other schools. Some simply didn't date in prep school. For some ABC students, the only social life they had took place when they returned home for summers and holidays.

Jeffrey Palmer, for example, when asked about his social life at Kimball Union, replied:

> At Kimball Union, there wasn't any. It was an all-boys' school. There wasn't any, at least on any basis that would allow me to maintain my sanity. There were dances, but this was 1965, 1966, and there wasn't a whole lot of mixing, at least openly. Obviously there were people sneaking off in the corner, but black people were not received in New England in the social environment very well at that time. So when the Glee Club visited the girls' schools, nobody ever said anything to me, but the reception was less than warm. But I had been in that situation before, so it didn't bother me.

Some students, however, especially those who entered prep school a few years after Palmer, when the number of black students had increased dramatically, did lead active social lives, primarily with other black students at their own or a nearby school. Many drew on the social network that sprung up among black students as a result of friendships made during the summer orientation program and at the various ABC conferences that were held.

Some said that while in prep school they dated white students. These relationships rarely progressed beyond the stage of casual dating. Christine Dozier recalled that the males at nearby Andover, both black and white, were challenged by the novelty of interacting with females of a different race:

> So there was a lot of that running back and forth. . . . We went to mixers and dances and things like that, but it was always on a very superficial level. Nothing real serious. And the guys were typical teenage guys, you know, one thing on their mind and they didn't care really if it was black or white. It was basically all the same to them, especially in that kind of prep school environment where you go to an all-boys' school or all-girls' school. It always ends up being the focal point of any mixer any time they get together. Socially, I didn't have those kinds of problems, and there wasn't really a lot of time for socializing. Intentionally, it was kept to a minimum.

Her former classmate, Cher Lewis, dated both whites and blacks while at Abbott Academy, but she too said of these prep school relationships: "None was intense and they were all short-lived."

Interracial dating, however, was not inevitably superficial, casual, or short-lived. At times, it could be rife with psychological, practical, and long-term complexities. One man recalled spending two prep-school vacations at the home of his white girlfriend. Because of that relationship and his friendship with other white students, he was given a hard time by the other black students; he said his wife still has "problems dealing with" the fact that he dated white women in prep school and in college.

Greg Pennington said that he and his black ABC friends at Western Reserve Academy dated both blacks and whites and that at times this led to uncomfortable situations. One night, he recalled, he and his roommate, Charles, who was also black, got a phone call from two white women they had been dating:

> They wanted to know if we wanted to go to a ball game with them, and I got on the phone and Beth says, "Do y'all want to go to a basketball game?" So I said yes and when I hung up the phone I said, "Ravenna, is that a black school or a white school?" We didn't know, but we decided to go. . . . We took off to this basketball game and there was one black basketball player on the court and all the stands were on one side. . . . During halftime I looked up and saw this group of black students with denim jackets and black leather gloves and shades on and everything. . . . Now at the time I was 160 pounds and my roommate was about 195 to 200 pounds and six foot five. So this group of black students as they walk past look up and see us with these two white girls and one of them says, "Hey," and he gave me the power sign. I looked at Charles to see if he wants to get involved with this potential altercation, and he looked every which way except at these guys, so I gave them back this power sign. . . . The guy says "That's all I wanted to know," and walked out. . . . I was more comfortable going in a white environment with a white date than I would have been going in an all-black or predominantly black environment.

Though Pennington found that his interracial activities were more likely to be challenged by blacks than whites, in some cases, not surprisingly, problems stemmed from the objections of white parents. Glenn Boxx, at the time of our 1987 interview a financial advisor for the Bell Telephone system in Chicago, recalled that when he was a student at the Shattuck School in Faribault, Minnesota, there was just one black female student at the nearby girls' school, and he did not date her. He found that the students did not seem to be uncomfortable with blacks dating whites, but their parents were. In fact, he dated one woman for a while in his junior year until, as he put it, "We got into a big row with her parents—well, not her parents, her father." He had vivid memories of the graduation ceremony that year. Shattuck was a military school, and traditionally the seniors turned their positions over to juniors for the ceremony. He was given a company to lead in the graduation march. As he passed the parade stand, giving orders to his company, he remembers staring into the eyes of the father of his former girlfriend, who was there to watch the ceremony. His girlfriend's father seemed surprised to see him in a position of such authority, sending his (mostly white) men through their military paces.

Many indicated that if they wanted to date they had to date whites simply because there were so few blacks in their schools. The following comment by Greg Googer, describing his experiences dating white women while a student at Andover, reflects the practical nature of these relationships (it also reflects how far he and other prep school students were from considering marrying the women they dated): "Dating at Andover was kind of hard. . . . I went out with some of the girls at Andover. There was a limited number of black females there. There was not always an opportunity to go out with them. Someone else would have ties with those people. Sometimes when you went to a dance you would go with a white female, or go alone. I chose not to just go alone. Sometimes, I chose to go to a dance with white people. . . . We all were really dating what was available to us. It wasn't that I was going to take this girl home and marry her and have mixed babies. It was no big deal. It was basically I had to have a date."

The wish for more social contact with other blacks was reflected in a number of anecdotes. Janice Peters recalled a mixer she and her Milton Academy classmates went to at a New England boys' school. She was one of just two or three black students at Milton; the school they were visiting had twenty or thirty black students. When she and the other black women got off the bus, all of the black students at the host prep school—gathered to see the arriving women—broke into applause. Similarly, Frank Borges recalled that he and the other black students at Millbrook loved to play sports against Windsor Mountain, a coed school in the Berkshires, because the school had some black women students: "We used to love to go up there to Windsor Mountain because for about two minutes we got to see a black female."

Though many indicated that they continued to date whites as well as blacks in college, by the time they left college, relatively few black ABC graduates continued to date whites. Some attributed this to less tolerance of interracial relationships in their working environments than in their college environments. Alan Glenn, for example, said that he had dated both whites and blacks while at Hotchkiss and at Brown but had not dated whites since graduating from Brown: "I haven't dated a white woman since Brown, not because I don't think I should but because I haven't run into any white women that I wanted to date. But I also think that is due to the fact that in corporate America I don't think that is readily accepted as it is in the academic world. Not at all, to be quite honest."

Our interview with a more recent ABC graduate, Anthony Ducret, the 1995 Groton graduate, helps to shed light on the transition from college to the working world in terms of dating partners. Even though Ducret attended prep school and college more than twenty years after most of the ABC graduates in our study, his description of who he dated while in college and who he has dated since graduating from college helps us to understand both the internal and external pressures on ABC graduates when it comes to interracial dating.

At the time of our interview in October 2001, Ducret was living in New York City after graduating from Wesleyan in 1999 as a double major in theater studies and economics. At Wesleyan he lived with a group of five guys, all of whom were black, a group that he still considers his "primary friendship group." His friendships at Wesleyan, however, extended beyond the community of color, and so, too, did his dating partners. As he explained it, "wherever my interests took me, I would meet people and, you know, you're in college—it's all about absorbing as much as you possibly can."

Both he and his roommates spent time with various groups of friends. Those who played baseball or lacrosse hung out with the guys on those teams. Tony spent time with his theater studies friends and with other members of the "secret society" he had been asked to join at the end of his junior year, The Mystical Seven. On a typical Saturday night while he was at Wesleyan, he might spend some of the evening at a party at the Malcolm X House, and some of the evening at another party with a group of students that consisted mostly of New Yorkers from the upper west side who had attended prep schools. He felt no pressure from his friends to socialize exclusively with students of color.

Although aware that some students of color, and especially African American women on campus, were unhappy when African American men dated white women, he basically applied the same approach he used with friendships to his choices of dating partners. As he put it, "My romantic interests always coincided with genuine shared interests, like we're studying something together, or we're in a class together, and this included people from the student of color community and people outside the student of color community. I didn't have a problem with meeting someone outside the student of color community and saying, 'I'm interested in you, romantically,' and being able to pursue that."

Since graduation, however, he has looked "more for women of color." He explains the change he has undergone in the following way:

A lot of things that you could ignore in high school and college come into sharper focus when you leave school. Given my background and my experiences that are really, really specialized, I feel that if I'm going to date a person seriously I need someone who can handle the complexity of who I am and part of that can come from just understanding what it's like to be ethnic, being able to sympathize with what that is, what that means, and how that's affected me.

I also think there's still a lot of negative energy attached to interracial dating. I have an [African American male] friend living in the city with his [white] girlfriend. He tells me that it's very, very hard to be out in public. Nothing overt. No one is going to come up to you and say anything, but you get looks, curious looks, and it feels uncomfortable. I know exactly what he means because there will be times when just doing my job I end up having to walk down the street with a co-worker who happens to be a white woman. Everyone assumes that when you walk with a woman in New York she's your girl. You get all these weird stares from people, and, I mean, if you're strong enough of mind you should be able to ignore the stares, but it is distracting and it wears you down. . . . These days, I just want somebody who can really understand and someone who I can feel comfortable with, where there's as little stress as possible. Relationships are hard on their own without having the external stress.

Anthony Ducret, then, identifies both internal needs and external pressures that make it less likely that he will date across racial lines now that he has left the relatively comfortable environment of the university campus ("You're in college—it's all about absorbing as much as you possibly can"). The internal needs are based on his desire that a potential partner can understand the unusual life he has led in which, as a young black male, he had left his single mother in Houston, Texas, to spend three years at Groton and then four years at Wesleyan. Simultaneously acknowledging that relationships are hard enough on their own, he wants to avoid the additional pressures externally created by a world—even in cosmopolitan New York City at the beginning of the twenty-first century—that make those in interracial relationships feel uncomfortable.

MARRIAGE

Before turning to a consideration of marriage among the ABC students, we wish to note a few relevant findings from the extensive literature on marriage patterns in American culture.

- Research by social psychologists and sociologists has shown that people are most likely to marry those who live nearby. This phenomenon, which social scientists have called "residential propinquity," holds for friendship as well as marriage patterns; it was first systematically applied to marriage in 1931 through a study of marriage license applications in

Philadelphia. At that time, one out of every four couples lived within two blocks of each other, and the proportion of marriages decreased as the distance between marrying partners increased. This pattern has been found more recently in cities throughout America (and in other countries).[2]

- People who marry tend to share many similarities, including religion, social class, attitudes, and values. They also tend to be of the same race. In spite of an increase in interracial marriages that occurred during the civil rights movement of the 1960s, the proportion of interracial marriages in the total population has remained quite small. As of the 1960 census, only 4 in 1,000 marriages were interracial, and only 1.2 in 1,000 were between blacks and whites. As of 1990, 28 marriages per 1,000 were interracial, and only 4.1 per 1,000 were between blacks and whites. The figures for overall intermarriages were actually a bit lower by 2000 (26 per 1,000 marriages), but slightly higher for black/white intermarriages (6.4 per 1,000). In the case of black/white intermarriages, in the various censuses since 1970, between 63 and 77 percent have included black men and white women.[3]
- Research on "marital timing" (the age at which people marry) indicates that both black men and black women marry later than white men or white women. Moreover, for women, black or white, those who enroll in four-year colleges or universities marry later than those who do not.[4]

As of our initial round of interviews between 1986 and 1988, about 60 percent of the ABC graduates had been married at one time or another (some more than once), but only 50 percent were currently married. Almost all—but not all—married other blacks, but no simple pattern emerged. Some married friends they had known growing up or had met when they returned home to visit or live. Some married people they had met in college or graduate school. Some married people they met once they entered careers. And some married whites. But not all patterns were equally satisfactory. We will examine each of these marriage patterns separately.

Marriage Partners from Back Home

Almost 20 percent of the ABC graduates we interviewed first married people they knew from their neighborhoods. One of these marriages ended seven years later when the partner drowned tragically in a boating accident. All the others ended either in divorce or separation.

Jeffrey Palmer, who left Steubenville, Ohio, to attend Kimball Union and then Yale, married a woman he had grown up with in Steubenville. They remained together for six years before divorcing. He continues to be somewhat puzzled by the whole relationship: "To tell you the truth, I don't know how the hell that happened. I have often tried to figure it out. . . . You would think there would be no rational reason that I would marry her. All of the sociological things—people say, 'Well, this guy has gone away, and done this, and this is where he is headed'—you put all those things in a line and it wouldn't equal me marrying her. But, at the same time, we were happy for a while and I was never sorry that I did it. But I go back and look at it and it seems bizarre. We didn't have anything in common."

Another of those we interviewed described his marriage to a woman from his hometown. After graduating from prep school and college, he returned to live in the town in which he had grown up. There he met and married a woman four years younger than he—she had just graduated from high school. They thought they could overcome their various differences, including their differences in age and education; they couldn't and divorced after five years.

Cecily Robbins, who grew up in Philadelphia and then attended Walnut Hill and George Washington University, did not marry someone from her own neighborhood, but she did marry a man with whom she had little in common. He had dropped out of high school and had very different views than she had. Though their differences were partly what attracted her to him initially, she found that ultimately these differences made it impossible for them to stay together. As she explained in our initial interview, shortly before the divorce was final: "He was a police officer when I met him. I had decided that all these nice little middle-class men in suits were a drag, and I figured why not become involved with someone who was more along the lines of a blue-collar person. His background was not anywhere near mine. That's one of the problems that we had. Educationally, sociologically, ideologically, politically—should I go on? I thought we were going to complement one another, but we did not. We ended up clashing a lot."

College and Graduate School Romances

Slightly more than one-fourth of the ABC graduates we interviewed met their partners while in college or graduate school. For instance, LaPearl Winfrey met her husband when they were both undergraduates at Oberlin. Despite the strains of a three-year period when she was in New York doing doctoral work in psychology while her husband and daughter remained in Chicago, their marriage has survived. She recalls with a measure of pride that although "nobody expected our marriage to last, we managed." In 2001, she told us that she and her husband had recently celebrated their twenty-seventh anniversary. Greg Pennington, also a psychologist, met his wife when he was an undergraduate at Harvard and she was an undergraduate at Wellesley. And Alan Mitchell met his first wife when they were both studying at Case Western Reserve (he was studying architecture, and she, having graduated from Wellesley, was working on a master's degree).

Some of the ABC graduates, almost all of whom were from backgrounds that included unmistakable poverty, married partners whose parents came from the black middle class. One of those we interviewed said that his wife's background was very different from his own. Her parents, both of whom worked, "knew what they wanted for their kids and they did everything they could to get them there." He added that as a result of her parents' efforts, "If you'll excuse the expression, my wife is a Black JAP [Jewish American Princess]."

Others saw such differences as potential problems and consciously chose to marry blacks who had economic backgrounds similar to their own. One of those we interviewed noted that while in college he had almost married a black woman who had a middle-class background, but decided against it. He had gone home with her to visit her family and found himself uncomfortably aware of how different her background was from his. He worried that she might not understand or be sympathetic toward his mother, who was struggling on her own—his parents were divorced—to make ends meet for a large family. He broke off the relationship. He later married another black woman he met in college who was from a family that, like his own, had struggled economically.

Though none of those we interviewed had married other ABC students, we did hear about such marriages. In one case, two ABC students fell in love while in prep school, applied to and attended the same university, and married during their undergraduate years. In another, perhaps more expected pattern, two people who met originally as ABC students during the summer program began to date seriously when they were students at the same college, fell in love, and married. In August 2000, the *New York Times* featured a story about the marriage between Althea Beaton and Malik Ducard, each of whom is a graduate of the ABC program. She attended Miss Porter's ("She's a Miss Porter's girl through and through" said one of her friends) and he was a student at Pomfret. They first met as undergraduates at Columbia University in the early 1990s, and subsequently ended up working next to one another at Young & Rubicam, the advertising agency. According to the *Times*, one reason she wanted to marry him was that he fit in so well with her family. "The men in my family had humble beginnings," she said. "They worked hard, studied hard and reached a level of success, and Malik is cut from that same cloth."[5]

Degrees First, Marriages Later

Many of those we interviewed—almost a third—did not marry until they were out of school and in the working world. For the most part, these ABC graduates, with their degrees (and often advanced degrees) from prestigious schools, married other people who were well educated. For example, Doris McMillon, the newscaster, married a Haitian physician, and Calvin Dorsey, who has degrees from Stanford and the University of Mississippi, married a black woman he met in Atlanta who was a third-generation college graduate. In some cases, ABC graduates met their husbands or wives through their work. For example, Jeffrey Palmer met his second wife (who graduated with honors from the University of Illinois) when he was in the advertising business; at the time of our 1987 interview, she was working as the creative director of a small, black advertising agency.

Marrying Whites

We have noted the relative infrequency of marriages between blacks and whites in America. Few black ABC students married whites, but they did marry whites more often than occurs in the country at large. We estimate that between 5 and 10 percent of the ABC graduates married whites.

Bobette Reed's marriage to Jeffrey Kahn is particularly intriguing because it highlights quite clearly both their differences and their similarities. After graduating from Williams College in 1973 with a degree in religion, Bobette Reed entered the Harvard Divinity School. While there, she worked at two jobs in order to support herself. The first was at the Divinity School Bookstore and the second was with the Harvard University police department. She started as a security guard for the police department and was soon promoted to a position in which she supervised the security patrol. It was in this capacity that she met Jeffrey Kahn. Not long before, Harvard's Fogg Museum had been broken into and valuable paintings had been stolen. Jeffrey Kahn—a student at the Harvard Business School—had set up a new computer system that was being used by the Harvard police. Like Bobette, he was working part time for the Harvard University police department to help pay for his schooling. Unlike Bobette, he had experience in criminal work as a former New York City policeman. And unlike Bobette, an Episcopalian soon to be ordained as a deacon, Jeffrey Kahn was Jewish. He had grown up in Hartford, had attended a New England prep school (Loomis), and had received his bachelor's degree from Yale.

Though a rabbi married them, there was never any discussion of Bobette's converting to Judaism. Bobette received counseling from her priest. She described their conversation: "When I went to my priest, he said, 'Bobette, is it the same God?' and I said, 'Of course it is.' He said, 'Well, what's the difference?' I said, 'You know what the difference is. The Jews believe that Jesus Christ is not the Messiah, and indeed, if there is a Messiah, he is yet to come.' And he said, 'Well, yes. Would you have any problems raising your children as Jews? Is there anything besides that that you do not believe in?' I guess if I were picky there would be some things, but I said 'No.' And he said, 'Well, then, I have no problem.'"

At the time of our 1987 interview, they did not yet have children. Bobette attended church every Sunday, and Jeffrey attended temple periodically (not every week, but more often than just during the High Holidays of Rosh Hashanah and Yom Kippur). Though it might appear that they had vast differences to overcome, Bobette's view was that they had many important things in common: "Even though we come from very different kinds of socioeconomic backgrounds, they're really not that different. When you look at the private school, when you look at the colleges, when you look at the graduate schools, they really begin to merge."

In 1997, Bobette and Jeffrey adopted twin daughters from China. When we spoke in August 2001, we reminded her that fourteen years earlier she had said that if she and Jeffrey were to have children, they would be raised as Jews. When we then asked in which religious tradition her daughters were being raised, she laughed and replied: "I'm true to form. They're Jewish."

Notably, Bobette Reed Kahn was not the only ABC graduate we interviewed who married a white, Jewish man. As we have mentioned in the opening chapter, Cher Lewis, born in Richmond, educated at the Abbott School, NYU, and the Columbia School of Business, also married a white, Jewish man. "We are of different religions," she explained when we interviewed her in 1987. "We celebrate some Jewish holidays, we celebrate public holidays. So we sort of do both." They, too, have twin daughters, three-and-a-half years old at the time of the 1986 interview. The children were attending a neighborhood nursery school run by the First Presbyterian Church ("We haven't told his mother the name of the nursery school," she confided), but they had just been accepted into a private nondenominational school for gifted children.

Fifteen years later, when we spoke with Cher Lewis in November 2001, she told us that she and her husband had separated and divorced in the mid-1990s, when the twins were in the tenth grade. The girls had attended Hebrew school, and, although Cher never converted to Judaism, she had been active in the temple to which they belong. Her daughters think of themselves as Jewish (one even lights candles on Friday nights), and, as Cher also was quick to note, "They have always thought of themselves as black."

Of the thirty-eight ABC graduates we interviewed between 1986 and 1988, three married whites, and two of the three married Jews. The third interracial marriage was between a black male and a white woman he met in college; about four years later they were divorced.

In order to gain a larger picture of the patterns we were interested in—not just marital patterns, but friendship and career patterns as well—we asked each ABC graduate to tell us about other ABC students he or she knew from the summer program, prep school, or college. This provided us with information about a much larger sample of ABC graduates—a few hundred instead of thirty-eight. On the basis of this larger but less direct sample, we can draw the same general conclusion that we have drawn from our interview sample: most black ABC students did not marry whites, but the rather small percentage who did is surely greater than the national figure. The indirect sample reinforces our estimate that between 5 and 10 percent of the black ABC graduates married whites. And this indirect sample also provides supporting evidence for our finding that when intermarriage did occur, the white partner was likely to be Jewish.[6]

Even with this expanded sample, our sample is too small to draw any clear conclusions about intermarriage between blacks and Jews, but these findings were part of an ongoing pattern we've alluded to earlier in the book indicating that many black ABC students have had especially good relationships with Jews at various stages of their lives. For many ABC graduates, teachers and counselors with whom they were close at their inner city schools, community sponsors and mentors, prep school, college and graduate school friends, and valued colleagues, have been Jewish. Jeffrey Palmer (who did not marry a Jewish woman—in any of his three marriages) provides what is perhaps an exaggerated but useful example of the point we wish to make. The key person back in Steubenville, Ohio, who encouraged him to pursue the ABC program was Art Kobacher, a successful Jewish businessman who owned a chain of shoe stores. Fifteen years after Palmer graduated from Yale, Kobacher persuaded him to open and manage some stores in Chicago (they were partners for two years before Palmer sold the business back to Kobacher, who has remained a lifelong friend). While he was working for J. Walter Thompson in Chicago in the late 1970s, Palmer became friendly with a Jewish colleague who twenty-five years later he considers his best friend (as he put it in our interview in June 2002, "we became good buddies—it's now been over twenty-five years, and he's probably my very best friend").

We agree with those social scientists who argue that people who are mistreated by a society develop a healthy skepticism about its culture and pretensions. They develop "double vision" and as a result may be more sensitive to and put off by sham and hypocrisy. Jews and blacks thus may share some common perspectives on American society that bring them closer despite other cultural differences.[7]

Still Unmarried after All These Years

As of the initial interviews from 1986 to 1988, about 40 percent of both the men and the women we interviewed had never married. For the most part, the men did not express concern about this but the women did.

Many of the men who had not married indicated that they had been so dedicated to their careers that they had not had the time for, nor were they willing to make a commitment to, marriage. Jesse Spikes is an example. "People used to ask me," he said, "'Why have you never gotten married?' I never had time. There were things I wanted to do, and there was no time in my life for this the way I saw it. There were things I had to do."

In what at times were painfully honest self-analyses, some of the female ABC graduates we interviewed indicated that because of loneliness, or the feeling that time was running out on their childbearing years, or both, they were reassessing their commitment to their careers. One made it clear that her commitment to her career, especially as a black woman, had taken its toll "in sleepless nights, in stress, and in breaking down of social life." The day we spoke with her, she acknowledged that she was "feeling a little lonely and alienated." As she explored the nature of her alienation, she eventually discussed marriage:

> At different points of my life I have felt different kinds of alienation. Initially, when I was first at prep school, I felt a kind of alienation from my parents. There have been other kinds of alienation. What I feel to the greatest extent now, oddly enough, even though I have a number of friends who are from that prep school world, and from [college], is that I feel a certain social alienation and I think I'll always have that. I'll never be here nor there. I'll never be a full member of that club. Yes, I can have friends that are from prep school and yes, I can have friends from college. We can have very warm relationships and we do. Some of my friends are married and I feel close to their husbands and children. But, on many levels, there are times when I just feel that I don't fit in. And yet, on so many other levels, I do feel like a part of that world, and that world is largely a white world. I've never talked so much about black and white as I have with you today. . . . Socially, I'm beginning to think about things now, like marriage. In some ways it would be very natural for me to marry someone who was white and of a certain class and educated. Some ways that would cause all kinds of difficulties and does create difficulties for me.

Another of the women we interviewed was also reassessing the nature of her social life. When asked if she was married, she responded by saying: "I'm single. Oh, God, sometimes I think I always will be. I hope to not always be. I'd like very much to get married." She had been involved with a man for ten years and was in the midst of asking herself (and presumably him) questions about the future of this relationship. Ten years earlier, she had met the man she refers to as her "preferred mate." They dated for three years while both were in the same city, but he subsequently moved. Despite the distance, they continued to see each other.

She acknowledged that for a long time the intermittent nature of the relationship had been just what she wanted because it allowed her to pursue her career, a career that required long working hours. But she wasn't so sure that long-distance love was what she wanted in the future. In her mid-thirties, she was thinking more and more about getting married. As a result, she was having second thoughts about the relationship and was "sort of aggressively pushing for some change." Recently, she had been seeing this preferred mate less often than in the past. Though they still talked on the phone a few times a week, they were seeing each other only every other month or so. As she put it: "Time is still an element, a major, major element. [He] is my preferred mate. As long as I have any hope of having him, then I don't really want to bother with anybody else. But at some point you cut your losses. That's a horrible thing to say, but ten years is a long time." (Within a few months of this interview, they were married.)

Among these ABC graduates, then, interracial friendships are relatively common and long lasting; interracial marriage is rare. Given the elite cultural styles of many of the ABC graduates, along with their frequent interactions with whites, the small number of intermarriages is one piece of evidence that class similarities cannot counteract racial differences as readily as they do religious ones, even at the top levels of the American social ladder. This finding reinforces what has been shown at the middle levels of American society, where Hispanics and Asian Americans are far more likely to marry Anglos than blacks are.[8]

The picture that is emerging, then, reveals that the further we move into adult life, the more difficult the integration process becomes. But what about the world of work and governance? How are the ABC graduates doing in their careers, and have any of them attained positions of power?

NOTES

1. The quotation from Myrdal is cited in Joseph R. Washington, Jr., *Marriage in Black and White* (Boston: Beacon Press, 1970), 8. In Washington's view, marriage between blacks and whites is "our fundamental fear." He goes on to assert "it is the American problem" (1, 4).

2. Zick Rubin, *Liking and Loving* (New York: Holt, Rinehart and Winston, 1973), 194.

3. These data are drawn from the U. S. Bureau of the Census, Current Population Reports, Series P20-537, "America's Families and Living Arrangements: March

2000," "Interracial Married Couples: 1960 to Present," and "Interracial Married Couples: 1980 to Present." See also Rubin, *Liking and Loving,* 197, George E. Simpson and J. Milton Yinger, *Racial and Cultural Minorities: An Analysis of Prejudice and Discrimination,* 5th ed. (New York: Plenum Press, 1985), 298–299; and David Heer, "The Prevalence of Black White Marriage in the U.S., 1960–1970," *Journal of Marriage and the Family* 35 (1974): 246–258; and Jerry A. Jacobs and Teresa Labov, "Sex Differences in Intermarriage: Exchange Theory Reconsidered," unpublished paper, Department of Sociology, University of Pennsylvania, September 1995.

4. Jay D. Teachman, Karen A. Polonko, and Geoffrey K. Leigh, "Marital Timing: Race and Sex Comparisons," *Social Forces* 66, no. 1 (1987): 239–268. Their finding that blacks marry at a "slower pace" than whites is based on longitudinal data from a national sample of twenty thousand respondents tested initially in 1972 and followed up in 1973, 1974, 1976, and 1979. See, also, Rosalind Berkowitz King and Jenifer L. Bratter, "The Path to Interracial Mate Selection: Choosing First Partners and Husbands Across Racial Lines," paper presented at the annual meetings of the American Sociological Association, Anaheim, California, August 2001.

5. Lois Smith Brady, "Vows: Althea Beaton and Malik Ducard," *New York Times,* August 20, 2000, 37. As of October 2002, Malik Ducard was executive director of business development and financial planning at MGM Studios in Santa Monica, California. He and Althea Beaton have a son, born in August 2002.

6. It is not surprising, then, that the first interracial couple described in *Newsweek*'s special feature "Colorblind Love" consisted of a black and a Jew—Chuck and Lois Bronz (Barbara Kantrowitz, "Colorblind Love," *Newsweek,* March 7, 1988, 40–41). An article in the *Wall Street Journal* points out that blacks and Jews have had close partnerships in the corporate world also. See Jonathan Kaufman, "As Blacks Rise High in the Executive Suite, CEO Is Often Jewish," *Wall Street Journal,* April 22, 1998, 1. Among the many prominent Americans whose fathers were black and whose mothers were white and Jewish are Lani Guinier (the law school professor whose nomination as the head of the civil rights division of the Justice Department was withdrawn by Bill Clinton after heated opposition from conservatives), Walter Mosley (the acclaimed mystery writer), James McBride (the author of the bestselling *The Color of Water: A Black Man's Tribute to His White Mother*), and jazz saxophonist Joshua Redmon.

7. See, for example, Karen Brodkin, *How Jews Became White Folks and What that Says about Race in America* (New Brunswick, N.J.: Rutgers University Press, 1998).

8. Thomas F. Pettigrew, "Integration and Pluralism," in *Modern Racism: Profiles in Controversy,* ed. Phyliss A. Katz and Dalmas A. Taylor (New York: Plenum Press, 1988); Jerry A. Jacobs and Teresa Labov, "Asian Brides, Anglo Grooms: Asian Exceptionalism in Intermarriage," unpublished paper, Department of Sociology, University of Pennsylvania, October 1995; and U. S. Bureau of the Census, 1960, 1970, and 1980, Subject Reports on Marital Status and 1991 and 1992 Current Population Reports, P20-537, "America's Families and Living Arrangements: March 2000," "Interracial Married Couples: 1960 to Present," and "Interracial Married Couples: 1980 to Present."

6

Careers

At the same time that Sylvester Monroe, Cher Lewis, and the other early ABC students were receiving the finest prep school and college educations the country has to offer, the job market for educated blacks was undergoing dramatic changes. Prior to the 1960s, career choices for blacks with advanced degrees were severely limited. Education was the major most frequently chosen by black college students, and black college graduates who did not pursue careers in education were most likely to go into social work. A select few went on to become doctors or dentists, and an even smaller number became lawyers; these black professionals typically attended traditionally black colleges and lived and practiced in black neighborhoods.

As black ABC students entered the job market in the late 1960s and early 1970s with undergraduate and graduate degrees from schools like Harvard, Dartmouth, and the University of Pennsylvania, they could not have been better positioned to take advantage of the increasing number of white-collar jobs in the changing economy and the employment opportunities created for educated African Americans by the civil rights movement. A new black middle class was emerging that was no longer based primarily in business and professions serving the black community, but in jobs in the larger society that previously had been closed to blacks. Blacks with advanced degrees were particularly sought after. According to a 1976 report prepared for the Carnegie Commission on Higher Education: "At the top of the educational hierarchy black workers with graduate training obtained increases in income far above those of comparable whites, with the result that the economic incentive for black investments in post-bachelor's study came to exceed that for white investments."[1] Here we see very clearly that the relationship between race and class seemed to be in for a dramatic change.

In addition to their excellent formal educations, ABC graduates had two other assets that gave them a strong advantage in the job market: the ability to talk with anyone about anything, and the ability to benefit from the access to influential people they had gained as a result of attending elite schools. In sociological terms, they acquired cultural capital (various forms of knowledge and skills) and social capital (useful interpersonal connections) due to the booster shot given to them by the ABC program.

During our interviews, a number of the ABC graduates referred to their ability to feel comfortable in a variety of settings. Some noted that they had developed this quality while they were ABC students. For example, William Foster, at the time of our 1986 interview employed by Xerox Educational Publications, and now a writer and an associate professor of English at Naugatuck Valley Community College in Waterbury, Connecticut, described his behavior with some friends of his wealthy white in-laws: "I have such eclectic taste in so many things. I mean, I'm able to converse with anybody on almost anything. I went to someone's house, a marvelous home, and I felt a little out of place until I saw they had some Oriental prints, and I was saying, 'Isn't this from the such and such dynasty?' The guy perked right up. It worked out well. I felt very comfortable."

Similarly, Eric Coleman, now a state senator and the assistant majority leader in the state legislature in Connecticut, emphasized that his experiences as an ABC student at Pomfret, and then as an undergraduate at Columbia, contributed to his ability to move comfortably in very different settings: "I feel like I can relate to a broad spectrum of people. I'm comfortable walking down Albany Avenue in Hartford, which is the commercial strip in what would be considered a ghetto, and I feel comfortable interacting with the Chamber of Commerce and the corporate community. Whether they are black or white, I don't think there are very many people who can feel comfortable in the spectrum of interactions that one finds oneself in."

Maccene Brown, a lawyer in Durham, North Carolina, explained how her prep school experience as the only black student in her class at Miss Hall's contributed to her ability to work effectively with and feel comfortable around whites: "When you've gone to school with people who are truly rich, you just don't get impressed with things as easily as other people are. . . . It made me wiser to white people in a lot of ways. . . . You tend not to put the people of another ethnic group on a pedestal. You feel that you can compete if you have to." She then added a very important and revealing comment that we heard echoed in other interviews: "You're comfortable in the presence of folks who are not of your own ethnic group—and a lot of black people are still not comfortable around white folks." Although black prep school graduates may be more likely to notice this discomfort, other blacks who are aware of it would probably be less likely to mention it to a white interviewer.

Greg Googer observed that his years at Andover helped him in "learning the games, the rules, of what to say, of what not to say, and how to say it." He went so far as to conclude, "I attribute most of the things I've learned to my Phillips Academy background." Perhaps there is no more important cultural capital for blacks than to feel comfortable interacting with whites on an equal basis; this is a major contribution of the ABC program to its graduates.

Thanks to the friendships they developed at prep schools and colleges, graduates of the ABC program also formed valuable connections; they had become part of a number of networks. For example, graduates of Choate knew Choate schoolmates who, like themselves, had entered the working world; moreover, they knew that because they had gone to Choate they could, with carefully placed phone calls or letters, gain access to thousands of Choate graduates they did not know personally. The director of development at Choate has stressed the valuable entree a Choate education provides: "There is no door in this entire country that cannot be opened by a Choate graduate. I can go anywhere in this country and anywhere there's a man I want to see . . . I can find a Choate man to open that door for me."[2] (That was thirty years ago, before Choate and Rosemary Hall merged—now he might find Choate women who would open doors for him.)

ABC graduates were also part of networks that included all those who had attended their colleges, and many were also part of law school, business school, or graduate school networks. Such connections can prove valuable for getting an interview for a job, getting the job itself, or gaining certain advantages once in a job. For example, Alan Glenn, who was working for Manufacturers Hanover at the time of our 1986 interview, described his ongoing friendship with a Hotchkiss classmate:

> One of my best friends from Hotchkiss is Mike Carroll. He's white. He's from a middle-class Irish background here in New York, and we became very good friends. He's now a writer for the American Banker. And we stay in contact, get together and go out for drinks every now and then, have breakfast or lunch, whatever the case may be. Sometimes it's mutually convenient because he works for the American Banker, so he feels he can grind me about what is going on here at Manufacturers Hanover, and I can grind him about what's going on in the banking industry in general. So it's mutually beneficial for both of us.

A corporate lawyer we interviewed described how the father of a former prep school classmate had become a valuable contact for him when he was interviewing for his current job. He had been invited for an interview at the largest firm in the city in which he grew up. Knowing that the father of a woman he had gone to prep school with was a partner at another large law firm in that same city, he called him up and told him of his forthcoming interview. His friend's father asked for his résumé and then arranged for him to be interviewed while he was in town. The ABC graduate ended up joining that firm.

The benefits of "old school ties" can continue throughout one's career. Eric Coleman explained that his having attended Pomfret and then Columbia University made his work easier as a legislator. "There are at least three people I can think of in the legislature who have Pomfret connections," he told us in our May 2002 interview. Two of the three had gone to Pomfret and one had been a faculty member, though none of the three was there when Coleman was a student. Still, he noted, "It's very easy to do things in the legislature with them. It's easy to converse with these folks who have Pomfret backgrounds. Somehow that creates a bond, a sense that you can help somebody who has had that same experience."

Similarly, he had a close friend as an undergraduate who is now a senior executive at a large insurance company in Hartford. When Coleman needs help from him, or from others at the company, it is easy to get it: "On the basis of a phone call, I can get help for something that I'm involved in in Hartford, say financial contributions or technical assistance or other some other kinds of resources. He's a very good and responsive colleague."

ABC GRADUATES AT WORK:
STARS, PROFESSIONALS, AND HIDDEN ABCERS

How effectively have ABC graduates used the formal educations they obtained and the cultural and social capital that accompanied their formal education? On the basis of our interviews with ABC graduates, in which they described not only their own careers but the careers of other ABC students, we have concluded that most fall into one of three categories: stars, professionals, and "hidden ABCers."

The Stars

By ABC stars, we are referring to people who have done exceptionally well in their chosen fields, people who have gained regional and, in many cases, national recognition for their success. These ABC graduates are on the cutting edge. Many have risen to occupational heights in fields that have long been dominated by whites.

More than a few of those we interviewed, and others we heard about, fall in this category. Sylvester Monroe, a former writer for *Newsweek* and *Time*, and, at the time of our interview with him in August 2001, the assistant managing editor at the *San Jose Mercury News*, is surely a star, as is Monique Burns, who graduated first from the Concord Academy and then from Radcliffe College, and who at the time of our 1986 interview was a senior editor at *Travel & Leisure* (she has since written for many magazines, and edited the *Fodors 2001 Guide to Seattle*). Bill Lewis, a managing director at Morgan Stanley, is certainly a star. Eric Coleman, a state legislator from Hartford, is a political star in his home state, as is Frank Borges, at the time of our 1987 interview the treasurer of the state of Connecticut (and, more recently, the CEO of an investment company, and the treasurer of the NAACP). Jesse Spikes, a graduate of Dartmouth, a Rhodes Scholar and a graduate of the Harvard Law School, now a successful lawyer in Atlanta, is certainly a star. So, too, is Jeffrey Palmer, a senior vice president at Pep Boys.

Many other stars have emerged from the ABC program in a variety of fields. They include Latanya Sweeney, who graduated in 1977 from Dana Hall, started at MIT, dropped out, founded and managed a medium-sized computer company for ten years, and then received her bachelor's from Harvard, and her MA and Ph.D. in computer science from MIT. She is now a professor at Carnegie Mellon University (her work on Internet privacy and bioterrorism surveillance has been featured in *Newsweek*, *Business Week*, *Consumer Reports*, and the *Wall Street Journal*). They also include John Reasoner, Jr., a 1971 graduate of Westminster who did his undergraduate work at Brown, and then went to the Brown Medical School, and is now the medical chief of staff at Evans Army Community Hospital in Colorado Springs. Reasoner has worked as the head physician at the Pan-American games, with the Olympic Training Center in Colorado Springs, and helped modernize the military medical system in the United Arab Emirates. Another star is Sandra Thomas, a 1980 ABC graduate of the Laurel School who attended MIT, earned an MD from Ohio State University, did a postdoctoral fellowship at the University of North Carolina, has many publications and done many presentations on asthma, and is now the director of epidemiology at the Chicago Department of Public Health. Yet another star is Dwight Hopkins, a 1972 graduate of Groton, who received his bachelor's degree from Harvard and then earned two doctoral degrees, one from the Union Theological Seminary (in New York) and the other from the University of Cape Town (in South Africa). A theology professor at the University of Chicago Divinity School, he has published extensively, served on numerous national and international committees, and received many academic honors.

However, rather than listing the occupational accomplishments of the many ABC stars we have interviewed and come across in our research, we have chosen to provide fairly in-depth profiles of two: Linda Hurley, who at the age of thirty-three became one of the highest-ranking women in minority banking in the country, and Harold Cushenberry, a judge on the Superior Court in Washington, D.C.

Linda Hurley Ishem

Linda Hurley Ishem's rise to ABC star status was not continuous and predictable. From the outset of her relationship with the ABC program, her path was unusual.

When she was about to enter the ABC program, her older brother was just completing the program as a boarding student at Kimball Union, a prep school in New Hampshire. His experience at Kimball Union had not been a good one, and he consequently counseled his younger sister to avoid boarding-school life. He even looked into the options available to her, suggesting that she continue to live at home with her mother and two younger brothers in the Franklin Field Public Housing Development in Dorchester, Massachusetts, while commuting daily to the Commonwealth School, a progressive private school in downtown Boston. She took his advice.

Although she liked the Commonwealth School enough to stay, she remained somewhat of a loner, partly because she was a commuting student and partly by inclination. There were about a dozen other black students, but many of them, like most of the white students, seemed to be from another world.

> It appeared that most of the black students there . . . were able to pay a significant portion of their way through. That put them in a radically different class. I lived in Dorchester in a housing project; they lived in Roxbury on something that's called The Hill. And even though you hear that Roxbury is a slum, there is a very elite section. I mean, one of my classmates was the daughter of a television announcer. Yes, she was black also, but I had about as much in common with her as I did with some of the whites there whose parents were professors at Harvard.

Academically, she recalls, she was a lazy student, not very likely to push herself. "If I could get by with reading every other chapter," she recalls, "that's what I did." Still, she did well enough to be accepted at both Wellesley and Wesleyan. She decided to attend Wellesley, partly because it was closer to home and partly because the campus was so stunningly beautiful. At Wellesley, she majored in psychology and black studies. She spent the summer prior to her junior year at the University of Ibadan in Nigeria, and her junior year as an exchange student at Spelman College in Atlanta, Georgia. Although not an academic standout, she did solid work at Wellesley. As graduation approached, she knew she was ready to leave the Boston area, but she was not at all sure where she wanted to be or what she wanted to do.

After a summer of partying in Memphis with a friend she had met while she was an exchange student at Spelman, Linda moved in with friends in Chicago, just to see if she liked the city. She took a job at Marshall Field's to help pay room and board. But four months later she was working at Continental Illinois Bank because she had learned that banks were a good place to work in Chicago. Though she did not realize it at first, she started out "grossly underemployed." With a liberal arts background, and no real business experience, she was trained in the personal banking area, the next step up from being a teller. Within a few months, she realized that would be a dead end.

So she went through the management-training program and was assigned to the New York regional office as a commercial loan officer. Over the next three and a half years, this accidental banker managed portfolios of corporate customers with annual sales of between $20 million and $2 billion; performed credit analyses; negotiated, priced, and structured loan agreements; marketed noncredit services; and managed leveraged buy-outs. Though Continental was encouraging her to specialize—one of her supervisors told her he wanted her to be "sharp as a pin and just as broad"—her inclination was to broaden her banking experience. By this time she wanted to be the CEO at a bank. She also knew that she would not become the chief executive officer at Continental, one of the ten largest commercial banks in the country at the time.

She therefore left Continental to work for Highland Community Bank, which is also in Chicago. As she put it: "I left a forty-billion-dollar bank to go to a forty-million-dollar bank." Though Highland is black-owned, that was not what attracted her. What did attract her was the opportunity to have broader responsibilities than were available at a larger bank. She was also drawn to this bank because of its mission. As she put it in an email that she sent us in October 2000: "I wanted to own or run a bank. But by September 1983, I'd discovered that I wanted more. . . . I wanted to give back to the community from which the bank drew its deposits. I wanted to do something more positive rather than enrich a few already wealthy entrepreneurs at the expense of jobs for working class people." She was given the title of vice president and director of marketing, and though her main responsibility was to bring in corporate business, she handled everything from local advertising to dealing with the Federal Reserve. In a feature article about her in the *American Banker* in 1985, she explained to the reporter that she kept her various responsibilities straight by having a separate notebook for each task. "People would say to me, 'You wear a lot of different hats,' and I'd say, 'No, I carry a lot of different notebooks.'"[3]

During her second year at Highland, this formerly "lazy student" entered Northwestern University's Executive Master's Program. After attending classes all day on alternate Fridays and Saturdays for two years, she received her MBA in June 1987, while serving as the number two person at her bank. Despite the extraordinary demands on her time during this period, she also remained active in professional and civic organizations.

In January 1987, she left Highland to join Seaway National Bank of Chicago, the nation's largest black-owned bank. Her appointment as a senior vice president made her one of the highest-ranking women in minority banking. At the time of our 1987 interview, she was vice chairperson of the board of the National Bankers Association and still looking forward to becoming the CEO of a bank. When asked if that meant that she would either stay in Chicago or move back to New York, she said it did not: "It can really be anywhere—and I'm not just looking at the minority banks. I almost don't care who owns it. I'd like an ownership interest, thank you very much. And I don't care who has it or anything like that. But even just looking at the minority banks, there are 109 minority-owned banks. That includes women, Hispanic, black, Asian. There are thirty-nine black-owned banks in thirty-two states. I mean, I could be anywhere."

But, in another unexpected turn in her career, she left Seaway in March 1988, and moved to Tacoma, Washington, where she married, had a son, and went to work in the public sector, first for the state government and then for the county. As she later explained, "Somewhere around this time I lost my passion for banking or it got sacrificed or abandoned and replaced by my need to make a difference. It seems by now I realized that there were many ways, besides owning and operating a bank, to potentially make a big, positive and lasting difference. I also realized that my skills and talents went beyond finance and were transferable to other disciplines." Soon she became the director for the Pierce County Community Action Department.

In April 1995, on the evening of her forty-first birthday, returning to her office after a meeting, her car was blindsided. She spent a week in intensive care, suffering both multiple physical injuries (which required seven surgeries) and a traumatic brain injury (which required eight months of intensive cognitive therapy). She was out of work for a year, but then returned to her job, where the department she directed won numerous awards. "I like where I am right now," she told us in an email message in November 1999. "I love my job and the daily opportunity it provides to make a significant difference in the lives of the most vulnerable and voiceless members of our community. . . . I like the way it leaves me feeling at the end of the day."

Although she liked where she was in 1999, Linda Hurley Ishem is a woman with many dreams, and another of those dreams moved to the forefront a year later. "I informed my boss and my staff of a lifelong dream of teaching at the university level, researching and writing public policy. I have completed my

eight-year obligation to County Executive Doug Sutherland, who is prohib-
ited by term limits from seeking another term. The timing is right for me to
return to school to pursue a doctorate in public policy." She was accepted into
a doctoral program at the University of Washington, took a ten-week statistics course as a transition back into academia, and began working on her
Ph.D. in the fall of 2001. As she wrote in another email:

> I'm not certain how my story fits into your book, but I'd love to share my story.
> I do find that no matter how uncommon my course has been and continues to
> be, mine is more often than not the only black face in the room. Being "the only"
> is in some ways an honor, a privilege and a humbling experience. It is also one
> of tremendous responsibility, because I never want to leave a poor impression
> and risk closing the door for others to walk through. I always work hard and am
> conscious of the fact that my performance may very well represent (to some ob-
> servers) much much more than the actions of one individual.

Harold Cushenberry

Harold Cushenberry, an only child, was in the eighth grade in Henderson,
North Carolina, in 1964 when his parents heard about the ABC program,
which was in its very first year. Unlike most ABC students, Cushenberry's
parents were public school teachers, and unlike most ABC students, once
Harold applied to participate in the ABC program, he and his parents visited
four or five schools to try to decide which would be the best one for him. Still,
as he looks back, he acknowledges that "This was as foreign to me as anything in my whole life, and, although my parents were both educated, it was
equally foreign to them—it was a leap into the dark." They decided on the
Taft School. He then spent eight weeks at Dartmouth in the first summer orientation.

Cushenberry graduated from the Taft School in 1968, from Harvard in
1972, and from the Georgetown University Law Center in 1975. After serving as staff attorney at the Federal Trade Commission for two years, and for
seven years as a trial attorney in the United States Attorney's Office, he was
appointed associate judge of the Superior Court of the District of Columbia
in 1986. At age thirty-six, he was the youngest of the fifty-one Superior Court
judges.

In contrast to Linda Hurley, there was remarkable continuity in the life of
Harold Cushenberry, Jr., in the fourteen years between our two interviews
with him. In March 1987, when we first visited Judge Cushenberry in his
chambers at the D.C. Superior Court, he was married, had two daughters, and
was living off 16th Street in an upscale black neighborhood known locally as
"the Gold Coast." As of May 2001, when we returned to watch him try a case

and then interview him in his chambers, he lived in the same house (and had the same home phone number). He looked very much the same, though in 1987 our notes included that his hair was "sprinkled with gray," and by 2001 it was more than "sprinkled" with gray.

During those years, he presided over jury and bench trials, rotating on a yearly basis in the civil, criminal, and family divisions. In 2000, he was reappointed to another fifteen-year term, and in 2002 he became the deputy presiding judge of the Criminal Division of the D.C. Superior Court. The day we visited him, he was conducting a trial in which a woman had accused her former lover of assaulting her. Throughout the emotionally intense cross-examination, Judge Cushenberry treated all parties, including the witness and the two lawyers, with unflagging courtesy, even as he made rulings (sustaining or overruling objections) and tried to provide guidance to the long-winded defense lawyer.

When we asked if he had ever considered giving up his judgeship to enter the more lucrative corporate legal world, Cushenberry said he had not: "I really haven't. I've been sort of blessed in a way. My wife's also an attorney, and I could have earned a lot more money in the private sector, but at some price . . . especially in terms of time with my kids and my family. . . . Our incomes together, because they have fortunately raised salaries for judges, it's fine. We can handle our expenses—we're not rich, but we can pay our tuition. We can qualify for enough money, and we can borrow enough to pay the rest."

Linda Hurley and Harold Cushenberry are but two of many ABC graduates we consider to be stars. It is impossible to know precisely what percentage of the early graduates would fall into our star category. On the basis of comments made by the ABC graduates we interviewed, including what they told us about others who participated in the ABC program, we estimate that 15 to 20 percent of the early graduates could be called "stars" but it is too soon to know for sure how many of the more recent graduates will fit into this category. Whatever the exact figure, far more ABC graduates, probably more than half, are in an equally important category, that of professionals, the second of our three.

The Professionals

Hundreds of graduates of the ABC program work as doctors, lawyers, professors, bankers, journalists, accountants, or in other white-collar jobs. We have chosen to call these people "the professionals." Some of them may be on their way to becoming stars, but by and large, they have joined the new black middle class, a class that now includes a much wider variety of occupational alternatives than ever before. In order to suggest the variety of experiences of those we are calling professionals, we will describe the experiences of four ABC graduates who fall into this category. As we will see, some of them have had to face obstacles, but their educations and their skills as professionals have helped them to confront these problems.

LaPearl Winfrey

After finishing the ninth grade in her hometown of Richmond, Virginia, LaPearl Winfrey attended the Masters School in Dobbs Ferry, New York. Three years later she entered Oberlin College, where she majored in psychology and graduated in three years. During her second year at Oberlin, she met her future husband, a black student from Chicago who had started at Oberlin in 1964, dropped out of school to go into military service, and subsequently returned to Oberlin. When he graduated, a year before she did, he returned to Chicago to work as an advertising representative for one of the newspapers there. She joined him in Chicago after she graduated, worked for a year, and then entered a master's program in psychology at Roosevelt University. After completing the program and working for another three or four years, she decided it was time to get her Ph.D. in clinical psychology.

Her husband thought he was going to receive a promotion that would send him to New York City, so LaPearl Winfrey applied to doctoral programs in the New York area. As it turned out, he did not get the opportunity to move to New York, but she was accepted at the State University of New York (SUNY) at Stony Brook. She decided to go anyway, leaving her husband and their two-year-old daughter in Chicago, and commuting back and forth to Chicago. After three years at Stony Brook she returned to Chicago, where, at the time of our first interview in 1987, she was completing her degree and working as a clinical psychologist in a practice with five other therapists (four women and one man), all of them black. In 1990 she joined the faculty of the Chicago School of Professional Psychology where she taught and continued a part-time clinical practice. By 1994, she had finished her Ph.D. and worked for seven months directing an adult outpatient component of a community hospital before moving to an outpatient center affiliated with the hospital.

As part of her practice, she and her partners did some work with corporations, which they called "workplace consultation," especially in the area of diversity. Among other things, they were running diversity-training programs for managers. The only other Ph.D. psychologist in our sample, Greg Pennington, also has done a great deal of diversity training, as has Bill Foster, who does programs in schools, corporations, and community agencies for the Anti-Defamation League of Connecticut. It makes sense that ABC graduates, with their boarding school experiences living with the children of well-off white people, would be drawn to and good at diversity training.

In 1995 Winfrey moved to Washington, D.C., to become director of training and associate professor at the Arlington campus of the American Schools of Professional Psychology. Then, in the summer of 2001, she and her husband left D.C. for her to take a position as the director of clinical training and professor in the School of Professional Psychology at Wright State University in Dayton, Ohio.

Calvin Dorsey

In autumn 1968, Calvin Dorsey, the youngest of six children, left Clarksdale, a city of 20,000 in northwest Mississippi, to attend the Mount Hermon School. After three enjoyable years there ("It was just a wonderful experience"), he attended Stanford University, where he majored in political science and minored in communications.

After graduating from Stanford, he returned to the South to enter a master's program in communications at the University of Mississippi. He earned his MA and then lived in his hometown of Clarksdale, where he worked first as a disc jockey and then started his own record promotion company.

He left Clarksdale to sell advertising for Cox Communications. After two years in Chattanooga, he was transferred to Atlanta. At the time of our first interview in 1986, he had been working for Cox in Atlanta for five years and was living with his wife in a renovated home they had recently purchased in a predominantly black neighborhood on the south side of the city. He did not, however, expect to stay with Cox Communications. When asked what he thought he'd be doing in five years, he responded: "In five years I won't be working for Cox. I'll be in my own business." His prediction was accurate. In 1990 he left Cox, and Atlanta, to move to Dallas, where he and some colleagues started the Summit Broadcast Group, which managed various properties, including some radio stations in Dallas. Two years later he went out on his own, founding and becoming president of Dorsey Management Services, which assists businesses in sales, management, and employee training.

Cecily Robbins

Cecily Robbins remembers very clearly and sadly the day she received the letter accepting her into the ABC program, because it was the same day her mother died. She didn't go away to school that year, but over the next year she and her father concluded that she should take advantage of the opportunity to attend a boarding school. Before she left her home in south Philadelphia to begin school at Walnut Hill in the fall of 1966, she participated in the summer program at Mount Holyoke.

Unlike a lot of ABC students, Robbins was from a family with many educated relatives. Both her grandmothers had gone to college and had been teachers, and there were many other professionals in her family. The computer screensaver in her office in Alexandria, Virginia, was covered with old photos of her mother's ancestors, elegantly attired West Indians, taken in the early 1900s. "There was never any question that any of us would be going on to college," she told us in our initial interview in 1986, "it was just a matter of how."

After graduating from Walnut Hill in 1969, Robbins went to George Washington University, from which she graduated in 1973 with a major in American studies. After working at a number of different jobs (including employment at the Environmental Protection Agency and the Small Business Administration), she became a senior administrator in the nonprofit world. At the time of our initial interview in 1986 she was the executive director of the Big Sisters program in Washington, D.C. She and her husband were separated, and about to be divorced, and she was raising her four-year-old son. After juggling the pressures of heading the program for eight years, she decided she needed a sabbatical. As she put it: "I had had it, in a word. I left. I was having a meeting with a couple of my board members and I said, you know what, I'm going to leave. So, from there I took what I call a self-subsidized sabbatical and lived very, very frugally. I was a stay at home mom who did consulting work on the side."

After a few years she went to work for the National Mentoring Partnership, a nonprofit organization that serves as a catalyst working with the various individuals, communities, states, or other organizations that have mentoring programs. In 1997, when they started a Web site, she reluctantly agreed to work on it, and then, as she put it, "I discovered, Eureka, I could be the magician around here, and now I'm sometimes referred to as the database queen."

Due to chronic sciatica, she is forced to use a special transit system for disabled people, and she uses a motorized scooter to travel around the spacious offices of the National Mentoring Partnership. She has groceries and other needs delivered through a service. She described her situation in the following way:

It doesn't stop me, it just slows me down. People look at me and they say, "You look fine." I don't care to talk about it. It's not that I won't, but I just don't dwell on it. I try to live my life as normally as possible. With the help of the computer it is very easy. I was raised to think that we all have our crosses to bear. So you know, you just keep getting up and doing what you have to do.

Doris McMillon

Doris McMillon's father was in the military, and the family moved a lot. When she was in junior high school in Detroit, her parents divorced, and her relationship with her mother was not a good one. Fortunately for her, one of her favorite teachers became a confidante who provided her with important emotional support ("I knew he genuinely cared about my welfare"), and, when he heard about the ABC program, he encouraged Doris to take the necessary test and apply. She was accepted, and as we recounted in chapter 3, she spent one year at Concord Academy where she did poorly academically before a sympathetic headmaster helped her to transfer to Cushing Academy.

After graduating from Cushing Academy, McMillon began college at Elmhurst College in Illinois. After two years there, she returned to Detroit, where she majored in communications at Wayne State. A professor helped her get a job at a local radio station, which led to a job with the NBC radio network in New York City, and, ultimately, to a career in communications.

In our initial interview, she said that she had just given a talk to a group of ABC students: "I keep trying to explain to the kids, 'This is an opportunity for you to meet the folks who are out there making decisions in the business world. I went to school with the Cartiers, the Pillsburys, the Rockefellers, the Fishers. Tony Fisher's family, the Fisher Brothers in New York—I think they've just built every high rise, every skyscraper, that's up on Park Avenue and Fifth Avenue. But I got a chance to meet those kind of people. Well, what I found out ultimately is that they get up in the morning and get out of the bed and go to the bathroom like I do. So it's no big deal. However, they are who they are, and if they can help you, they will.'"

Doris McMillon gave a casebook description of how to draw on various networks to obtain a desired job. McMillon had heard that Worldnet, a worldwide telecommunications network that is part of the United States Information Agency (USIA), was about to expand. At the time she was hosting a half-hour evening talk show for the Black Entertainment Network. The network was about to go on "hiatus" from June to September, so she knew she would have some extra time. She turned first to her pastor. She recalls saying to him, "There's a job coming up. Now we can pray about this job. But do you have any connections?" It turned out he did. He called Reverend Garrett, a special assistant to then Vice President Bush, who in turn called Mel Bradley, a special assistant to President Reagan. After meeting with Doris McMillon, Bradley sent a letter and one of her videotapes over to Charles Wick, the head of the USIA, asking him to take a careful look at her.

This was not the only message Charles Wick was to receive about Doris McMillon. A few days later, McMillon happened to run into Bill Gray, a black congressman from Philadelphia whom she had interviewed on her show for the Black Entertainment Network. She told him that she had applied for a job at the USIA, and the next day, Gray called Wick to recommend McMillon. She also mentioned her interest in the USIA job to a member of her Tuesday morning prayer group, Rosemary Tribble, the wife of Senator Paul Tribble, who wrote Wick "a glowing letter of recommendation," as did Jim Quello, a commissioner for the Federal Communications Commission whom she had known since her radio days in Detroit. After all these recommendations came into the USIA, the next thing she knew, McMillon was broadcasting news around the world for Worldnet.

As her career was taking off, she married Raphael Bacin, a Haitian physician who was at the time of our initial interview running for the presidency of Haiti. In that interview she told us: "I'd prefer not to be first lady of Haiti, and it's touched off a great strain on our marriage." There were other strains on the marriage as well, including the fact that she was spending the week in Washington, D.C., working in television, and then would join her husband, his two daughters by a previous marriage, and their own daughter on weekends at their home in Kingsport in Great Neck, New York. She described her commute in the following way: "On Friday, I hop in my car and drive to New York. Sunday morning, at 11:00, I hop back in my car and I drive back to Washington so I can chill out and get ready for Monday morning."

At the time of our first interview, McMillon had become a devout Christian (as she put it in our second interview, fourteen years later, "When you met me in 1987, I was about a year into my new relationship with Christ"). Her goal was to become a television evangelist. "The Lord," she said, "did not put me into this profession to do bad news. Gospel means good news."

Not long after our initial interview, the marriage fell apart, she lost her job with Channel 7 in Washington, and she found herself in debt. As she described it in our 2001 interview: "After I left Channel 7, I'd really hit rock bottom, personally, financially, I mean things had really gone into the hole because I lost my job, my marriage went down the drain. There I was $100,000 in personal debt and I felt that I was down so low, I had to look up to see my feet. So, it was then that the Lord got my undivided attention."

She's continued to work in media, and she's continued in her evangelism ("When I go out, wherever I work, I tell everybody I know"). Her business card describes her as a "Media Consultant and Trainer," and indicates that she is available for "Voice-Overs, Video Conferences, Industrials, Commercials, News Anchoring and Reporting, Media Training, Voice Coach, Emcee, Motivational Speaker." Over the years, she has worked in radio and in television, for NBC News, WABC-TV, Fox Television, WJLA-TV, the Black Entertainment Network, CNN, and the U.S. Information Agency's Worldnet. She has also played the role of a reporter in a number of movies, including Clint East-wood's *In the Line of Fire*, and Wesley Snipes's *Murder at 1600*. The night of our interview, she appeared in the final 2001 segment of the popular television show *West Wing*.

McMillon, like Cecily Robbins, has had serious health problems in recent years. In her case, rheumatoid arthritis has given her immense pain, unrelieved by the numerous surgeries she has undergone:

> The last four and a half years have been healthwise very trying for me because I have been dealing with rheumatoid arthritis. I've had some lady screaming at me because I have handicapped parking. She's screaming at me, "You're not handicapped." I said, "Lady, you don't know my pain." I have it in my feet and I have it in my hands and you know there's a lot of swelling. I've had like six surgeries and so it's been day in and day out in dealing with pain. But, you know what? I'm still walking, moving, breathing and as long as I have a breath in my body, my mother's voice is in my head. She says, "If you're not dead, go to work."

Though the pain is day to day, she remains "optimistic and upbeat about what's to come." She plans to continue reporting, and working as a media consultant, but her primary focus is, as she puts it, "on spiritual things."

These four professionals—a psychologist, a management consultant, an executive in the nonprofit world, and a newscaster (who is also a "media consultant and trainer")—suggest the range of occupations of ABC graduates who fall into our "professional" category. They all received BA degrees from good schools, all have earned good money, but none is wealthy (while married, Doris McMillon was). And, as is true for many people who reach the age of fifty, they have faced various kinds of adversities and landed on their feet.

The Hidden ABCers

It was Linda Hurley Ishem, one of our stars, who used the term "hidden ABCers" in our initial interview to refer to "people who won't come forward because they don't feel they've lived up to the standards of ABC." The most poignant example she had of such a person was her older brother, who attended the Kimball Union Academy, dropped out of college, and became a successful dancer in Europe. She described him in the following way:

> He is living a very happy and successful life, but is it what ABC prepared him to do? Well, probably ABC didn't care, but there is this image we have that I am supposed to be the next black Einstein, if you will, or something because I've been given the chance. But there are a whole lot of people who are so afraid to identify themselves as ABCers because they felt, "I'm the ABCer who fell in the

crack," or "I'm the one that didn't conform," or "I'm the one who never even finished the ABC program." And I think that's unfortunate. There's no reason for us to have pressure on us for the rest of our lives just because we got this opportunity and somehow didn't live up to our interpretation of what it was trying to do for us. . . . I talk to my brother sometimes about Kimball. We used to go up there to visit and he used to come home all the time. But there is still this pain, and Jesus, my brother has been out of high school forever.

"Hidden ABCers," then, constitute a third category, along with the stars and professionals. It includes those who dropped out of the program, either during the summer program or after starting prep school, those who have not been successful, and those who by most standards have been successful but, like Linda Hurley Ishem's brother, do not feel that they have lived up to the expectations of the program. For various reasons, these ABC graduates have chosen not to maintain contact with the program.

In the course of our interviews, we heard about various ABC graduates who had not followed the traditional path to success. One name came up twice: Spencer Armstead. His name was first mentioned during our interview with Barry Greene, a banker in Richmond, who went to junior high with him. A few months later, Doris McMillon mentioned Armstead while listing the names of other black ABC students who had been at the Cushing Academy when she was there. She didn't have an address for him, but provided the name of someone at Cushing who might know more about him. That person told us Armstead was indeed in Richmond, where he was working as a chauffeur, and gave us his address and phone number. After a few letters and phone calls, we drove to Richmond to interview Armstead.

Spencer Armstead . . . but, now, Spencer Edward Jones III

When we met Spencer Armstead, a stocky, five-foot, six-inch former halfback with a light complexion and a close-cropped beard, we asked him, as we asked each of those interviewed, whether he minded if we taped the interview. Like all but one of those interviewed, he agreed. When we then asked whether he preferred that we use his name or refer to him anonymously, he said he didn't mind if we identified him, but pointed out that he had legally changed his name five years earlier. He wrote his new name—Spencer Edward Jones III—on the file folder on which we had written the name Spencer Armstead.

Earlier than he can recall, his parents had split up and his mother had married Andrew Armstead. Though Spencer knew his real father was named Jones, he grew up using his stepfather's surname. In spring 1966, when he was in the tenth grade, he was asked to participate in the ABC program.

That summer, Armstead attended the summer program at Carleton College. Like so many who went through the summer program in those early years, he has very fond memories of that summer. He worked hard and learned new things, but mostly he remembers the intense camaraderie that developed over the eight weeks he and the other students spent in Minnesota. The parting scene was particularly memorable:

> When it was time to go, everybody cried. I mean, everybody. The tough guys. It was real moving. Because we were so raw, and we were away from home, many for the first time, it was like, why couldn't we just take this whole group and go to one school? It was like nobody wanted to leave, people were pulling each other apart, and the advisors and stuff were crying. It was very, very moving.

His experience at Carleton was so positive that three years later, when he graduated from Cushing Academy, he decided to go to Carleton. Like other ABC students who had attended the summer program at Carleton, he chose to return there for college in part because of Fred Easter, a black administrator who ran the summer program. Armstead recalls Easter as "beyond unbelievable," someone who would challenge students to take full advantage of the opportunity they were being given: "He was the disciplinarian. The big guys, he was the one who would go up to 'em and collar 'em and tell 'em: 'Look here, man, don't blow this.' He'd say: 'You got brothers back in the ghetto, turning junkies and whatever, and here you are, you got all this, white folks are going to take care of you, pay for this, all you got to do is learn.' You could relate to him."

The transition from Cushing to Carleton was dramatic. At Cushing, Armstead had been a star athlete (a halfback on the football team, a guard on the basketball team, and an outfielder on the baseball team), popular, and a decent, though not particularly good, student. In his view, you had to be "really dumb" to get poor grades at Cushing because your behavior was monitored so carefully that at the slightest drop in performance, teachers would be on your case, pushing you to do your work. As he put it: "The academic part of it, I could keep up. I wasn't at the head of the class, but I wasn't a dummy, I could keep up. I never got bad grades. Really, if you got bad grades at Cushing you was really dumb, because the teachers . . . lived in the dorm. If you was messin' up, the teacher would come knock on your door at eight o'clock after dinner, and sit down with you, and say 'Now what's the problem?'"

At Carleton, however, no one was monitoring him on a daily basis, and the temptations were many: it was the late 1960s, and there were lots of drugs available; there were women living in the same dorm; and you didn't even have to go to class if you didn't want to. "Carleton was just like a country club. It's a great school—I have nothing but the best to say for it. It was so liberal—I mean, women were living right next door to me. That blew my mind after coming from Cushing. . . . So I just got there and said, 'Wow.'"

By his senior year, he was asking himself a lot of questions about how he wanted to live his life. He had gone to see some recent graduates who were out in the working world and realized that the lives they led were not what he wanted for himself: "It was like they had no freedom. They were already locked into nine-to-five junior executive jobs, they already had the ulcers, they already were in debt over their heads. It frightened me, and I realized that's not what I wanted to be."

He decided he also didn't want to be in college, so during his senior year he dropped out. He spent the next few years

hanging around and traveling, some in Minnesota, some in Denver, Oakland, Reno, Vegas, Tijuana, I had a ball. It was a collection of us. About three or four of us just up and left school, and we formed what you could call, I guess, a little mutual admiration society. It was that dropout mentality. A couple of them lived out there, so we just kind of hung around, and when things died there, we went somewhere else. It was fun times. We were our own people, didn't have any responsibilities. Whenever we'd want gratification for what we were doing, we'd go back and see some of these people who had graduated. These guys, they were, like, "Well, I can't drink but one beer because I got to go to bed at nine o'clock cause I got to be up by six to go to work at eight."

By 1975 he was back in Richmond, and by 1976 he was in jail. Over the years, he had, as he puts it, "been in and out of trouble," but he had never been to jail. One night he and some of his buddies got into a fracas outside a neighborhood store, and when a policeman came, his friends ran and he didn't. When the policeman pulled his gun, Armstead blew a fuse: "He didn't need to pull his pistol. When he pulled his pistol, that's when I went off. I said, 'I'm going to take that pistol from you and whip your ass.'" The policeman immediately put out an all-points bulletin. Within minutes, a slew of other police had arrived, and after what Jones now calls "a little tussle," he was arrested and subsequently convicted for disorderly conduct and resisting arrest. He spent the first half of the bicentennial year in jail.

He came out of jail with plans to fight a legal battle associated with some property he had inherited from his grandmother, to get and keep a job, and to stay out of jail. He did all three. Richmond was in the process of a renewal project that involved tearing down the commercial, industrial, and residential property in his neighborhood. When all but three houses, one of them the house he had inherited, had been torn down, Armstead decided to sue the city. He lost the initial rounds at the local and state levels but won at the federal level; the city had used federal money for its project but had not prepared the required environmental impact statement. Because of the outcome of the lawsuit, the city of Richmond had to rebuild the community it leveled, and Spencer Jones became chairman of the Fulton Project Area Committee. The city, he told us, had to go through his organization. As he then put it, "I'm trying to rebuild a community."[4]

He also achieved the occupational stability he sought. At the time of our interview in 1987, he had had his professional chauffeur's license for more than ten years and was the head taxi driver for an upscale Richmond transportation company that provided both limousine and taxi service.

He had also stuck to his third goal: he had not returned to jail.

Jones did not regret his participation in the ABC program. In fact, he told us that, like the many ABC graduates who became "stars" and "professionals," he had benefited from the experience. And once again, the emphasis was on interpersonal skills and self-confidence in dealing with whites: "I feel like I'm a better person from the ABC program. I think that the main thing that helped me was that [the program gave me] my ability to handle or understand white folks. . . . The experiences that I learned in the ABC program helped me to deal with what I wanted to do in life."

More specifically, he was convinced that his ABC experience helped him in his legal battles to save his house and in his role as head of his neighborhood organization. As he put it:

Everybody told me when I first started, "You'll never beat City Hall." I knocked them on their ass. That kind of strength came from all the people I've been dealing with: the ABC students, Carleton students. . . . All you gotta do is walk through that door. Just cause it say for white only, you go through there, see what's happening and face issues and people face to face, they have to deal with you. They knew what I was talking about and they knew I was right. It was the urban renewal thing. They just leveled the whole community, right? The oldest community in Richmond. And I got up in front of City Council and started making noises, and they said, "Hey, we got to listen to him." And they found out where I had been educated at and it was a thing of like, "He didn't graduate but he ain't no dummy."

I've always been real appreciative to the ABC program for giving me that opportunity. I could have been a lawyer. That's what I wanted to be. But it wasn't because of what ABC did that I didn't become a lawyer, it was because of what I wanted to do after I saw what being a lawyer could turn you into. . . . I don't think I cheated the program. I believe in my mind that I'm a success, though not by traditional standards. I think that I've succeeded because my mind is straight now.

According to his half-sister, and the records of the Richmond newspaper, he has met his main goal of staying out of jail. As of August 2002, he was driving a cab (the chauffeuring company he worked for went out of business), but we were unable to get in direct contact with him. He is but one hidden ABCer, and though his experience differs in some ways from that of others in this category, his account reminds us that some ABC students did not "make it" in traditional terms but still feel that they benefited from participating in the program.

What percentage of those who participated in the ABC program fall into this category of hidden ABCers? Linda Hurley Ishem estimated that it might be as high as 40 percent. We think it's probably closer to a third, but we have no way of knowing with certainty. We stress, again, that this is not a category of failures. Indeed, we agree with Spencer Jones's self-evaluation that he is anything but a failure. There are others in this category who by any objective standard (including academic degrees or income) have done quite well, but who feel they have not lived up to expectations. According to most standards, many are leading successful and productive lives. When we add them to the stars (15 percent to 20 percent) and the professionals (50 percent), we conclude that the vast majority of those who participated in the ABC program emerged as productive members of society.

ACHIEVING SUCCESS, RESISTING AUTHORITY

Both the complexities of human achievement and the relatively small size of our sample make it difficult to pinpoint the factors that have led ABC students to become stars, professionals, or hidden ABCers. How did Doris McMillon, who had a very troubled relationship with her mother and who flunked out of the first prep school to which she was assigned, become a highly successful television commentator, seen not only nationally but internationally? And what led her former classmate, Spencer Jones, to find himself, in the first half of 1976, a college dropout in a Virginia jail? What caused Linda Hurley to change from a "lazy student" at the Commonwealth School and Wellesley to an ambitious banker, willing to go to school for two years on weekends to earn her MBA? There are no simple answers to these questions. Human behavior is influenced by situational factors, personal qualities, and congenital temperamental patterns, all interacting and sometimes changing dramatically in their importance over the span of a lifetime. However, some patterns seem to be related to particularly high or low levels of achievement on the part of ABC students.

Most ABC students were the first members of their immediate families to attend college. However, those whose parents had gone to college, even if they did not graduate, seem to have had a distinct advantage. Moreover, whether or not their parents had gone to college, those who thrived in the program and afterward were especially likely to have had parents who emphasized education and who liked to read. Linda Hurley Ishem's mother, for example, never attended college, but she had been a schoolteacher in rural South Carolina. Linda's mother remained "very academically focused." She encouraged her children to read and saw to it that they had dance, acting, piano, and violin lessons.

Similarly, Jeffrey Palmer's father, a postal worker with three years of college, was widely read and, as his son put it, "one of the brighter people I've ever met." Palmer also noted that his grandmother, though not formally educated, "read extensively." Monique Burns mentioned that her father, whose last year of formal education was the eighth grade, worked as a printer and loved to read. "I suppose," she told us, "being a printer, the written word was very important to him, so he gobbled up all kinds of books on history and philosophy and literature, and he educated himself." In some cases, other relatives, such as aunts and uncles, provided important role models.

Social psychologist Thomas Pettigrew has suggested a concept that may help account for the encouragement received by Hurley, Palmer, and several other successful ABC graduates. He argues that within the black economic lower class there has always been a "hidden middle class," comprised of poor people who have middle-class values and participate in activities typically engaged in by members of the middle class. Psychologist LaPearl Winfrey described her background in a way that fits this concept very well:

> I always found myself in a rather curious kind of position, because I think the typical picture of an ABC student is someone who came from a very poor and very deprived family, and I don't seem to fit that mold at all. I was very poor but I don't think I was deprived in that sense. I think that without ABC many people would not have gone to college and never taken a foreign language and would have wound up farming in the back woods of Georgia or someplace. . . . My family was very poor but it was middle class in a sense. We had piano lessons, and we went to camp through church and that kind of thing. Education was very, very much stressed in my family, and I never even considered that I would not go to college.

Also noteworthy was the frequency with which ABC stars and professionals mentioned individuals at their local junior high schools or in their communities who played important roles as mentors in encouraging and supporting them when they needed it. Bobette Reed Kahn spoke fondly of a favorite English teacher and of an assistant principal at her junior high school in Cleveland, both of whom encouraged her to consider the ABC program and helped her with what turned out to be a difficult interviewing process. As we noted in the previous chapter, Art Kobacher, a businessman in his hometown of Steubenville, Ohio, had been extremely important at various stages of Jeffrey Palmer's life, encouraging him to pursue the ABC program and later going into business with him. Linda Hurley Ishem referred gratefully to a guidance counselor at her junior high school who was "an incredible resource" for her family and who guided her older brother and herself into the ABC program.

A "hidden middle class," role models, and mentors, although significant, do not go far enough in explaining the success of many ABC students for several reasons. First, it is important to note that most of the siblings of ABC students did not attend college. Those who did, almost without exception, went to local schools, not selective ones. If being from a hidden middle-class family were enough, many more of these siblings should have gone to college. Second, most black families put a strong emphasis on the value of education; there are many more families that stress the importance of education than there are successful black students. Finally, there is some evidence that even students from the black middle class itself have more trouble in school than their white counterparts. All this suggests that something may be undercutting the strong emphasis on education in most black families, whether middle-class, hidden middle-class, or lower-class. One clue to the problem may be found in those ABC students who did not do well in school and who have not been successful by traditional white cultural standards.

We found that those who were particularly rebellious and who had the most difficulty accepting authority were most likely to run into trouble in school. The late 1960s and early 1970s were years of considerable youthful rebellion, of course, and many ABC students challenged the status quo; indeed, many were challenging the status quo by their very participation in A Better Chance. But some students were more rebellious than others. As we indicated in chapter 3, some of those who dropped out of the ABC program were individuals who were unable or unwilling to adjust to the prep school regimen. As banker Ed McPherson said of one of his friends who left Andover during his first year there, he "was the kind of person who would only accept Andover on his own terms."

Three of those we interviewed emphasized that their rebelliousness had made their experiences more difficult, even though they graduated from their prep schools. Recall Christine Dozier, the only ABC graduate we interviewed who did not go directly on to college. Not only did she have conflict at Abbott Academy, as we discussed earlier, but she remembers that during the summer program one of the Mount Holyoke students on the staff recommended that she be dropped from the program "because I had a very independent and aggressive attitude. I was very outspoken and in the small school environment that I was going to, I might be perceived as being very rebellious. And she was very astute in recognizing those things, because it was true. It was like putting a firecracker in Abbott."

Another ABC graduate we interviewed had been fired from his job, had difficulty finding another, and had recently been thrown out of his mother's house. He was living with a friend (but looking for his own place) and supporting himself by parking cars for an expensive restaurant. Looking back on the conflicts he had in prep school, college, and in various jobs, he said: "I don't tend to do well with authority. . . . I'm funny about who I take orders from." And Spencer Jones also recounted earlier run-ins with people in authority before he went to jail. For example, after playing basketball during his first two years at Carleton, he left the team because he and the coach had "differences in philosophy": "I liked to show off on the basketball court. You know, play that ghetto ball. He didn't want me to play that." Jones also had run-ins with Fred Easter, whom he met during the summer session at Carleton College and so liked and admired that he decided to attend college at Carleton. Even though Easter was black, he was in a position of authority, and this meant, as Jones put it, "Sometimes you hated him because he was 'the man.'"

If the tendency to develop "attitude"—that is, an oppositional identity—is one frequent reaction to racism, then it may be that the ABC program had an effect on achievement that goes beyond alleviating the obvious impacts of racism on many low-income African Americans, such as resource-poor local schools, lack of funds for college, and lack of future job opportunities. Perhaps the program helped some of these students avoid or overcome the rejection of academic achievement that is often incorporated into an oppositional social identity. Thus, the program helped to deal with the less obvious but no less important ways in which racism attacks the psychological integrity of its victims. If so, the ABC program shows that any tendencies toward an oppositional identity are far from immutable if they are placed in a fundamentally different structural context that allows for the development of a more academic social identity.

In this chapter we have argued that many ABC graduates have become successful middle-class professionals, and some have become stars. However, being a productive member of society as a professional, or even a star, is one thing. Reaching the very highest levels of power is another. In the next chapter we explore another one of the questions that animated this research—can African Americans with an upper-class style and education make it to the top in corporate America? Can they become part of the corporate elite, the less than 1 percent who are major corporate executives or sit on the board of directors of large corporations?

NOTES

1. Richard B. Freeman, *Black Elite: The New Market for Highly Educated Black Americans* (New York: McGraw-Hill, 1976), 37.

2. Peter S. Prescott, *A World of Our Own: Notes on Life and Learning in a Boys' Preparatory School* (New York: Coward-McCann, 1970), 67.

3. Andrea Bennett, "Building Up Bank Unity for Big Business Bids: Linda Hurley Harnesses Minority Bank Power," *American Banker* (August 23, 1985): 25.

4. See "Fulton Roots," *Richmond News Leader*, November 19, 1977, 1.

7

Blacks in the Corporate Elite

When the very first fifty-five ABC students were in the midst of the summer program at Dartmouth in 1964, a historic announcement appeared on the business pages of the *New York Times*. Samuel Pierce, a forty-two-year-old Republican corporate lawyer with undergraduate and law degrees from Cornell, became the first African American ever to serve on the board of directors of a major corporation. The company was U.S. Industries, where the maverick CEO, a Democrat who supported unions, decided to integrate the board because of his liberal racial values. A few days later, W. T. Grant, a nationwide chain store whose lunch counters were being picketed by civil rights supporters, announced that it, too, had a new board member, sixty-two-year-old Asa Spaulding, the president of North Carolina Mutual Life Insurance, the largest black-owned business in the country. These appointments were the first small indications that someday it might be possible for ABC graduates to rise to the top of the corporate world, but the pace was very slow throughout the rest of the 1960s. By 1971, there were only ten more African Americans on *Fortune* 500 boards. All were men, all were well educated, and almost all came from economically privileged families.

Then, in the years 1972–73, at a time when many of the first ABC students were beginning to graduate from college and head for graduate schools or the business world, there was another spurt in the appointment of black directors, bringing the total to sixty-seven men and five women. Although the figures were not much different ten years later, there was a jump to 118 by the beginning of the 1990s, when the early ABC graduates were well established in their careers, and then a slow climb to nearly 200 by the year 2000, a little less than 3 percent of all directors at top companies. Unlike most white directors, who join boards as part of their work as executives in major corporations, most of these black directors entered the corporate elite from other career paths, such as universities and the government. Once they had proven their mettle, they were soon also asked to serve on additional boards (on average, these men sat on 1.9 boards, and these women sat on 2.4 boards). However, these averages underplay the role of a few prominent black directors, such as lawyer Vernon Jordan, a personal advisor to President Bill Clinton in the 1990s, one of only two directors who sat on ten corporate boards in the late 1990s.[1]

At the same time that boards were being integrated in the mid-1960s, the opportunity structure in the corporate sector also began to open up at the entry level. Before that time, African Americans with strong educational credentials in business or economics had a very difficult time obtaining jobs with large corporations. As revealed in a longitudinal study of seventy-six top-level black corporate executives in the Chicago area by sociologist Sharon Collins, fewer than half of her twenty-nine interviewees who entered the labor force before 1965 were able to find positions in the white private sector. Those who were hired by mainstream corporations were often given jobs well below their educational level, such as stockroom clerk or billing clerk. Most had to begin their careers in government, black businesses, or black community agencies. The only good corporate jobs were provided by companies that were subject to government oversight. The president of an insurance subsidiary of a major corporation, who held an MBA from a prestigious university, explained to Collins how he finally landed his first job as an accountant with a large government contractor:

> I wanted to be in the investment banking community, but there was no opportunity at all. I finally settled on a job as an accountant at [an aerospace firm]. [The] company stacked the roster, they wanted lots of graduate degrees and they wanted minorities, despite the fact that there were not the obvious or blatant kind of regulations. And I was [underutilized], not doing work [at] the level of an M.B.A.[2]

For those in Collins's study who entered the job market after 1965, there were many more corporate offers, including jobs that provided opportunities to interact with white employees or customers. These opportunities were clearly the result of increased government involvement in the economy due to the civil rights movement. The most visible of these government pressures came from the Equal Employment Opportunity Commission created by the Civil Rights Act of 1964, but they also included new federal contract compliance policies, new federal purchasing guidelines, and the expansion of the social services sector. In fact, a significant number of the new corporate jobs were in affirmative action or personnel departments that dealt with government agencies, or else in public relations or community relations units that interfaced with black communities.

In the long run, however, it turned out there were still limits to how far executives of the early civil rights generation could rise. The fact that many of them were doing what Collins calls "racialized" labor, such as personnel supervision of black employees, or community relations work with black communities, meant they were often shunted into dead-end jobs with little or no opportunity for further advancement. Indeed, many such jobs were eliminated in the 1980s when social turmoil diminished and conservatives took over the White House. When Collins interviewed most of those still in the corporate sector for a second time in 1993 and 1994, they expressed far less optimism than they had a few years earlier. None of those in Collins's study who were once touted in corporate circles as potential CEOs ever made it to the top.

By 1987, only one black, Clifton Wharton, the son of America's first black ambassador, had become a CEO, and he did so by an atypical route at an atypical company. Wharton graduated from Harvard and then earned a Ph.D. in economics from the University of Chicago in 1958. After working with an economic development agency financed by the Rockefeller family, he served as president of Michigan State University from 1970 to 1978 and as chancellor of the State University of New York system from 1978–87. During this time, as is often the practice with university presidents, he became a director of several corporations. Thanks to his university administrative experience and corporate contacts, in 1987 he became the CEO of TIAA-CREF, the company that manages pension funds for educators. It was the world's largest private pension fund and the third-largest insurance company in the country. Wharton served as CEO until 1993, when he became deputy secretary of State in the Clinton administration, at the time the highest-ranking African American in the Department of State.[3]

Such was the corporate world that ABC graduates would encounter as they began their climb up the corporate ladder in the 1970s and 1980s. By and large, those we interviewed in the late 1980s expressed strong satisfaction with their entry-level jobs. Indeed, many, especially those with law degrees or MBAs from prestigious universities, indicated that they were much in demand when they entered the job market. However, when we asked about their current level of satisfaction and their future plans, most of them lowered their voices, sometimes asked not to be quoted, and stated that they were thinking of leaving their current employers. In a number of cases, when we tried to call these people back a few months later to ask further questions, we learned they already had left. For example, when we asked one ABC graduate what it was like working for a major New York bank, he responded:

It has its ups and downs. Being black in corporate America is no picnic. Regardless of how well you are educated or how strong your background, there are still biases and prejudices in corporate America. . . . I don't feel I've been treated as I should at [company at which he was employed]. When I went into the training program, I was near or at the top of my class. Every position that I have been put into, I've always been told I've done well. I've been told that I've done well verbally but when it comes to putting it on paper, it loses something in the translation. Then it is always explained to me as, "Well, you have to realize that I'm a tough grader" or this or that and it doesn't float. You tell me how great a job I do, say that on paper. . . . I see many blacks leaving the corporate ranks.

When we tried to call him a year later, we were told: "He's somewhere out in California."

Some of those we interviewed indicated that they were shocked when they first encountered racial prejudice where they worked. After encountering little to no racism at Citibank, Cher Lewis was stunned by the level of racism when she took a job at Chase Manhattan. "I got a lot of crap. I was told I would never have gotten so far if I had not been black. Someone actually said in front of me once, 'This is what happens when you let these type of people work here.' This was meant for me to hear. It was mean. I also heard 'You're making it difficult for the rest of us, we don't work that way,' like only immigrants and struggling people work that hard."

Monique Burns, at the time of our 1986 interview an editor at *Travel & Leisure*, told us that she had not experienced prejudice at Concord Academy or at Radcliffe, but she did when she entered the working world:

> I was the first black editor here. There was one other that had lasted about six months. I understood quickly why. I was treated as someone who was not as skilled as my colleagues, even though I was (and in some cases I was more skilled). Someone had lost a Cross pen, and I had been given a Cross pen by my brother. This woman's pen had her initials on it, mine didn't. She came into my office and started talking about this stolen Cross pen. She picked up my pen and looked at it. I felt hurt, and I don't think she would have done it otherwise, but she had heard that black people steal. It was incredible because I thought the people I was working with were pretty intelligent, and I was just amazed to find these prejudices. . . . I didn't have these experiences in prep school. . . . I hadn't really encountered it in college—it may well have been there, but I didn't notice it.

In those initial interviews, some made it clear that they were planning to go out on their own at some point. As we noted in the previous chapter, in 1986 Calvin Dorsey told us: "In five years I won't be working for Cox [Communications], I'll tell you that. I'll be in my own business." Another had this to say about his plans: "I see a plateau for myself that I may have reached already, not only in this organization, but in any large corporation. . . . I don't see a long-term career for myself in the large corporate world, because I think that requires certain compromises that I am not willing to make. So, I'm going to have to at some point strike out on my own. . . . One has to have the capital to jump into something like that, and I'm not in that position yet and won't be for another several years."

This same person noted that his "bitterness level" had increased as a result of his experience in the corporate world. As an example, he told the following story:

The president of this [corporation] is a good-old-boy. I don't know if you know him or not, his name is . . . and his family is very big, I think with . . .—his father or grandfather was head of . . . one of the big Southern colleges—but anyway that is just background. . . . Our [corporation] has been getting a lot of press, because we're doing very well, we're going through some structural changes which the market seems to really like. There was an interview with him and he was not quoted, but an anecdote was told about him. They were trying to get a flavor for the type of individual he is, and in the article they said here is a man who refers to blacks as "coloreds," sometimes correcting himself and sometimes not. Now it was not a direct quote; however, having met the man and having heard some of the internal anecdotes about him, things that he has reportedly said and done, I believe it. And what bothered me more was that after this came out he issued no statement to the population as a whole or the black officers in this [corporation] to try to smooth what he had to have known would be ruffled feathers. That disturbs me a bit. Therefore, I wonder. If indeed that is how he feels, and if indeed he is now trying to mold this bank into the image that he wants it to be, what is to say that his lieutenants and their lieutenants are not going to share these types of attitudes? And, therefore, what's in this for me?

Jeffrey Palmer, a graduate of Kimball Union Academy, decided to leave a large elite institution for a black company. He recalled the irony of some of the changes he had made since his undergraduate days as a student activist at Yale. After receiving his MBA from the University of Chicago, he was hired by Needham, Harper and Steers, an advertising agency and assigned to work on the Recipe Dog Food account. "It was so bizarre," he laughed. "One day I had hair out to here and was saying 'Power to the people!' and the next day I had a job selling dog food." He "was doing very well" at Needham but after five years had not become a supervisor. When the J. Walter Thompson Company offered him a job as an account supervisor, with a substantial pay increase and significant responsibilities to run the Quaker Oats account, he accepted.

He also experienced success at J. Walter Thompson, but, after a while, he became dissatisfied there, too: "I was on the fast track at Thompson. They put me in all these special things that they had going for their rising stars. . . . I was at a retreat one time and I was talking to the chairman of the board of J. Walter Thompson and he said, 'Well, why are you thinking about leaving?' And I said, 'It's very simple, actually. When I came into this company, I looked up and saw the ceiling. The white guy that came in the door right next to me looked up and saw a skylight. Quite frankly, I'm having to bend over to stay in this room I'm in. And it's time for me to move on.' So, he understood that. I told him, 'I can't have your job. How high can I go? Either I'm dissatisfied today or I'm dissatisfied tomorrow.'"

So, after three and a half years with J. Walter Thompson, Palmer left to work for Burrell Advertising Agency, the largest black-owned agency in the country. At the time of our 1987 interview he was in business for himself as co-owner and president of the Accent Printing Company, which employed forty people. He had no doubt that he made the right decision: "When I went into the advertising business in Chicago as an account executive, there were—in all of the agencies in Chicago, particularly the ones up and down Michigan Avenue, the cream of the crop in the agency business—there were three black account people in the entire agency business. I was the first black account person ever to work at Needham, Harper and Steers. In 1987, eighteen years later, there are three black account people on Michigan Avenue. And there is one at Needham, Harper and Steers." But as we shall see, Jeffrey Palmer's departure from corporate America did not turn out to be a permanent one.

DOWNSIZED AND OUT

Some ABC graduates did not leave the corporate world because they experienced discrimination or were staring at a glass ceiling. They left because of downsizing at a point when they thought their careers were still on the rise.

Born in Baltimore, Jennifer Casey Pierre entered the ABC program in 1968. After successfully completing the summer program at Carleton College, she attended the Baldwin School outside of Philadelphia. Because of her interest in engineering, she decided to attend Carnegie-Mellon University in Pittsburgh, a school known for math, science, and engineering. When she found her first physics course boring, she decided to switch her major to math and to minor in business.

While a student at Carnegie-Mellon, she spent her summers working for General Foods. As a result of that work, she won a minority fellowship that paid for her to attend Columbia University's Graduate School of Business. After receiving her MBA in 1977, she went to work for General Foods in White Plains, New York, as an assistant products manager. In 1981, after two years with General Foods and two years with the American Can Company in nearby Greenwich, Connecticut, she accepted an offer from R. J. Reynolds in Winston-Salem, North Carolina.

At the time of our first interview, she had been working for Reynolds for six years and had been promoted twice, first to assistant manager and then to brand promotion manager. When we spoke with her in 1994, she had been at Reynolds thirteen years, survived numerous downsizings ("the downsizing has become what I consider standard operating procedure"), and was the only black female in management in her "section" of the company. In 1997, after sixteen years with the company, in yet another round of downsizing, her position was eliminated. Since that time, she has worked in the public sector, first with the city of Winston-Salem, and then, starting in January 2000, with United Way of Forsyth County.

When we interviewed Kenneth Pettis in 1986 in his New York office at Bankers Trust he was vice president and "team leader" of the Global Syndications Group, which managed primary and secondary asset sales within the bank's New York division. He first heard about the ABC program as a junior high school student in Chicago. Although neither of his parents had attended college, his uncle Ernest had gone to college after his discharge from the navy. "In my family," he recalls, "I was always the one. . . . I was Kenneth who was like Ernest, Ernest being my uncle who had gone away to college. People had expectations for me." Knowing that he was scheduled to attend a high school with one of the worst reputations in the city, he was enthusiastic when a counselor asked him if he would like to go away to a prep school. He had never been east of Gary, Indiana, and had never been on an airplane until 1970, when he flew east to participate in the summer program at Williams College in Williamstown, Massachusetts ("the smallest town I'd ever seen").

After four years at the Taft School and four more at Brown University, where he majored in economics, Pettis was ready to enter the business world. While at Brown, he had held many jobs, including student manager of the college bookstore, projectionist for the film society, and housekeeper for a family in Providence. As he made his plans for what he would do after graduation, he knew one thing: "I decided I wanted some of the things I'd seen. I decided it was time to start making some money."

Employment recruiters were streaming into Brown looking for ambitious young talent. Pettis received several offers, but decided to go with Bankers Trust, mainly because they offered the most money, but also because he believed they had a good training program and because the people he spoke with from Bankers Trust were "enthusiastic." A year after completing the twelve-month training program, he was promoted to assistant treasurer; then, two years later, to assistant vice president. He was again promoted two years later, this time to vice president, the position he held at the time of that first interview. Pettis stayed in banking for twenty years—eight years with Bankers Trust, four and a half years with Chase Manhattan, seven years with Barclay's Bank, and a year with J. P. Morgan.

Having seen many downsizings, in which he watched his fellow workers receive bad news, and sometimes having to deliver it to them himself, his own position was eliminated in a downsizing. He decided that he'd "had it with corporate America," and that he "didn't want to do finance anymore." Instead, he converted a longtime hobby, furniture restoration, into a business: on June 27, 1999, he purchased a franchise from Furniture Medic. Two years later, when we talked by phone, he indicated that his small business was doing well, that he had two part-time employees, and that he did not miss corporate life at all. "I'll never make as much money as I did in banking," he said, but he was happy with his decision. His wife of sixteen years, a black graduate of Smith College, was helping him with the office work. He sits on the board of the Community Coalition on Race, a community organization dedicated to maintaining integrated housing in Maplewood, New Jersey, where he lives with his wife, his thirteen-year-old daughter, and his seven-year-old son.

Downsizing also played a role in the corporate career of Vest Monroe, but not because he was downsized out of his job. In 1999, he left *Time* magazine to become assistant managing editor for National and Foreign Business News at the *San Jose Mercury News*, one of thirty-two newspapers in the Knight Ridder chain. Starting with a large staff and ample budget, he looked forward to building a top-notch business section in the newspaper that serves the fabled Silicon Valley. About a year after his arrival, much to his surprise and dismay, he was asked to identify which people to lay off as part of the downsizing Knight Ridder was undergoing, and to continue to produce high quality news with far fewer resources. During our interview with him at the newspaper in August 2001, Monroe unexpectedly told us that he had voluntarily accepted the company's buyout, and would be leaving the *Mercury News* in just a few weeks, because downsizing made his work, and the quality of the work of his unit, less meaningful:

I only have two more weeks here. I took the buyout. Nobody forced me. I did it because of what had happened here. When I came here, I had sixteen jobs to fill in business alone. Now, in less than a year, I was being asked to identify people for layoffs, for downsizing. I have the third-largest business department in the country. My business travel budget for fifty-five reporters was cut from $29,000 a month to $6,000 a month. I can't send anybody anywhere. I turned fifty years old a week ago Sunday. I have been in this business for thirty years, since I was twenty years old. I did not come here to manage downsizing.[4]

MEMBERS OF THE CORPORATE ELITE

Of the many tens of thousands who start careers in corporate America each year, only a very few make it to the top, or even close to the top, so it would not be surprising if few or none of the relatively few ABC graduates in the corporate world ever became CEOs. However, there are a handful of early ABC graduates who are highly successful in the corporate world in the face of extremely stiff competition. They are members of the corporate elite by any standard.

As we noted briefly in chapter 1, Jesse Spikes is one of the more inspiring ABC success stories in the corporate world. He went from a share-cropper's family in Georgia to a Dartmouth BA in 1972, a Rhodes Scholarship, and then a Harvard law degree in 1977. After a year as a law clerk for a federal judge on the U.S. Court of Appeals, and another year as general counsel for the black-owned Atlanta Life Insurance Company, he took advantage of an opportunity provided by his work for the black mayor of Atlanta, Andrew Young, and became a lawyer for the Al Bahrain Arab African Bank, a bank in the Middle East with international investments. Although the job gave him a chance to see the world and maybe bring some investments to Atlanta, the primary attraction was the opportunity to make much more money than he was currently making, which would allow him to do more for his parents, ten siblings, and his many nieces and nephews.

The work was interesting and lucrative, but life in the Middle East proved lonely. Even after the business pace slowed down a bit and he moved from Bahrain to Cairo, Egypt, Spikes still found himself feeling isolated.

> The people were very friendly, very nice, but not very open to outsiders. I think that part of my situation was being single. People tend to socialize in coed, family groupings, and a single, foreign male really has no place in that social setting. So I found that most of my social life there was with friends who came over from the States to visit. I met a number of people from the American Embassy, or people who were there doing other things, and I belonged to a sporting club. I was learning to play tennis, and so the people around the tennis court were people I started to spend time with. So, yes, it was lonely and I think toward the end that was the thing that really made me decide to give it up.

He earned enough working in the Middle East to afford a long break when he returned to Atlanta in December 1985, and for the next ten months spent most of his time with family and friends (especially with his mother, who passed away five months after his return). Almost a year after he returned from the Middle East, Spikes decided to join the Atlanta law firm of Long,

Aldrich and Norman, where Oliver Lee, a Dartmouth friend who had also been an A Better Chance student, was a partner. He also began to represent Andrew Young again. When Young ran unsuccessfully for governor in 1990, Spikes was his general counsel. About the time of that election, Young was on an airplane with Evander Holyfield, an Atlanta native who had won the heavyweight boxing championship a few weeks earlier. When Holyfield told Young that he was seeking a business lawyer to represent his interests, Young recommended Jesse Spikes.

Spikes became Holyfield's lawyer, and that opened up a new area of legal work for him. As he explained to us in an interview in 1994, "As a result of that, some of the other sports figures in town came to me, so we got into sports law. Then that spilled over a little bit into entertainment . . . so I've represented some artists as well. So since 1990 I have very heavy emphasis on the sports side of the corporate law practice."

By 1994, Spikes was the only black among the forty-four partners at Long, Aldridge and Norman (Oliver Lee had left to join another Atlanta law firm). Five years later, the firm had grown to 190 people with almost sixty partners, and Spikes was one of two black partners.

So, after leaving a small Georgia town outside Atlanta to enter the ABC program, and after a journey that took him to New Hampshire, Nairobi (Kenya), Oxford (England), and Cambridge (Massachusetts), Detroit, Bahrain, and Cairo, Jesse Spikes has settled in Atlanta, working in a corporate law firm, surrounded by his large extended family, active in his church and in his community.

Bill Lewis, mentioned earlier in the book as a graduate of Andover and Harvard and an investment banker at Morgan Stanley, is another rising star in the corporate world. At the time of our 1987 interview he had been with Morgan Stanley for seven years, and his title was vice president. How had things gone for him at Morgan Stanley? "Great. Promoted. Top of my class. Making a lot of money. Having a lot of fun. Working in the mergers and acquisitions department." He had no worries about a glass ceiling:

This is a service business. Your performance is gauged with others around you. There are a lot of subjective factors—it's not like we're making widgets on a production line where somebody can come by and monitor your performance. We're doing analysis, providing services. . . . In any sort of service business, interpersonal relationships are major in determining how successful you are. . . . I, fortunately, have been able to develop sufficient relationships and do a sufficiently good job to be promoted right along and to do well. Whether that will continue or not, who knows, but to date I haven't had any problems. . . . I certainly haven't received any indication that I'm capping off, but I don't know. Call me in four years.

When we interviewed Lewis in October 2001, his career had indeed continued to flourish at Morgan Stanley. He became a managing director in 1988 (in seven years, faster than anyone ever had at Morgan Stanley), and during the 1990s he also served as head of the worldwide corporate finance department, head of the worldwide real estate department, and co-head of worldwide mergers. Shortly before our interview he had been named head of the global banking department. His clients have included such major corporations as Sara Lee, Union Carbide, Phillips Petroleum, Dial Corp., Whirlpool Corporation, Weyerhaeuser Company, and AMF. Both inside Morgan Stanley and in the larger financial community, Lewis was recognized as hugely successful. In 1997 a *Fortune* magazine feature titled "The New Black Power: The Players" referred to him as "a managing director on the rise." A July 2002 article in *Fortune* on the "50 Most Powerful Black Executives in America" ranked Lewis number thirteen on the list.[5]

Though we did not ask him for details about his income, one of our informants (a managing director at another financial investment company) put Lewis's income in the 1990s in the following context:

In the first half of the 1990s a young Morgan Stanley managing director would have earned in the range of $1.0 million to $3 million [annually] with a lot of folks in the $1.5 to $2.5 million range. In 1997–1998 the industry was booming . . . the years 1998, 1999, and 2000 were unbelievable. Let me give you an example. One of Morgan Stanley's principal competitors has approximately 200 managing directors in the Investment Banking Division. In 1999 and 2000, 70 of the 200 received total compensation where the first digit was 3 or more—meaning $3 million or more, with the range being $3 million to $10 million.

From the time of our first interview to the time of our second interview, therefore, Bill Lewis had become a multimillionaire. When the *ABC Alumni Newsletter* for fall 2000 listed the names of those donors who had given $1,000 or more to ABC in the previous fiscal year, Lewis was third on the list of "special impact" donors with a gift of $250,000, right after Oprah Winfrey at $10 million and the Goldman Sachs Foundation with a three-year $1.2 million grant.[6] Similarly, Lewis has been quite generous to his prep school alma mater. In addition to gifts totaling more than $100,000 to the art gallery at Andover, he and his wife contributed between $100,000 and $500,000 to create the "William M. Lewis, Jr., '74" endowed scholarship. More recently, as Lewis explained to us in our 2001 interview, he has supported "organizations that are looking to better the lot of African Americans," including the National Urban League (where he serves as treasurer) and the NAACP Legal Defense and Educational Fund.

Like Bill Lewis, Frank Borges had a very positive experience at a large financial institution, but unlike Lewis, he decided to leave in order to run a smaller one. After graduating from Millbrook School and Trinity College, and finishing law school at the University of Connecticut, he worked for Travelers Insurance Company from 1978 to 1986. After serving two terms as the treasurer of the state of Connecticut (it's an elected position) from 1986 to 1993, he became a managing director of Financial Guaranty Insurance Company, a subsidiary of G. E. Capital (in turn, a subsidiary of G. E.). In 1998, he was recruited to become the president of Landmark Partners. In our interview with him in April 2002, he told us he had been successful at G. E., did not feel discriminated against because of his race, and had not been seeking other opportunities. Still, the chance to run a company and to work in an entrepreneurial environment with the potential for growth appealed to him. When we asked him if his decision to leave G. E. was related in any way to some awareness on his part that the opportunities for moving up the corporate ladder might be limited because he was an African American, he acknowledged that the possibility of his becoming chairman of G. E. at some point in his career was "remote," but he went on to say that such considerations were only, as he put it, "in the back of my mind." So, as of April 2002, he was running a full service alternative investment firm that employs forty people and, according to his bio, "has formed 14 funds focused on venture capital, buyout, mezzanine and real estate partnerships totaling $3.8 billion."

Another of those we had interviewed in 1987 emerged near the top of a *Fortune*-level company. This one surprised us because he had told us that he had left corporate America when he thought that his upward mobility was likely to be limited because of race. Yet, as of June 2002, when we interviewed him in Philadelphia, Jeffrey Palmer was a senior vice president at Pep Boys. Palmer spent five years, from 1987 to 1992, as president and owner of TAS Graphics, a printing company with plants in Chicago and Detroit that did work for various *Fortune* 500 companies, including Hallmark, Ford Motor Company, American Airlines, and Dupont. Although the company was quite successful—he bought it as a $12 million company, and five years later it was a $22 million company—he decided to close it. The primary reason was the arrival of a union. It was the largest nonunionized shop in Detroit, and, as he put it, "the union came after us really hard and strong." When the union came in "it increased our costs so much that we were no longer competitive and so we ended up closing it down." Moreover, with plants in both Chicago and Detroit, and with the time and energy he put into running the business, he found that he was working seven days a week and spending almost no time with his family.

Rather than starting another entrepreneurial venture, Palmer decided to go back into corporate America. He became senior vice president and group account director at Uni World Group in New York City, "depending on who you're talking to either the number one or number two largest minority owned advertising agency in the United States." He ran that agency until 1996 when he received a call from a headhunter encouraging him to apply for a position at Circuit City in Richmond, Virginia. After interviewing there, he accepted a job as vice president of advertising and marketing, overseeing a staff of about 150 people. Two and a half years later another headhunter called and told him about a job at Home Depot. He visited the corporate headquarters in Atlanta, liked what he saw, and became a vice president, directing the entire advertising department for this $40 billion corporation. At Home Depot he oversaw a staff of 250 people located in ten divisions dispersed throughout the United States, Canada, Puerto Rico, and South America.

Palmer stayed two years, commuting from Atlanta to New York City on weekends to see his wife, a creative director for *Essence* magazine (he had done a similar commute from Richmond while with Circuit City). Then, one of the two headhunters got back in touch with him, and in December 2001, he began work as senior vice president of marketing and advertising at Pep Boys in Philadelphia (for this job, he takes the train to and from New York each day). Though Pep Boys is smaller than Circuit City or Home Depot (in 2001 it was number 606 on the *Fortune* 1,000 list, whereas Home Depot was number 23 and Circuit City was number 155), Palmer is closer to the top of the corporate hierarchy. At Pep Boys, along with the president and the other three senior vice presidents (of merchandising, store operations, and administration), he sits on the executive committee that runs the company on a day-to-day basis.

The most important ABC graduate in the corporate world, Deval Patrick, has yet to be mentioned in this book. His rise to the corporate elite reveals how the ABC program places capable young men and women onto a track that can lead to the highest circles in America. Born in Chicago in 1956, his father, a baritone sax player, abandoned the family to join up with a jazz band when Patrick was four years old. Patrick, his mother, and his sister lived in a low-income neighborhood where he was attending the local public school when one of his teachers recommended him to ABC. He graduated from Milton Academy in 1974, went to Harvard and then Harvard Law School. After working for the NAACP Legal Defense and Educational Fund, he joined a prestigious corporate law firm in Boston, Hill & Barlow.

Patrick came to national prominence when Bill Clinton nominated him to be the assistant attorney general in charge of the civil rights division of the Department of Justice. Unlike Clinton's previous two nominees, Lani Guinier and John Payton, both of whom faced such strong opposition that Clinton withdrew his nominations, Patrick won bipartisan support and was confirmed easily.[7] As head of that division from 1994 to 1997, Patrick directed the work of 240 lawyers. In August 1995 his wife and two daughters moved back to Milton, Massachusetts, and he commuted back and forth from Massachusetts to Washington, D.C. In early 1997, he returned to private practice as a partner with another Boston law firm, Day, Berry & Howard. Significantly, in 1997 he also became the first ABC graduate to serve on the board of a major corporation when he was invited to join the board of directors of UAL.

Shortly thereafter, Patrick moved to the center of the battle over racial fairness in corporate America when he was asked to chair a task force created as part of the settlement in a huge racial discrimination suit against Texaco. As chair of the Independent Equality and Fairness Task Force, he had responsibility for helping Texaco create and implement a human resources program that would ensure fairness and equal opportunity for all employees. It had to report annually on Texaco's progress to the Federal District Court for five years. After submitting two such reports to the Federal District Court, Patrick resigned from his role as chair of the task force and accepted a position as Texaco's vice president and general counsel. From February 1999 to April 2001, he headed Texaco's legal department, which has more than seventy lawyers in offices around the world.[8]

In April 2001, Patrick left Texaco to become executive vice president and general counsel at Coca-Cola, where he and four other senior vice presidents join the president of Coca-Cola on the executive committee. According to the *Atlanta Journal and Constitution*, Patrick received $1 million to compensate him for payments he would have received had he stayed at Texaco. He has a five-year contract that pays him a base salary of $475,000.[9]

There's also a younger generation of ABC graduates, from the 1980s and early 1990s, who are moving up in the corporate ranks. Dwayne Gathers, for example, attended a Harlem school that had a long tradition of sending children to independent schools through ABC and other programs. He graduated from Deerfield in 1980 and Dartmouth in 1984, and then completed the management-training program at a major New York bank, where he worked in the energy and minerals division. Banking took him into the international area, and from 1991 to 1993 he worked in the State Department as a special assistant to the assistant secretary of State for African Affairs, where he became so conversant with African economic and political issues that he ended up doing projects for the Agency for International Development and serving as a United Nations election observer in South Africa's first racially open election in 1994. In 1995 the governor of California appointed him as the first director of the state's new Office of Trade and Investment in Johannesburg, providing advisory services to California companies of all sizes seeking business opportunities anywhere on the African continent. By January 2000, he was president of his own international business development company, The Hanover Group, with headquarters in San Francisco and affiliates in Australia, Brazil, The Netherlands, and South Africa. Most of his clients are foreign trade promotion councils and companies that want to operate in the American market or make deals with American companies. Gathers is on the board of trustees at Deerfield, and he is on the advisory board for Africa of the Overseas Private Investment Corporation. During our interview in August 2002, he said that he likes the independence of having his own business and does not foresee working for a large corporation in the future.

Stepping back from the specific careers we have examined in this chapter, our findings on ABC graduates in the corporate world are mixed. For many, there is a sense of discouragement based on a perception of racial discrimination. For a few, however, there is continuing optimism as they move up the corporate ladder, within a few steps of the top. The career of Jeffrey Palmer, who got out when he saw the glass ceiling in 1984 and ended up in the innermost circle of power at Pep Boys, shows just how complex the situation can be. It is therefore time to see how our findings fit with those of other researchers.

BLACKS ON THE CORPORATE LADDER

The negative message we heard from many of the corporate executives we interviewed—the slights, the downsizing, the outright racism—has parallels in the findings of black investigators who have studied the careers of black executives in corporate America. In three different survey and interview studies, two based on data gathered in the 1970s and the third based on data gathered in the mid-1980s, sociologist John Fernandez found blacks and Hispanics reporting that they were being passed over at the middle levels of corporations. Moreover, they provided him with numerous examples of individual, cultural, and institutional racism.[10]

As already noted, Sharon Collins also found that many of the black executives she interviewed in Chicago were on shaky ground. One-third of the top executives in her study who entered the labor force after 1965 were recruited for dead-end positions in personnel or public relations, even if they had such technical skills as accounting or engineering. More generally, she found in 1986 that 38 percent of her seventy-six interviewees were doing "racially oriented" work in their present position or had done so in the last job they held before leaving the company, meaning work in which they interacted primarily with black customers, civil rights agencies of government, or black communities. Not only were many of these jobs dead ends, they were being downgraded or eliminated in an atmosphere of social apathy and intense foreign economic competition. "The lack of a strong push by government on the one hand, and the need to reduce staff costs on the other, will eradicate these positions," she concluded.[11]

However, two-thirds of the black executives were not doing racially oriented work at the time they were interviewed by Collins. One-third had always held positions where they interacted primarily with nonblacks, and one-third had been able to escape from racially oriented jobs, usually because they had gained generalizable experience and skills through sales or marketing to black customers.[12] Nevertheless, Collins is not optimistic that many blacks will rise to the top in major corporations because of the persistence of racism inside and outside the corporate community.

Support for this pessimism can be found in the work of management consultant Edward W. Jones, Jr., a former assistant to the president of AT&T. In a survey conducted in the 1980s of hundreds of black managers with MBAs from five of the highest-rated business schools, more than 90 percent said they had encountered subtle forms of racism and felt they had less opportunity to advance than whites; two-thirds had the strong impression that many whites in corporations persist in the belief that blacks are intellectually inferior.[13]

More recently, in 1998, the Joint Center for Political and Economic Studies surveyed 750 black professionals in corporate America. Although most expressed optimism about their own professional futures in America's largest corporations, 81 percent said discrimination in their jobs was common. When asked to rate how well "corporate America" was doing in terms of promoting blacks on an equitable basis, 40 percent said "poor," 33 percent said "fair," 18 percent said "good" and 1 percent said "excellent." Tellingly, 78 percent said that they believed top black executives are "often in those positions for appearances sake." Almost two-thirds (64 percent) advised black youngsters to pursue careers as entrepreneurs, far more than the 24 percent who encouraged them to enter the corporate world. And more than two-thirds (68 percent) said they wanted to do what former ABC students Calvin Dorsey, Alan Mitchell, and Ken Pettis have done—start their own businesses.[14]

But just as was the case for the ABC graduates we have written about, there is also evidence that other African Americans have made some remarkable strides within the corporate community in recent years. Significantly, Deval Patrick, formerly with Texaco and now with Coca-Cola, is not the highest-ranking African American in a large corporation. Between 1999 and 2001 black males became the CEOs at American Express, Maytag, Avis, Merrill Lynch, AOL Time Warner, and the Federal National Mortgage Association (known as Fannie Mae). When Wharton of TIAA-CREF is added to the picture, this means that seven African Americans have made it to the very top. These men, all between the ages of forty-five and fifty-six at the time of their appointments, come from both middle-class and low-income backgrounds. What they share in common with each other and the ABC graduates high up in corporate America are excellent educational credentials (four of the seven have been to Harvard either as undergraduates or to attend the business or law schools). All but Wharton worked their way up the corporate ladder through a variety of management positions, and some have government experience as well.

Furthermore, as *Fortune* magazine put it in a July 2002 feature story on the "50 Most Powerful Black Executives in America," there may be "more on the way." The article noted that the Executive Leadership Council, a networking organization of primarily senior black executives in *Fortune* 500 companies who are "no more than three steps away from CEO," had 275 members as of that date, compared with nineteen members when it was founded in 1986. Although there are several thousand executives within three steps of the top in *Fortune* 500 companies, the 275 may represent from 3 to 5 percent of the total.[15]

As we have noted, all seven of the African American CEOs are men. Only eleven of the "50 Most Powerful Black Executives in America" identified by *Fortune* in 2002 are women, none is in the top nine (Oprah is number ten), and seven of the eleven are in the bottom half of the list. As the article's author puts it, "rather than running big-ticket mainstream divisions or companies, they tend to drive more entrepreneurial businesses, often creating the businesses themselves." Ella L. J. Edmondson Bell, a professor at Dartmouth's Tuck School of Business and the coauthor of a book on black women executives, only half-jokingly refers to the *Fortune* list as "the brothers list."[16] Along the same lines, three-fourths of the members of the Executive Leadership Council are men.[17]

There have been very few women of any color who have become CEOs of *Fortune* 500 companies. The first was Katharine Graham who took over at the *Washington Post* (which her father had owned) when her husband committed suicide in 1963. Almost forty years later, in January 2002, with the appointment of Patricia Russo to head Lucent Technologies, there were six women CEOs of *Fortune* 500 companies. Unlike the African American men who have become CEOs, whose origins are quite varied in socioeconomic terms, the women CEOs have been born into privileged economic circumstances, and all but one are white (Andrea Jung, who became CEO of Avon in November 1999, is Chinese American).[18]

CONCLUSION

The high-level corporate executives and corporate lawyers discussed in this chapter, whether from the ABC program or some other pathway to the top, represent a remarkable achievement that did not seem to be in the cards as recently as 1998. Combined with the appointment of an African American, Colin Powell, as secretary of state in 2001, it may be that there has been a breakthrough for African Americans.

But is there reason to think there will be continuing increases in African Americans in the corporate elite during the next decade? What about the corporate pipeline? Have the top business and law schools increased their enrollment of African Americans? Are there a growing number of young black executives who are poised to join the handful who have made it to the top? Are Dwayne Gathers and other young ABC alumni who are doing well in the executive ranks of corporate America the exceptions or the rule? We discuss these questions in the final chapter as part of our more general discussion of whether progress will continue for black Americans. But before that, it is necessary to see how the children of ABC graduates are faring.

NOTES

1. For a more in-depth treatment of the first blacks to serve on *Fortune*-level boards, see Richard L. Zweigenhaft and G. William Domhoff, *Diversity in the Power Elite: Have Women and Minorities Reached the Top?* (New Haven: Yale University Press, 1998), 78–103.

2. Sharon M. Collins, "The Marginalization of Black Executives," *Social Problems* 36, no. 4 (1989): 320.

3. See "Clifton R. Wharton, Jr." *Current Biography Yearbook* (1987): 598. Gerald H. Rosen, "TIAA-CREF: Declining Returns," *Academe* 78, no. 1 (1992): 8; and Lee A. Daniels, "Abrupt Exit: Racism, Leaks, and Isolation Drove Clif Wharton to Resign from State Department," *Emerge* (February 1994): 28–33.

4. In March 2001, Jay Harris, the fifty-two-year-old publisher of the *San Jose Mercury News*, and an African American, resigned from his position in protest of the budget cuts forced upon the newspaper by Knight Ridder. According to the *Washington Post*, "Harris, 52, stunned the newspaper world March 19 by resigning with a public blast at Knight Ridder for attempting to impose deep budget cuts so the *Mercury News* could maintain a 22 percent profit margin during an economic downturn." A few weeks later, he received a standing ovation and "something approaching a hero's welcome" when he spoke to the American Society of Newspaper Editors. Howard Kurtz, "Newsroom versus Boardroom: Ex-Publisher Decries Emphasis on Profits," *Washington Post*, April 7, 2001, C1, C14.

5. Eileen P. Gunn, "No Boundaries," *Fortune* (August 4, 1997): 77; Cora Daniels, "50 Most Powerful Black Executives in America," *Fortune* (July 22, 2002): 65.

6. *A Better Chance News* 2, no. 2 (Fall 2000): iii.

7. Steven A. Holmes, "Street Survivor via Harvard: Deval Laurdine Patrick," *New York Times*, February 2, 1994, A12.

8. As of October 1999, Texaco was one of ten *Fortune* 500 companies with legal counsel who were minorities (nine of the ten were men). See Darryl Van Duch, "Minority GCs Are Few, Far Between," *National Law Journal* (October 18, 1999): 1ff.

9. Henry Unger, "Ex-Coke President Got $3.5 million; Stahl's Separation Deal Also Gave Stock Access," *Atlanta Journal and Constitution,* May 2, 2001, 1C

10. John R. Fernandez, *Black Managers in White Corporations* (New York: Wiley, 1975); *Racism and Sexism in Corporate Life: Changing Values in American Business* (Lexington, Mass.: Lexington, 1981); and "Racism and Sexism in Corporate America: Still Not Color- or Gender-Blind in the 1980s," in *Ensuring Minority Success in Corporate Management*, edited by Donna E. Thompson and Nancy DiTomaso (New York: Plenum Press, 1988), 71–99. For a discussion of individual, institutional, and cultural racism, see James M. Jones, "Racism in Black and White: A Bicultural Model of Reaction and Evolution," in *Eliminating Racism: Profiles in Controversy*, edited by Phyliss A. Katz and Dalmas A. Taylor (New York: Plenum Press, 1988), 127–131.

11. Collins, "Marginalization of Black Executives," 329.

12. Ibid. For a more complete presentation of all Collins's findings, see her *Black Corporate Executives: The Making and Breaking of a Black Middle Class* (Philadelphia: Temple University Press, 1997).

13. Edward W. Jones, Jr., "Black Managers: The Dream Deferred," *Harvard Business Review* 86, no. 3 (1986): 84–93; see also Jones, "What's It Like to Be a Black Manager?" *Harvard Business Review* 51, no. 4 (1973): 108–116; and Joe R. Feagin, *Race and Ethnic Relations*, 3rd ed. (Englewood Cliffs, N.J.: Prentice-Hall, 1989), 228.

14. See Shelley Branch, "What Blacks Think of Corporate America," *Fortune* (July 6, 1998): 140, 142–143.

15. Cora Daniels, "50 Most Powerful Black Executives in America," *Fortune* (July 22, 2002): 63. The 3–5 percent estimate is our best guess. Jeffrey Palmer informs us that when he worked at Home Depot (number 23 on the *Fortune* list in 2001), there were fifty to seventy-five people within three steps of the CEO. Presumably there are fewer at smaller companies, so we have ventured a speculative guess at an average of twenty executives within three steps of the top.

16. Daniels, "50 Most Powerful Black Executives," 74.

17. The 75 percent figure was provided by Joann Stevens at the Executive Leadership Council in a phone interview on July 29, 2002.

18. For a discussion of women in the corporate elite, see Zweigenhaft and Domhoff, *Diversity in the Power Elite*, 41–62. For a more detailed comparison of the class backgrounds of the African American men and the women who have become CEOs, see Richard L. Zweigenhaft, "The African Americans in the White Establishment: How and Why Did They Get There?", paper presented at the annual meetings of the American Sociological Association, August 14, 2000, Washington, D.C. See also Claudia H. Deutsch, "Xerox Moves Up an Insider to Be Its Chief," *New York Times*, July 27, 2001, C4; and Simon Romero, "Lucent Finally Chooses a Chief Executive," *New York Times*, January 8, 2002, C1.

8

The Children of ABC Graduates

Although the growth of the black middle class has been substantial since the 1970s, there are nonetheless two reasons to be concerned about whether that growth will continue in the future. First, children of the black middle class achieve less academically in school than their white counterparts, perhaps in part because they are susceptible to the pull of street or ghetto culture in the context of continuing racial stigmatization.[1] Second, the children of the black middle class are less likely than the children of the white middle class to maintain their middle-class status. They are also less likely to be upwardly mobile.[2] Central to these patterns, though not the only factor, middle-class blacks have far less wealth than whites in the middle class. As two sociologists who have compared the wealth of black and white Americans put it, "an accurate and realistic appraisal of the economic footing of the black middle class reveals its precariousness, marginality and fragility." To the extent that ABC graduates, as newly arrived members of the black middle class (or even as newly arrived members of the black upper middle class), are in a "precarious" and "fragile" position, their children may be in an even more precarious and fragile one.[3]

The educational careers and early adult lives of children of ABC graduates may provide a unique angle on these issues. For one thing, their ABC-graduate parents received excellent educations and are well aware that (as was true for them) their children might be criticized by their peers for doing well in school and are at risk of slipping into an oppositional stance toward school authorities. Furthermore, these parents have the potential to help their children in a way that many black middle-class parents cannot because prep schools and Ivy League universities routinely give admission preferences to "legacies," as the children of graduates are called. Thus, ABC parents are able to provide their children with high expectations, role models, middle-class values and tastes, and ready-made educational networks, the latter a powerful form of social capital.

Although the educations and early careers of ABC children are of considerable interest, our conclusions have to be tentative for two reasons. First, our sample of ABC graduates has relatively few children due to the emphasis they put on their careers and the fact that many married late (or not at all). The twenty-three ABC graduates with whom we've spoken in the past few years have a total of only thirty-nine children. These small families are impressive evidence in and of themselves for the upward mobility of ABC graduates. Second, because many of those we interviewed married late, or married more than once, some of their children were still below age sixteen in 2002. This chapter, then, draws primarily on what twenty-three ABC graduates told us about their twenty-seven young adult children (though, as will be seen, we also have information on the children of other ABC graduates who were not in our original sample).

Our findings are based on responses to three general questions. First, to ascertain how they felt about their prep schools and to get a sense of whether ABC graduates viewed their prep school educations as a resource for their children, we asked them in our initial interviews if they would send their children to their prep school alma maters, and, if not, to other private schools. Second, we asked them in those initial interviews, and then again in the more recent interviews, about their children's educational experiences (including how decisions were made about where they went to school). Third, when relevant, we asked what their children are doing now that they are out of college.

THE LEGACIES

The ambivalence and complex feelings that can be triggered for ABC graduates by having their children become legacy students can be seen in a frank article in the *Choate Rosemary Hall Alumni Magazine* by Byron Haskins, an ABC student who graduated from Choate in 1972. Haskins, who has two master's degrees (one from the University of Michigan in general psychology and the other from Western Michigan in counseling psychology), works for the state of Michigan as an area administrator in the Department of Social Services. The article he wrote for the Choate alumni magazine, titled "A Mission Together: Establishing a Legacy," explains how his son became the first African American legacy student at Choate. Haskins felt mixed emotions about his experience at Choate because he had "endured quirky and traumatic lessons." He recalls that he had "arrived to silent acclaim and smoldering racism both bred by a gradually unveiled cultural ignorance." For the most part he had "repressed" the question of whether he would send any of his children to Choate. However, in the spring of 1995, he received a phone call from Tim Bradley, an old Choate buddy a year behind Haskins in the class of 1973, and more importantly, also an ABC student, one of only a small number of blacks at Choate in the early 1970s. After attending Tufts, Bradley became the keyboardist for Grammy award-winning singer Jody Watley. After years as a musician, and then starting a business in which he composed and produced music sound tracks for recruiting videos for prep schools and colleges, he returned to Choate to work in the admissions office and teach music production and technology. Bradley called Haskins to encourage him to consider sending his children to their alma mater. He then mailed Haskins a video that he and Andy Greenspan, a Choate classmate ("one of my best friends at Choate, and he has remained so throughout my life") had made about the school. Haskins's children were entranced by it—according to Haskins, "the kids watched the video over and over."

"Eventually," wrote Haskins, "the subliminal message took hold," and he took his daughter, already a high school sophomore, and his son, a few years younger, to visit the campus. "After agonizing debates, we decided that my son would apply for admission to the class of 2000." He applied, was accepted, and became the first African American legacy to attend Choate Rosemary Hall. Haskins draws the following conclusion in his article:

> Stephen symbolizes commitment to include people of color in the inner court of generational Choate families. This is a "glass ceiling" not often mentioned in diversity literature, but quite a thick and well protected one. When immigrants come to America, the first generation often struggles to lay a foundation for their children's and grandchildren's success. The African American community has often only dreamed of such an experience. My opportunities were avant-garde; my dream and my mission, a foundation. Unfortunately, I cannot say with assurance that the sky is the limit for Stephen, but he is better equipped to build an American life. And as long as there are those in institutions like Choate Rosemary Hall who also take up the mission Stephen and I now share, so will his privileged cousins be ready for his joining a successful American life for all.[4]

Stephen graduated in 2000 and went on to Yale.

Unlike Haskins, Ed McPherson, an Andover graduate, knew early on that he'd be pleased if his children were to attend his alma mater. When we asked him in 1987 if he'd consider sending his daughter to Andover, he answered, without hesitation: "Sure. My oldest daughter. She's already been there two or three times. I'd be glad to send her there if she wanted to go." By the time she was fourteen, McPherson—like many others we interviewed—had left the corporate world and was working in the public sector as coordinator of the

Faculty Development Institute at Virginia Polytechnic Institute in Blacksburg, Virginia. Although he was not sure how he would pay for her to go to Andover, she applied and was accepted. Then, in a turn of events that would certainly please the three headmasters who created the program back in 1962, she won the scholarship set up by Bill Lewis, the Morgan Stanley managing director who graduated from Andover two years after Ed McPherson.

When she graduated from Andover in the spring of 2000, she had won awards for her musical talent and for her compassion toward others. She had also been co-chair of the organization for African American and Latino students, the Af-Lat-Am Society, which her father had chaired thirty years earlier. In the fall of 2001, she entered the class of 2005 at Oberlin College.[5]

Ed McPherson noted in our 2001 interview that several faculty who had been at Andover when he was a student were still there when his daughter arrived, and they helped her with her transition to life at Andover: "They looked out for her, and talked to her, and helped her to feel comfortable and part of the school community." Here we see in clear focus the kind of benefits that prep school legacies have been receiving for generations. Ed McPherson, already a loyal alumnus who had served on the alumni council and had attended a number of reunions, became an even more loyal one. His second child, also a daughter, was only twelve at the time of our 2001 interview, but she was considering applying to both Andover and Exeter.

Just as Ed McPherson encouraged his daughters from a young age to think about following their dad to his alma mater, so, too, has Bill Lewis made it clear to his three young children (age nine, six, and two when we interviewed him in October 2001) that they should consider attending Andover. He told us, "I'd be thrilled if my kids go to Andover." When we asked if his wife (who graduated from a private school, the New York High School for Music and Arts) was as eager for them to attend Andover, he replied: "It's impossible for any sort of non-Andover person to be as comfortable as the Andover person would be, but I think she could ultimately get her arms around it. Let's put it this way: she doesn't object to me leaving Andover catalogs in the kids' rooms."

Like other ABC alumni, Deval Patrick has been on the board of trustees of his prep school alma mater, and he is among the ABC graduates who have provided their schools with legacy students. Patrick and his wife own a house in Milton, south of Boston, the town in which Patrick went to school as a student at Milton Academy. During the two years that he worked in Washington as assistant attorney general in the Clinton administration, and in his subsequent work with Texaco and Coca-Cola, Patrick commuted back to Boston while his family remained in Milton. Both of Patrick's daughters are legacy students at the school. When he gave the 2002 Martin Luther King lecture at

Milton (telling the students that "If you don't understand something you might be standing in the wrong place"), his daughters were among the students in the audience.

As the prep schools continue to try to include students of color in their predominantly white student bodies, the children of the more than ten thousand ABC graduates represent a sizable population of potential black legacy students. We have already noted that many prep schools selected early graduates of the ABC program when they integrated their boards of trustees. Moreover, the prep schools have also drawn from the increasingly large pool of ABC alumni as they have sought to diversify their faculties and administrations. We have mentioned Jay Farrow, a 1975 Westtown graduate who is now the associate head at that school, Tim Bradley, who graduated from Choate in 1973 and now teaches music and is the associate dean of admission there, and Michael Gary, a 1982 Pomfret alum who is now director of admissions at Exeter.[6] A quick perusal of prep school Web pages reveals ABC alumni in various roles at their own alma mater (for example, Samuel Washington, who graduated in 1981 from Lawrenceville, became an associate dean of admission at that school in 1999) and at other schools (to cite just two examples, Leander Magee, who graduated from Western Reserve Academy in 1976, has been teaching math and coaching baseball and basketball at Deerfield since 1980, and Charles Thompson, an ABC student who graduated from Middlesex in 1986, is the director of academic technology and the head of the computer science department at St. George's). Having their children attend their prep schools, then, as legacy students is but one of the many ways ABC students have benefited from, and contributed to, the prep school world—a world now far different from the world the early ABCers inhabited.

OTHER PRIVATE SCHOOLS

Many ABC graduates have chosen to send their children to private schools in their own hometowns. For example, Judge Harold Cushenberry and his wife reluctantly concluded that the public schools in Washington, D.C., were "pretty awful" and that they would send their two daughters to private schools. In our May 2001 interview, he explained that they never really considered sending the girls to Cushenberry's alma mater, Taft, in part because of the cost and in part because there were good schools nearby. As Cushenberry put it: "I enjoyed my experience at Taft, I really did, but we had the opportunities here to have an educational experience as good as Taft, and obviously not as expensive. Taft is close to what we now pay for college tuition." After a few years at other private schools, both went to Holton Arms, an exclusive girls' school in Bethesda, Maryland. At the time of that interview, the older daughter had graduated from Holton Arms and had just completed her junior year at Princeton, and the younger daughter was finishing the tenth grade. In order to ensure that the girls would develop social relationships with other African Americans their age, and, as Cushenberry put it, "stay rooted in an experience that was real, for Holton Arms could be artificial," the Cushenberrys also arranged for them to join the local chapter of Jack and Jill of America, a national organization for black youngsters from the families of educated black professionals. Cushenberry's wife had been a member in her hometown.[7]

At the same time, the Cushenberrys did not want their children to think of themselves as better than others. As he put it in our interview, he wanted them to have opportunities, but he wanted them to stay "grounded":

> I remember awful things kids did in prep school. We had people who waited on us all the time, and we had kids who'd throw eggs at the staff, who, just because they were so privileged in life, didn't really think about anyone who did a menial job. They were just people who cleaned up for us. I didn't want my girls, no matter what environment they were in, to ever be like that. I want to make sure they stay grounded even though they have opportunities.

Doris McMillon's daughter also attended an exclusive and costly private school in the Washington area, the Washington International School, until McMillon ran into personal financial difficulties and her daughter had to transfer to the local public high school. Her two older daughters ("inherited when I got married") have graduated from college (one from Dartmouth, the other from the University of Pennsylvania). At the time of our interview, the third daughter was at the Tisch School of the Arts at NYU.

In 1986, when we asked Cher Lewis about the possibility of sending her twin daughters to boarding school, she replied, "I would love for them to go, but my husband says no way they're going to turn preppy." When the time came to choose a secondary school, they settled on Saint Ann's, a private school in Brooklyn (so whether or not they avoided the fate of becoming "preppies" depends on one's definition of "preppy").[8] As of the fall of 2001, one was studying film at New York University and the other was a sophomore at Oberlin.

In a number of cases, the children of ABC graduates attended a mixture of schools, both public and private. Cecily Robbins's son, as she put it, "just about sampled every kind of school that there was to sample." He went to a Quaker preschool, to a private school affiliated with the National Cathedral (Beauvoir) through the first grade, and then attended the D.C. public schools through middle school. After one not very happy year at a Catholic school, he transferred to Parkmont, a small alternative school where he spent his high school years. It was a place where students receive a great deal of personal attention ("The headmaster, he doesn't go by the name of a headmaster, the director there was watching him like a hawk"). At the time of our 2001 interview, her son was about to complete his first year at Syracuse University.

MAGNET SCHOOLS

One way that public school systems have competed with private schools is to create "magnet schools" that select outstanding students from a larger geographic area than the neighborhood. Some, like the well-known Bronx School of Science, the New York High School for Music and Arts (which William Lewis's wife attended), or the Boston Latin School, have been around for a long time. Others have been created more recently, at times to comply with court-ordered pressures to maintain certain levels of integration in the schools. For example, a 1983 settlement agreement to integrate the schools in and around St. Louis led to the creation of twenty-seven magnet schools. According to Amy Stuart Wells and Robert Crain, sociologists who have studied this court-ordered experiment in depth, the magnet schools, "with themes ranging from visual and performing arts to Montessori . . . were quite successful at attracting students. . . . Because the city's magnet schools are perceived to be superior to the all-black or integrated schools, many black and white parents are eager to enroll their children in the magnet schools. Waiting lists for the most popular magnet schools are long." Both the students who transferred into the suburban schools and the students in the magnet schools outperformed those students who remained in the nonmagnet inner city schools.[9]

Some ABC graduates told us that they and their children had considered both private schools and public schools, and they had chosen public magnet schools rather than private schools. LaPearl Winfrey's description of shopping for schools for her daughter, and the weight she and her husband gave to her daughter's wishes, was not atypical. Winfrey had taken her daughter to her twentieth prep school reunion at The Masters School, but her daughter didn't want to leave her friends and go away to school ("I'm saving that for college" she told her mother). So they began to consider local alternatives. In our 1994 interview, Winfrey summarized their choices, and their decision, in the following way:

There were several schools we had looked at, both a couple of private schools and the public schools, and we kind of wound up with two magnet schools in the city [Chicago]. My husband and I wanted her to go to one school, and she was kind of leaning toward the other school. Interestingly, she had what I thought was a good rationale. The one school that we wanted her to go to was closer to home. It had a good reputation for the program that she was going to enter as a good college prep program. The other school was farther away, would kind of push her a little bit because it wasn't a neighborhood school. It drew from all over the city and would expose her to a wider variety of kids and give her a way to spread her wings a bit. That was her rationale. We relented, and she went to the other school.

It seems to have been a good choice. She graduated from the magnet school and won a full scholarship to Talladega College, from which she graduated with a degree in mathematics. As of June 2001, she was working on her Ph.D. in math at the University of Pittsburgh.

Like LaPearl Winfrey and her husband, Greg Pennington and his wife considered various private school options for their daughter and son and ended up choosing magnet schools. Though he had "mildly pushed" his alma mater, Western Reserve Academy, the suggestion never took hold. At the time we spoke, in June 2001, his children (fifteen and thirteen) were in magnet schools within the public school system in DeKalb County outside Atlanta (the family moved there from the city because of their belief that the public schools were better than those in Atlanta).

Fred Williams took his son to visit the prep school he had attended, the Berkshire School, in Sheffield, Massachusetts. He had no particular agenda, other than to let his son know all the options available to him. As he put it in our first interview with him in 1988: "I tell them to do what they want to do. Just like I tell them to do anything else in life. I don't believe in dictating anything to my kids at all. I believe in letting them know what things are out there."

A day or two after they returned to their hometown of Durham, North Carolina, his son informed him that he wanted to go to the North Carolina School of Science and Mathematics, a highly competitive statewide magnet school located in Durham (the students are from all over the state, and most board at the school). Williams acknowledged that his son might have perceived the visit to his prep school as subtle pressure ("Maybe he chose to go because I had just taken him up to visit my prep school, and it seemed like Daddy wanted him to go to a prep school"), but he totally supported his son's choice. After graduating from the School of Science and Mathematics, he did attend his parents' college alma mater, Duke, and then went on to earn a master's degree in biology from the University of North Carolina in Chapel Hill.

PUBLIC SCHOOLS

Finally, many of the children of ABC graduates have attended local public schools. In 1987, Eric Coleman's response to our question about sending his children to boarding school indicated that he was ambivalent about it, and that his wife had serious reservations.

> I presented that proposition to my wife and she says no. Very quickly. I would still have to give that some thought. When we were students at Pomfret, part of our discussions would be around the same question. And, back then, the prevailing response was no, under no circumstances, no way. Right now I haven't resolved that question. I think I would like to at least present the option to my sons or daughter and to see how they would feel about it. I can't say yes or no to the question. There are both positives and negatives to the experience and if I thought they were well equipped to not be irreparably damaged by the negatives, I would probably say yes.

When we spoke with him fourteen years later, Coleman told us that by the time his children reached secondary school, the topic never came up. Although he would not have been against their going to Pomfret, he knew they were not interested. All three of his children attended the local public school in suburban Bloomfield, Connecticut (outside of Hartford), though when his oldest son had some problems in school, Coleman and his wife decided to enroll him in a nearby Catholic school for his final two years. That son went on to graduate from Central Connecticut State University and (as of May 2001) was a counselor in a group home (he also plays football for an Arena football team). A second son graduated from Hampton University with a major in English (he was working as an assistant director of residential life at Central Connecticut State University), and the third child, a daughter, was an honor roll student studying communications at North Carolina A & T.

Alan Mitchell's three sons grew up in Oberlin, Ohio, where they attended the local public school, Oberlin High School. After graduating, the first son attended Morehouse College (and then went into the navy), the second son attended Oberlin College, and the third was still at Oberlin High School at the time of our interview in July 2001. William Foster's twenty-four-year-old daughter graduated from public high school, and then from Shenandoah University in Winchester, Virginia, where she majored in drama and communications. In the summer of 2002, Jennifer Casey Pierre's fifteen-year-old daughter looked at the Salem Academy, a local private school in her hometown of Winston-Salem, North Carolina, applied, and was accepted, but decided she'd rather attend the local public high school.

AVOIDING THE GANGS OF L.A.:
SYLVESTER MONROE'S SON GOES TO ST. GEORGE'S SCHOOL

At the time of our first interview with Sylvester Monroe, in Washington, D.C., in 1986, he had a sixteen-year-old daughter and an eight-year-old son who lived with their mother in Chicago (she had grown up in the same housing project as Monroe). Monroe had encouraged his daughter to consider a prep school, and even went so far as to get her to apply to Milton, but despite her good grades, her test scores were low and she was not accepted. She attended a public high school in Chicago, and then graduated from Morris Brown in Atlanta with a major in marketing. She, her husband, and three children live in Nashville, where her husband works for Dictaphone, designing and installing telephone systems for companies in the Nashville region.

A few years after that first interview, Monroe left *Newsweek*, and Washington, to work for *Time* in Los Angeles, and his eleven-year-old son came to live with him. Initially, Monroe had no thoughts of sending his son off to prep school because he didn't think a person should have to leave home to get a good education. In Los Angeles, however, while enrolled in the local public school, his son had two unhappy experiences that led both of them to reconsider the possibility of the son attending St. George's. Sylvester described these incidents in the following way:

He had come to live with me in L.A. in 1990. He was then in the seventh grade, and we lived on the west side where gang problems were not oppressive. In that first year he was a latchkey kid. The school was very near, and he'd come home and be pretty much alone for two to three hours. He'd always call me when he got home, and he'd sometimes ask if he could go right up the street about a half a block to the McDonald's. So he goes to McDonald's one day and he's got on a red T-shirt and a pair of red shorts. He gets stopped by an older kid on a bike who says "You in a gang?" And he says no. "Then what are you doing with all that red on?" And he says "I'm going to kick your butt . . . you got any money?" My son says "No I don't have any money, I just have this thing for a free sandwich at McDonald's." "Give it to me." He takes it and says "Where do you live?' And he smartly points in the opposite direction of where he really lives. Everything works out, but it shakes him up. He goes home and takes everything red and blue out of his wardrobe (red was Bloods, Crips was blue).

He settled down, got some friends and things were fine. Then one day he's playing basketball in Rancho Park, which is very near where I live, very upscale part of town. Over the hill come a group of guys with guns, shooting, and everybody scrambles. It's pandemonium. They're looking for somebody specific who was at that park at that moment. It scares the bejesus out of him.

As it turned out, Monroe had been asked to deliver the commencement address at St. George's that very spring (the spring of 1991), so he asked his son if he wanted to go with him and take a look at the school. They stayed at the home of the headmaster and his wife. The headmaster was also the basketball coach. One morning during their visit, Sylvester asked the headmaster's wife where his son was, and she told him that he and her husband were out shooting baskets. The headmaster-coach was suitably impressed with him, and his son was suitably impressed by the school and by the headmaster's skill at the game of Horse ("Dad," he said to Sylvester, "I've got to come back here, that old white man beat me!"). He applied, was accepted, and received a scholarship that paid for most of the cost of attending St. George's (then $15,200 a year). When he came home for Christmas that first year, he told his father that he loved the school: "I'm so glad to be at St. George's School. When I hear tires screeching, I don't duck. I don't worry about what color I'm wearing. I can just be a kid."

CONCLUSION

The children of ABC graduates have grown up in strikingly different circumstances than their parents. First of all, not only was their ABC parent well educated, but in most cases the other parent, too, had graduated from college and some had advanced degrees. Many of the partners of ABC parents came from middle- or upper-middle-class backgrounds. For example, Greg Pennington's wife and her two sisters, the daughters of a pharmacist, all attended Wellesley; Bill Lewis's wife, the daughter of a judge, attended the University of Pennsylvania and Stanford Law School; Calvin Dorsey's wife, a graduate of Clark University, was a third-generation college graduate; the father of Cher Lewis's husband owned an insurance agency. The children of ABC graduates, for the most part, grew up in households where one or both parents were professionals, and, in many cases, one set of grandparents were well-educated professionals; their experiences, therefore, were solidly middle class or upper middle class.

Among other things, this meant that they grew up with different expectations about the educations they would receive. Although some of the ABC graduates told us that they were raised with the assumption that they would attend college, this was not universally the case. Early on, however, their children expected that they, too, would become well educated like their parents (whether or not they attended prep school). Cecily Robbins told us that her son "was a tot when he asked, 'Mommy, when am I going to sleep away school?'"

Middle-class status also meant participation in various cultural activities like art, ballet, learning to play musical instruments, and, in some cases, membership in social organizations for middle- and upper-middle-class blacks (as we've noted, Harold Cushenberry's daughters participated in the Jack and Jill Club). It also meant that many had the opportunity to travel widely. Jennifer Casey Pierre, whose family had to hire someone to drive her from Baltimore to Philadelphia in order for her to attend the Baldwin School because no one in her immediate family owned a car, noted that her children's experiences had been quite different. "My kids have traveled extensively," she told us in May 2001. "I mean, we went to Hawaii two years ago, they've been to Montreal, they've been to Toronto, to St. Croix, Trinidad, Tobago, the Bahamas, St. Martin—they've been a lot of places and met a lot of people." Along these same lines, consider the following excerpt from an essay written by Andover legacy student, Ryan McChristian, the son of 1973 ABC graduate Tim McChristian:

> During winter of sixth grade my parents gave me some good news. We were going to spend our Christmas break in Thailand. I raised an eyebrow. For most people this would have been the most astounding thing in their lives. Not me. My dad received an overseas assignment from IBM in the winter of my fifth grade. Ever since then we'd been living in Japan. IBM paid for all of our expenses. Our four-bedroom apartment, private school tuitions, and even our return flights home were all paid for by the company. Because of this my family was able to take vacations to foreign countries all over Asia. By that time I had already been to Singapore and Hong Kong! So when I heard we were going to Thailand I was happy but not totally surprised.[10]

Even if they have not attended boarding schools, or grown up in integrated neighborhoods, the children of ABC graduates have attended integrated schools and, earlier than their parents, they made friends with white children. Many of the ABC parents we spoke with noted that their children's friends were of diverse backgrounds. Doris McMillon proudly explained that her daughter had remained friends with classmates from Washington International School and from Wakefield High School: "She has a broad range of friends. I mean, nobody is a stranger to her." Cecily Robbins told us: "My son's friends are mixed. They're not all black. My son started out at a Quaker school, and he's one of Dr. King's children. You know, judge me not by the color of my skin but by the content of my character. That's what he did. He's had female friends, he's had gay friends, he's had white friends, he's had black friends, Hispanic friends." Cher Lewis described her daughters' friends in the following way: "They hang out with everyone. It's almost like an ad. When they say they're bringing a friend home, it could be someone of any color, age, or class background."

Due to their different experiences, and because the times are different, the children seem to have made different choices when faced with some of the same pressures as their parents. Harold Cushenberry, for example, like many others we interviewed, as an undergraduate hung out almost exclusively with African Americans. Cushenberry later came to question himself on this matter. Thirty years later, his daughter, an economics major at Princeton, faces some of the same pressures. He described her situation, and his reactions to her situation, in the following way:

Her friends are really across racial lines, and that's been great. I think both our girls have had that exposure, and one of the things that was most disappointing about Princeton—a wonderful school, but I saw something repeated that I thought we'd gotten away from in the sixties, which was the self-segregation. My daughter took a lot of flak because she is fairly immersed in all things that Princeton has to offer. She's in an a cappella women's singing group and they travel a lot and sing together. She has tons of white friends. But a lot of the black students at Princeton really don't associate very much. They don't get involved very much in a lot of the activities of the college. They sort of hang together. They eat together. They stay together. She tries to manage both worlds, this duality that black folks have always faced, keeping one foot in both places sometimes. It can be very uncomfortable doing that. She hasn't had any overt problems or pressures to sort of declare herself one way or the other, and she's managed to get through it. She's very comfortable with who she is, which is one of her strengths. She loves opera and she doesn't like rap music, so she's different in that regard. But she's comfortable with who she is. She loves plays— that's just her.

It depends on your background. I know a lot of kids who are just not comfortable in an environment that is all segregated. At Harvard I chose not to do a lot of things I did in prep school, and some of it was [because I felt that] "I've met this challenge." When I went to prep school, I didn't feel as confident about my abilities. But I did extraordinarily well, and I was a leader, so I felt I didn't have to prove anything anymore, and therefore I probably did isolate myself more. In hindsight, I think (and I've impressed this upon her) that I should have participated more in the broader range of opportunities that Harvard had. I did well academically. I always studied hard. I didn't lose track of what I needed to do. But I didn't fully take part in all the rich things that Harvard could have offered me because it was a different era—Black Power, and all that stuff. So I've encouraged her, despite whatever pulls there are in another direction, to enjoy her college years, and to really take advantage of the university. And she's been able to do that.

Cher Lewis told us that her daughters, like Cushenberry's daughter, had felt pressure from black students to be racially exclusive in their friendships, and especially in their dating relationships. In particular, her daughter who attends

Oberlin felt these kinds of pressures from black women. Cher described her situation in the following way:

> There's something called the "Black House" at Oberlin. In her first year, she felt such pressure that she questioned her identity (though she told me, "I know who I am"). This year some of the black girls have been upset that there's a shortage of black men. Last year she couldn't even have had a discussion with them. This year she's been able to discuss these kinds of issues.

The experiences of Cher Lewis's daughter at Oberlin are similar to those of Cushenberry's daughter at Princeton, but they differ in one important way. Though both are black women, Cher Lewis's daughter also is Jewish and has a white father. Her experience reflects both some of the ongoing pressures young blacks face and some of the complexities of identity for biracial children.[11]

Sylvester Monroe described his son's experiences as radically different from his own, and different from that of Cushenberry's daughter at Princeton and Cher Lewis's daughter at Oberlin. Even before he attended St. George's, but also at St. George's and as a college student, his son's friends were from many different ethnic and racial backgrounds. Monroe contrasted his own experience with his son's in the following way:

> When he was in middle school, when we lived just south of Westwood, he would talk about his friends — Sebastian, Kareem, a couple of other guys — and I always just assumed that these kids were black. I had no reason to assume that they were anything, but I just assumed they were black. And so one day I said bring your friends over. And his friends came over and they were like this rainbow coalition. Kareem actually is from Belize, and Sebastian is Peruvian, there was another kid who was white, and another who was Latino. When these kids are together, and I watch them, race is never an issue.

As far as Monroe could see, his son's friends at St. George's, and in college, were of all backgrounds (at the time of our 2001 interview with Monroe, his son was living with a white girlfriend). As Monroe put it, for his son and his friends, "race is so unimportant in their relationships. They are aware of racial issues and whatnot, but in their relationships it's almost never an issue."

Still, as we noted in chapter 5 on relationships when we quoted Anthony Ducret, a 1995 ABC graduate of Groton who went to Wesleyan and now lives in New York City, interracial dating can be more difficult after college than in college because of both internal and external pressures. Although interracial marriages between blacks and whites have increased over time, they remain relatively rare.

By all indications, the children of ABC graduates have been successful in school. Some have completed or are working on graduate degrees, almost all who have reached their mid-twenties are college graduates, and many have attended prestigious colleges and universities. It is notable that many of them have attended traditional black colleges, which are often favored by members of the black middle class. If educational level is used as an index, there is very little evidence of downward mobility in this group, even though the schools they have attended have not always been as prestigious as those attended by their ABC parent. As for those who have joined the working world, the evidence indicates that most are now young professionals in middle-class jobs. It appears that any pull to an oppositional identity can be overcome when there are solid support networks.

NOTES

1. See, for example, Ronald F. Ferguson, "A Diagnostic Analysis of Black-White GPA Disparities in Shaker Heights, Ohio," in *Brookings Papers on Education Policy 2001*, edited by Diane Ravitch (Washington, D.C.: Brookings Institution Press, 2001), 347–414; see also Jason W. Osborne, "Unraveling Underachievement Among African American Boys from an Identification with Academics Perspective," *Journal of Negro Education* 68, no. 4 (1999): 555–565. In *The Shape of the River* (Princeton, N.J.: Princeton University Press, 1998), William G. Bowen and Derek Bok found that even when they controlled for SATs and socioeconomic status, the black college students at academically selective colleges and universities had lower grades and lower graduation rates than other students, which they refer to as "the most disturbing finding" in their work (xivi).

2. Mary Patillo-McCoy, *Black Picket Fences: Privilege and Peril Among the Black Middle Class* (Chicago: University of Chicago Press, 1999), 21; see also Bart Landry, *The New Black Middle Class* (Berkeley: University of California Press, 1987).

3. Melvin L. Oliver and Thomas M. Shapiro, *Black Wealth/White Wealth* (New York: Routledge, 1995), 92–93.

4. Byron Haskins, "A Mission Together: Establishing a Legacy," *Choate Rosemary Hall Alumni Magazine* (Winter/Spring 2000): 50–51. Haskins's son was not the first ABC legacy student. As early as October 1986, the program reported the following in a publication called the *Abcedarian*: "Mildred McLain (Commonwealth School, '68) is the first known ABC graduate to have a child who is also an ABC alumna. Moreover, Mildred's daughter, Azania Robinson, also attended Commonwealth School" (3).

5. See Edward McPherson, "Heartfelt Reflections: Thoughts on Af-Lat-Am's 30th Anniversary," *Prism: The Newsletter of the Multicultural Affairs Committee of the Phillips Academy Alumni Council* (March 1999): 4. As further evidence that the world we are studying is a small one, just as Bill Lewis was a friend of Ed McPherson's at

Andover, Lewis's wife, Carol, was a friend of McPherson's when both were undergraduates at the University of Pennsylvania.

6. Of course, the prep schools have also hired African American alumni who were not ABC students. For example, Lorene Cary, a 1974 graduate of St. Paul's, returned to that school to teach English and subsequently sat on the school's board of trustees. She describes her involvement with the school in her memoir, *Black Ice* (New York: Knopf, 1992).

7. See Marianne Rohrlich, "Feeling Isolated at the Top, Seeking Roots: Jack and Jill Clubs for Middle-Class Black Children Are Newly Fashionable, as Families Feel Cut Off in Nearly All-White Suburbs," *New York Times*, July 19, 1998, 1. Among the members of Jack and Jill have been Ronald H. Brown, former secretary of commerce, actresses Lynn Whitfield and Phylicia Rashad, and the wives of former Mayor David Dinkins (of New York) and former Mayor Andrew Young (of Atlanta). See also Lawrence Otis Graham, *Member of the Club* (New York: HarperCollins, 1995), 58.

8. On a list of the one hundred "top feeder schools" to Harvard, Yale, and Princeton, St. Ann's School ranked number sixteen, right after St. Paul's and a few places in front of Hotchkiss. See Reshma Memon Yaqub, "Getting Inside the Ivy Gates," *Worth* (September 2002): 97.

9. Amy Stuart Wells and Robert L. Crain, *Stepping Over the Color Line: African American Students in White Suburban Schools* (New Haven, Conn.: Yale University Press, 1997), 145–146.

10. This essay appears on the Web at www.andover.edu, "The Essays of Ryan McChristian."

11. For insightful research on intraracial diversity and intraracial conflict and their effects on racial identity among African American college students at elite, predominantly white, liberal arts colleges, see Sandra S. Smith and Mignon R. Moore, "Intraracial Diversity and Relations Among African-Americans: Closeness Among Black Students at a Predominantly White University," *American Journal of Sociology* 106, no. 1 (2000): 1–39; and Mignon R. Moore and Sandra S. Smith, "'We Need to Know Who's With Us and Who's Not.' Intraracial Conflict, Race Consciousness, and What It Means to Be Black," paper presented at the annual meetings of the American Sociological Association, Chicago, August 16, 2002. For some readings that provide valuable insights on biracial children of black and white parents, see Maria P. P. Root, ed., *Racially Mixed People in America* (Newbury Park, Calif.: Sage, 1992); Claudine Chiawei O'Hearn, ed., *Half and Half: Writers on Growing Up Biracial and Bicultural* (New York: Pantheon, 1998); and James McBride, *The Color of Water* (New York: Riverhead, 1996).

9

Mobility, Social Class, and Racial Identity

Why has the ABC program been so successful in helping many of its graduates move from economic poverty into professional and managerial roles? What do the experiences of early ABC graduates tell us about the relative importance of race and class in the lives and the identities of African Americans? And will the progress continue for the black community in terms of a growing percentage of both men and women in the professions and the corporate elite? These are the questions we address in this final chapter drawing on our own findings as well as those of many other investigators.

WHY ABC HAS WORKED SO WELL: CULTURAL AND SOCIAL CAPITAL AS WEALTH

At the end of chapter 6 we suggested several reasons for the educational success and occupational mobility of those ABC students who seem to have done exceptionally well. We concluded that they were likely to have come from middle-class backgrounds (their parents, for example, were teachers) or from a hidden middle class. In many cases, there were important role models in their families, schools, or communities. We noted how often white teachers, counselors, and supporters from the community were significant in their transitions from their hometowns to their new lives at prep school. We also pointed out that unlike their less upwardly mobile counterparts, inside and outside the ABC program, they were able to resist the pull of an oppositional identity that worked against doing well academically and thriving in predominantly white elite schools.

Here we wish to look further at some of the reasons why the ABC program has been successful, shifting the emphasis from those individuals who were upwardly mobile to the factors that may account for the general success of the program. First, in addition to providing excellent secondary educations, and, when needed, orientation and remedial programs to overcome disadvantaged educational backgrounds, the ABC program and its member schools provide students with a new social identity. At the very outset, by a selection process that is clearly competitive, the program identifies them in a way that emphasizes their abilities and potential. Moreover, especially in the early years of the program, when there was a substantial summer transition program, but even today when there are multicultural specialists and on-campus groups at the schools that help students fashion new identities, the ABC experience in prep school serves to expand the former, narrower definition of what it meant to be a black teenager in America. ABC students were, and are, black and proud, but now they become black Andover students and proud, black Choate students and proud, ABC students and proud. These new identities help explain why ABC students have been able to resist the pull of oppositional culture, especially when they face the difficult and sometimes daunting task of going home.

As part of their new identities, they acquire elite cultural capital, the various forms of knowledge and skills typically acquired by those in the white elite. Those who have this cultural capital have a great advantage over those who do not (just as those who have access to economic capital—money— have a great advantage over those who do not). In the Middle Ages, for example, the small percentage of people who could read and write had access to knowledge that was unavailable to the masses, and this helped them to maintain their status and their power. Similarly, today, growing up without any knowledge of or skills with computers puts one at a major disadvantage in the modern economy, a problem often referred to as "the digital divide."[1] As we have noted in previous chapters, it became clear in our interviews that graduates of the ABC program had acquired elite cultural capital, and they were well aware of its value. The knowledge and skills acquired included the nuts and bolts of academia (for example, the ability to write, speak, and think more effectively), but it also included the ability and the confidence, as one put it, to "converse with anybody on almost anything."

ABC students also acquire social capital, the interpersonal connections that can be used to advance one's career (using social capital is often referred to as "networking" and in the old, pre-feminist days, such connections were routinely called "old boy networks"). Again, throughout the book we have provided examples of ABC students who made friends at their prep schools with whom they later went into business (Sylvester Monroe's son is one such example, and Tim Bradley, who has done the soundtracks for videos produced by a Choate classmate, is another), or who in some way were able to help out when needed (Doris McMillon told us that she had become friends with Alida Rockefeller when they were both at Concord Academy, and that "I can call her and say, 'Alida, if you can't help me with this, will you tell me who can?'"). The accumulation of social capital that began in prep school continued as ABC graduates went on to elite colleges and to graduate and professional schools.

By the time they emerged as young adults, then, with prep school, college, and often postgraduate degrees, ABC graduates still may not have had much money, especially when compared to their prep school classmates, but they had "wealth" in the form of cultural and social capital. This, we believe, is especially important in understanding the overall success of the ABC program. As researchers have carefully demonstrated, there is an enormous gap between the wealth held by blacks in the middle class and the wealth held by whites in the middle class. One comprehensive comparison found that, on average, "whites possess nearly twelve times as much median net worth as blacks, or $43,800 versus $3,700."[2] There are many reasons for this gap, including past impoverishment and continuing pay discrimination. In addition, blacks are not as likely to be able to accrue wealth through the accumulation of equity in their homes, one of the key sources of wealth for a great many white Americans. Blacks still face discrimination in obtaining home loans, they pay higher interest rates, and homes purchased in white or mixed neighborhoods may stagnate in value in the face of white flight. Obviously, this wealth gap means that in times of trouble—illness in the family, losing one's job, or having unexpected expenses—those in the black middle class are far more vulnerable than those in the white middle class. And, of course, such a gap tends to grow larger even if both groups receive the same return on their investments. A 10 percent return on $10,000 versus $100,000 soon leads to an even wider wealth differential.

The gap in wealth between blacks and whites is even more noteworthy when one considers a recent study that shows that if wealth is held constant, black children are as successful academically as white children. Unlike previous studies, which only looked at parents' education or occupation and income, this study included the amount of accumulated wealth (that is, property, assets, or net worth) held by the family.[3] This striking finding underscores the importance of wealth, because studies comparing black and white students, which do not control for wealth, have shown, time and time again, that black middle-class children do not perform as well academically as white middle-class children.[4]

It is our argument that the ABC program basically reduces the very important wealth gap by providing its students with considerable cultural and social capital. In a word, the ABC process provides students with the cultural and social capital they would have had if they had been part of wealthy families. In the long run, cultural and social capital are likely to lead to economic capital, and in some cases a great deal of it (remember multimillionaire Bill Lewis, who has given hundreds of thousands of dollars to the ABC program and to Andover). Most ABC graduates have not become multimillionaires, but going through the program moved all of them closer to an equal footing with white elites.

Thus, the careers of the ABC graduates show that upward mobility is possible when African Americans are given scholarship support at elite schools. Their style, manner, and expectations for the future indicate that it does not take generations to adopt middle-class, upper-middle-class, and even upper-class outlooks and personas. A private school education starting at ages thirteen to fifteen can lead to the acquisition of valuable knowledge and skills, and can lead to the confidence, the motivation, and the connections to make maximum use of that knowledge and those skills. Furthermore, as noted at the end of the previous chapter, the educational and occupational achievements to date of the children of ABC graduates suggest that it is possible for African Americans to maintain at least a black middle-class status when the resources and support networks are available to back up parental expectations.

The ABC program, then, helped move young African Americans into the black middle class (and, in some cases, to higher levels of the class hierarchy), and now we see that the concepts of cultural and social capital enhance the usual definitions of middle class, which tend to rely solely on education, occupation, and income.[5] But what does all this mean in terms of the relative importance of race and class?

RACE, CLASS, AND IDENTITY

Is race still as salient for African Americans as it was in the past, and as some theories continue to insist? Or is class now a stronger factor than race in shaping the consciousness of well-educated blacks who have professional credentials or elite corporate positions? Contrary to those who argue about whether race or class is now more important in the social identities of blacks who have joined the elite, and who assume that an increase in the importance of one means a decrease in the importance of the other, we think that the importance of both race and class have increased. It is not a situation of either/or, but of both, and the result may be that what being black means in this new era has been redefined.

Ironically, the increased importance of race develops in those settings that would seem to make class the more salient factor. To begin with, being one of just a few blacks at a prep school led many ABC students to think more about what it meant to be black in the United States than they had previously. Thus, even while they were learning upper-class styles, they were also becoming more race conscious. For example, Greg Pennington thought that his years at Western Reserve Academy made him "blacker": "I think I got a lot clearer on my cultural identity. . . . When you're in a homogeneous community, you don't think about what it means to be black, so especially coming from this black school to this prep school environment, that pretty much forced me to spend a lot of time thinking about what it meant to me to be black, and especially what it meant to be in that kind of environment. I became much blacker having gone to Western Reserve."

Similarly, Cher Lewis noted that in her black community in Richmond she never experienced racism directly. Only at the Abbott Academy did she have to acknowledge that some people didn't like her because she was black, although (as we mentioned in chapter 7) she did not experience more blatant racism until she entered the corporate world in the early 1970s. She was married to a white, but she does not minimize the importance of race in her life—the title of the book she has considered writing is "Black in a White Family."

Jennifer Casey Pierre, who grew up in a black neighborhood in Baltimore, recalls that she became especially aware of her blackness when she went to the Baldwin School:

> When I was growing up I did not realize that I was black. Television was a major influence in my life and most of the actors I saw on TV were white, so I used to have this vision of someday getting married and some white guy on this horse, you know, blond hair, would come by and get me. Well . . . when I went to Baldwin, I was a black militant. . . . Upon arriving at the school, the other ABC student from Richmond . . . and I mixed a solution of Tide and vinegar to get the chemical out of our hair so we could return to the natural hair form.

Eric Coleman also thinks that his ABC experience made him more conscious of being black, and more committed to "represent" the views of blacks. As he explained in our interview in Hartford in May 2002: "I think it made me more conscious of being black, not that I was ever not conscious of it. I always knew I was black. But I think that the exposure to a point of view different from my own sort of reinforced my values, and emphasized a sense of responsibility and obligation to be, I don't know, I'm not trying to say pioneer, but, in my interactions with my white counterparts, to make sure they are aware that there is another point of view."

For those who started out working in business settings, interactions within corporations also tended to heighten race consciousness because of the "triple jeopardy" blacks face there.[6] First, they encounter the negative stereotypes held by many whites about their job skills. Second, there is the assumption by most whites that they are "tokens," hired only because of affirmative action. Finally, they must cope with their "solo" role—being the only black employee in their company or at their level. Faced with this triple jeopardy, black employees become even more self-conscious and more race-conscious.

Nor do we see an attempt on the part of ABC graduates to leave the black community behind. Most live in exclusively or predominantly black neighborhoods. Some have been involved in careers that directly serve a black clientele. For example, Cecily Robbins directed the Big Sisters program for Washington, D.C.—most of her work was with black adults and children. Similarly, LaPearl Winfrey's psychological practice in downtown Chicago, before she left for teaching positions in Washington, D.C., and then in Dayton, Ohio, was with a group of black therapists, and most of her clients were black women. Others have done volunteer work that reveals their ongoing commitment to those in the inner cities—Jennifer Casey Pierre, for example, was a county court volunteer in Winston-Salem while she worked for R. J. Reynolds Tobacco Company, an activity that involved her with many black children who found themselves in legal trouble. And Eric Coleman, who has a large minority constituency in his legislative district in Connecticut, continues to see himself as a progressive politician who represents the views of African Americans (as well as other people of color, working people, children, and women).

In our Internet-assisted search for ABC graduates from the 1970s, 1980s, and 1990s, designed to supplement our findings on the ABC graduates we interviewed, we have found many who are working in the black community in a variety of capacities. Some are teachers, some are counselors, some are coaches, and some work in minority business development or human relations. And some attribute their commitment to the black community to lessons they learned as ABC students. For example, Willie Ratchford, a 1971 ABC graduate of the public school program at North Andover High School, and since 1994 the executive director of the Charlotte-Mecklenburg Community Relations Committee in North Carolina, told one interviewer that he decided on a career in human service because of what he considered the message he received from ABC. As he put it, "'Get all the education you can,' they told us, so you can give it back to your community."[7]

Even in those we have identified as especially successful in the corporate world, we see an ongoing commitment to the black community. When we look at a millionaire like Bill Lewis of Morgan Stanley, we note that he is the treasurer for the National Urban League, gives his money to the NAACP Legal Defense and Educational Fund and ABC, and says that he is in general looking for ways to help the black community. The same can be said for

Frank Borges, who is the treasurer for the NAACP, and for Jesse Spikes in Atlanta, who remains active in his church and in the community. Deval Patrick, of course, came to national attention because of the work he did as the Clinton administration's chief civil rights enforcer (according to the *New York Times*, he played a key role in Clinton's refusal to renounce affirmative action). Right after he graduated from the Harvard Law School, Patrick worked for the NAACP Legal Defense and Educational Fund. He currently sits on the board of the A Better Chance program.[8]

Participation in the ABC program certainly did not reduce the black consciousness of one of its most famous graduates, Tracy Chapman, the singer-songwriter sensation who burst upon the scene in the late 1980s. From a low-income family in Cleveland, Chapman won an ABC scholarship to Wooster School in Danbury, Connecticut, and spent three years there, graduating in 1982. She then went to Tufts University, where she majored in anthropology and graduated in 1986. She played her guitar, wrote songs, and developed her unique style during her prep school years. One of her best-known songs, "Talkin' 'bout a Revolution"—which included inspirational phrases stating that "Poor people gonna rise up and take what's theirs" and "Finally the tables are starting to turn"—was written during her senior year at Wooster School.[9]

In a comprehensive study of black graduates of elite colleges that provides extensive evidence of the positive effects of affirmative action, William Bowen (a former president of Princeton University) and Derek Bok (a former president of Harvard University) found that the black graduates participated at a substantially higher rate than white graduates "in community and civic undertakings." They conclude that their findings "bear out the assumption of selective institutions that minority students have unusual opportunities to make valuable contributions to their communities and the society."[10] Our findings about black ABC graduates very much support their conclusions.

Although we believe that race remains paramount in black interactions with the white community, we also believe that class has become even more important within the black community. That is, once the ABC graduates acquire prep school and Ivy League credentials and styles, it is very hard for many of them to go home again to their low-income neighborhoods. It is noteworthy in this regard to recall that with only one exception, every marriage by an ABC graduate to someone from "back home" ended in failure. However, to say that many ABC graduates are no longer completely comfortable in their original class setting is not the same as saying they are uncomfortable with other blacks. Instead, they become part of the new black middle class in terms of their neighborhoods, church affiliations, and voluntary groups. Thus, we believe that one major effect of the ABC program, whether this was intended or not, is to strengthen the black middle class (and, in the process, increase the class stratification within the black community).

WILL THE PROGRESS CONTINUE?

Our findings on both ABC graduates and their children demonstrate that progress can continue for African Americans under the right circumstances. But are those necessary circumstances still generally present? Two slightly different emphases lead to very different conclusions. The first view argues that progress will continue because job markets are now fundamentally fair, focusing primarily on the educational training and occupational skills that African Americans are able to obtain due to antidiscrimination legislation that resulted from the civil rights movement. Since African Americans are now able to obtain these necessary prerequisites, future progress can be expected. The upward mobility of some blacks into the professions and in the corporate world, which we discussed in chapters 6 and 7, are often cited as evidence that "market-mediated" factors now determine black occupational mobility. If the most capable applicants for jobs are African American, according to this perspective, they will be hired and they will be promoted.[11]

Furthermore, adherents of this viewpoint argue, there are more and more qualified African Americans entering the workforce every year. The 2000 Census reported that fully 79 percent of African Americans now finish high school (in 1980, only 51 percent graduated high school). An increasing percentage of blacks also are graduating from college: in 1970 only 5 percent of those twenty-five years and older had completed college, but in 2000 that figure had increased to 17 percent. These increases are reflected in a larger black middle class, and in the increasing number of skilled, white-collar, managerial, and professional jobs that more and more blacks hold. As we noted in chapter 7, a handful of African American men became CEOs of major corporations in the late 1990s, and the Executive Leadership Council, which consists primarily of African Americans in senior executive positions in *Fortune* 500 companies, now includes 275 members, compared to the nineteen members when the organization was founded in 1986.[12]

On the other hand, there is also evidence that calls this sole emphasis on market mechanisms into question. After all, those who make decisions within the market system are human, and thus susceptible to the same stereotypes and biases humans demonstrate in other domains. Moreover, there is reason to question whether the very real gains that have taken place are as sizable as the market-oriented emphasis suggests. The educational gains by African Americans, for example, have closed the gap at the high school level, but not at the college level. That is, whites, too, are more likely to complete college than they were thirty years ago (in 1970, 12 percent of whites over the age of twenty-five had completed college; by 2000, that figure rose to 28 percent, so the gap between blacks and whites with college degrees was greater in 2000 than it was in 1970). Similarly, the fact that some African Americans have become CEOs of *Fortune*-level companies is important, and the fact that there are many African American senior executives within three steps of the CEO level is encouraging, but in both cases these represent a very small percentage of CEOs and of senior executives at *Fortune*-level companies. There is also the fact, noted early in the first chapter, that blacks are still underrepresented in managerial and professional positions in the private sector. And when one looks at all black and white workers, one finds that black workers continue to earn less than white workers, even when education is controlled for. For example, in 1998, black male college graduates earned 72 cents for every dollar earned by whites with comparable educations. This suggests that the job market is not evaluating them fairly.[13]

Although there can be no doubt that there is less overt racism today than in the past, there is also considerable evidence that more covert forms of racism still persist that make many blacks feel uncomfortable or unwanted in white settings. Various researchers have labeled such covert forms of racism as "symbolic racism" or "modern racism." In covert racism, traditional American values are blended with anti-black attitudes, such that symbolic or modern racists tend to express antagonism toward blacks' demands ("Blacks are getting too demanding in their push for civil rights"), or resentment over alleged special favors for blacks ("The government should not help blacks and other racial minorities—they should help themselves"), or denial of continued discrimination ("Blacks have it better than they ever have before"). Subtle racism is also uncovered in various kinds of social psychology experiments that have revealed "aversive racism," in which people express egalitarian beliefs, but also hold unacknowledged negative feelings about blacks. The resulting ambivalence means that they avoid blacks, especially when the norms are conflicting or ambiguous.[14]

The evidence for such subtle forms of racism is important because it reveals the persistence of stereotypes about blacks and demonstrates that these stereotypes affect behavior, often at an unconscious level. These stereotypes, in turn, may account for the fact that blacks are the most excluded group on one of the most sensitive indices of acceptance, place of residence. According to a study of the 2000 census, blacks have the highest rate of residential segregation by far, a rate that has shown only slight decline since 1990.[15] Thus, residential segregation continues to reveal a form of what some sociologists have called "American apartheid."[16] Residential segregation is made even more ominous by the fact that it helps to ensure school segregation. More black students attend predominantly minority schools today than in 1976.[17] Additionally, the rate of intermarriage between whites and African Americans remains at a very low level, but the rates have climbed dramatically for all other people of color. One study found that the odds of whites marrying Filipino Americans, Native Americans, Cuban Americans, Chinese Americans, Japanese Americans, Puerto Rican Americans, and Mexican Americans were far higher (at least six times as high) than the odds of whites marrying African Americans.[18]

The sizable body of research demonstrating continuing covert racism, as well as the ongoing patterns of residential exclusion and low rates of intermarriage, suggests that blacks still face subtle and not so subtle discrimination. These factors lend credence to the argument that education and job skills may not be enough to sustain a vulnerable black middle class—more vulnerable than the white middle class, as we've noted, because it has so much less wealth to fall back on. The continuing income differentials between blacks and whites lends support to a viewpoint that doubts that markets alone can bring about racial equality. According to this perspective, many of the gains by blacks at the higher levels of society have been mediated by political forces, especially black social protest and the resultant government enforcement of fairness in labor markets. If this politically mediated view of black occupational mobility is correct, then job markets have not been deracialized to the degree claimed by adherents of the first viewpoint, and the movement of blacks into the corporate world may decline without renewed political mediation.

Since the civil rights era of the 1960s, this political mediation has come from the federal government by means of strong backing of incorporation by a wide range of government programs, including the Equal Employment Opportunity Commission (EEOC) and the federal contract compliance commission. During the Reagan–Bush era, however, the government began to pull back from such programs. Budgets were cut and people philosophically opposed to the programs were put in charge of them. The laws often were not enforced. Nonetheless, there was still a small amount of progress for African Americans in some areas, which suggests that something else must be going on if the political mediation perspective is correct.

We believe that a set of private-sector programs have helped to make up for the decline in government support, thereby countering the prejudices that might lead to discrimination against African Americans in the upper levels of the occupational and class structures. These programs, which begin in elementary school in some areas of the country, and carry through to corporate internships for black college students, are funded in large measure by the major corporations. The corporations in effect enter into partnerships with the educators who come to them with programs to prepare low-income students of color, but especially African Americans, for leading prep schools. The partnerships are also aided by significant donations from the hundreds of large charitable foundations the corporate rich influence through financial donations and directorship positions.[19] These programs add up to a corporate-mediated supplement to the necessary, but declining, government support. They are a mechanism to ensure at least some African American representation at the higher levels of American society. They are kept in place for many reasons, including potential lawsuits for racial discrimination in the workplace and the increasing purchasing power of black consumers.

A Better Chance is an ideal example of a corporate-mediated program. As we demonstrate in some detail in appendix 2, ABC was founded by the headmasters of three elite private schools, one of whom, Charles Merrill, was an heir to the Merrill Lynch fortune. Their plans were financed in good part at the outset by the Rockefeller Foundation, at the time one of the two richest and most powerful foundations in the country. ABC then received a major boost from two years of government funds provided by the Office of Economic Opportunity, but became almost completely dependent on corporate and foundation monies again when the government funds dried up. Even today, at a time when ABC alumni and Oprah Winfrey are supplying an impressive amount of ABC support, officers from American Express, Philip Morris, Salomon Smith Barney, and AOL Time Warner sit on the ABC board, and its list of donors in recent years includes the corporate foundations for American Express, Coca-Cola, Goldman, Sachs, the Limited, Pepsi-Cola, International Paper, Morgan Stanley Dean Witter, Bristol-Myers Squibb, J. P. Morgan Chase, and Texaco.

Thanks in part to the example of ABC, a number of similar programs have been created for specific regions or cities. Many of them are listed, with connecting links, on the ABC Web site at www.abetterchance.org. Taken together, as many as one thousand African American graduates of these programs may attend elite universities. For example, there's the Baltimore Education Scholarship Trust in Baltimore and the Independent School Alliance for Minority Affairs in Los Angeles, both of which receive funds from private schools and foundations to identify and help prepare low-income children of color for attendance at schools in the area. Some programs focus on students at a very young age. Early Steps, founded in 1986 by an association of private day schools in New York City, places about 125 students in kindergarten and first grade in forty schools each year. Its first students are just now beginning to go to college at schools such as Harvard, Vassar, Tufts, Howard, and Georgetown. Half of its funding comes from member schools, the other half from foundations.

The Black Student Fund in Washington, D.C., was started in 1964 by Lydia Katzenbach, the wife of the then attorney general, placing students in forty-two private schools in Maryland, Virginia, and the District of Columbia with the help of foundation grants and personal gifts. It has served over two thousand students, 84 percent of whom have earned at least a BA. The chair of the organization in 2001, Karen Hastie Williams, sits on the boards of three major corporations, including Continental Airlines, and she is a trustee of the Fannie Mae Foundation (chaired by Fannie Mae CEO Franklin D. Raines, one of the four *Fortune*-level African American CEOs as of August 2002). Raines, in turn, is a trustee of the Black Student Fund. The foundation gave the program $250,000 in 1999, and $75,000 in 2000.

Prep for Prep is perhaps the largest and most comprehensive of the new programs. Created in 1978 as a pilot project under the auspices of Columbia University's Teachers College, it takes in about 150 fifth graders and 60 seventh graders in New York City each year for a fourteen-month program to prepare them for placement in thirty-six private day schools and ten boarding schools.

The program includes two intensive seven-week summer programs as well as after-school classes one day a week and Saturday classes during the school year. It sponsors a leadership institute and offers counseling services. Its program of summer job placements is meant to introduce students to the business and professional worlds. Alumni participate in a summer advisory program to help create what is called the "Prep Community," a support group and sense of group identification. Seventy-five percent of the children complete the program and go to college.

By 2001 Prep for Prep had worked with just over 2,300 students—714 are college graduates, 609 are in college, and 1,000 are working toward high school graduation. The overwhelming majority of its students go to top private and public schools; half are from Ivy League universities, including 113 who graduated from or are attending Wesleyan University, 96 from Harvard, and 91 from Yale. Other top schools attended by Prep for Prep students are the University of Pennsylvania (80), Columbia (79), Brown (63), Amherst (46), Cornell (38), and Williams (37).

The program is directed by Wall Street lawyers and financiers. The chair in 2001, Martin Lipton, is a name partner in the Wall Street firm of Wachtell, Lipton, Rosen, and Katz. The president, John L. Vogelstein, is the vice chair of the board of directors of the investment bank E. M. Warburg, Pincus, & Co., and is on the board of directors of three other corporations. The program received $1.7 million from twenty-seven foundations in the late 1990s, including $400,000 from the Dana Foundation, $300,000 from the Hayden Foundation, $225,000 from the Starr Foundation, and $150,000 from the Picower Foundation.

The Steppingstone Foundation has developed a program in Boston that shares many elements in common with Prep for Prep. Started as a tutoring program in 1990, it now has a fourteen-month program for children in the fourth and fifth grades, who are prepared through two six-week summer sessions, Saturday classes, and after-school classes once a week for acceptance into both private and elite public schools for the sixth and seventh grades. Slightly fewer than one hundred of its students are now in college and five have graduated. As with Prep for Prep, the board of trustees includes lawyers and business executives and receives much of its funding from foundations.

Once African American students are in college, there are programs that encourage any interest they may have in going to law school or business school. A joint program between major corporations and the Harvard Business School is one good example of how African Americans are recruited for the business community. For almost twenty years, the Harvard Business School has sponsored the Summer Venture in Management Program (SVMP), a weeklong program designed to expose talented minority students to management in the business world. The participants are "underrepresented minority U.S. citizens" who have completed their junior year of college, have been hired as interns during the summer by sponsoring companies (generally *Fortune*-level companies), and nominated by those companies to spend a week at Harvard Business School learning what a high-powered business school is like. Participation in the program does not guarantee subsequent acceptance into the Harvard Business School, but it does allow the school to identify and encourage applications from highly qualified individuals.

Corporations also have joined with nonprofit organizations to provide scholarships and experiences for African American college students who are considering careers in the corporate world. In 1970, Father Frank C. Carr, a white Catholic corporate executive, quit his job and founded INROADS, an organization dedicated to "increase the number of people of color in corporate management in the U.S. and to help change the way people of color gained entry into the business world." He launched the program in his hometown, Chicago, by placing twenty-five college student interns in seventeen corporations. Today, INROADS is an international organization with sixty offices that serves approximately six thousand college students working as interns in over nine hundred companies.

Once they have their MBAs in hand, the potential business executives can take advantage of the many networking opportunities offered by the National Black MBA Association, which receives some of its financial support from partnership arrangements with four hundred major corporations and universities across the country. These companies and universities pay anywhere from $3,500 to $15,000 a year to be listed as potential employers of black MBAs in the association's employment center, as well as place advertisements in the association's magazine and have a booth at its annual conventions. These partnership funds are supplemented by grants from several corporate foundations, such as the $55,000 from the DaimlerChrysler Foundation, the $45,000 from the General Motors Foundation, and the $20,000 from the Detroit Edison Foundation that are listed in *The Foundation Grants Index 2002*. Founded in 1970, the association expected as many as thirteen thousand participants at its twenty-fourth annual convention in 2002.

Taken as a whole, this kindergarten to graduate school pipeline may produce several thousand potential members of the corporate community each year, if successful graduates of public high schools who receive MBA and law degrees are added to the prep school graduates. However, this does not mean these programs are large enough to ensure a fair chance for more than a tiny fraction of all African Americans without much more help from the government at the national, state, and local levels. At best, the corporate-funded organizations seem to be holding the line at the point that was reached when the politically mediated support for blacks began to decline. For example, despite all these programs, the percentage of master's degrees awarded to blacks has been flat at about 6.5 percent since 1977, which demonstrates a significant underrepresentation. A shorter time series available from the government for master's degrees in business reveals a slight but steady increase between the 1994–95 and 1999–2000 school years. During these six years, the percentages of black students receiving business degrees rose from 5.2 to 7.1 percent.[20]

It is perhaps revealing that the Harvard Business School has not increased its percentage of black students despite the summer program that it conducts to screen and recruit underrepresented minorities. We say "perhaps" because the admissions office would not give us any information on this issue, suggesting it is a sensitive one for the school. The admissions office does provide the percentage of international students (35 percent for the class that entered in the fall of 2002), and the percentage of "minority" students (19 percent in 2002), a term that includes African Americans, Asian Americans, Hispanic Americans, and Native Americans. This minority percentage is not very helpful, but a *Business Week* interview in August of 2000 with the school's managing director of admissions included a figure for "underrepresented minorities," which (as someone in the admissions office explained to us) includes African Americans, Hispanic Americans, and Native Americans, but not Asian Americans. The *Business Week* estimate for "underrepresented minorities" at the Harvard Business School was 8 percent. This suggests, then, not only that the percentage of African Americans at the Harvard Business School is seen as a sensitive matter by the admissions staff, but also that the numbers have remained fairly small, probably about 5 percent. We base this estimate of 5 percent on an interview with a 1995 African American graduate of the Harvard Business School who is active in recruiting minority students for the school; it is his sense that the percentage remained fairly flat throughout the second half of the 1990s, probably between 4 and 7 percent.

As the careers of Frank Borges and Deval Patrick show, some of those who reach the highest levels in corporate management have been trained as lawyers. The trends on black lawyers, therefore, are relevant, and they are not promising. In July 2000, the American Bar Association released a study revealing that minority representation was lower among lawyers, and among partners in law firms, than in many other professions. In 1998, blacks and Hispanics made up 7 percent of the nation's lawyers (the study did not look separately at blacks and Hispanics), compared to 14.3 percent of the accountants, 9.7 percent of the physicians, 9.4 percent of the college and university professors, and 7.9 percent of engineers. As for partnerships in law firms, which are the key positions when it comes to power and influence, only 3 percent of partners were black or Hispanic. The minority partners tended to be at the bottom of the management and compensation hierarchies within the law firms. Moreover, minority law school enrollment grew only 0.4 percent between 1995 and 2000, the smallest five-year increase in twenty years.[21] Notably, the percentage of African American students at the Harvard Law School was higher than these national patterns (and apparently higher than at the Harvard Business School): according to the Law School Admissions Council's most recent "Guide to ABA Approved Law Schools," 8.5 percent of the current students are African Americans.

When we add all these numbers up, it seems that between 5 and 7 percent of the young executives who enter the corporate pipeline are of African American descent. Because of the inevitable attrition along the way through the normal process of competition for fewer and fewer slots, it seems unlikely to us that the number of blacks at the top will increase beyond its current low level—less than 1 percent—in the near future. There is also the fact of the continuing triple jeopardy within the corporate hierarchy—negative stereotypes, the assumption that African Americans were hired as tokens, and the difficulty of functioning in the "solo" role—which will keep the percentage lower than it might otherwise be.

Even some of those we spoke with who were near the top were not encouraged by the small numbers of African Americans they see at the middle and senior management ranks of the corporate world. As Jeffrey Palmer put it, acknowledging both the changes that have occurred and the distance that remains, "There have certainly been major changes in terms of black CEOs. I know most of those guys and they're very, very good guys. The thing that is disappointing is that while there has certainly been a recent plethora of black guys taking over corporations, you look at the number of senior management people even within those same organizations and there are very very few. This is true even in my own organization here [Pep Boys] and it was true at Home Depot, where one other person and I were the only two African American officers in a company that had three hundred officers."

Although the number of African Americans at or near the top is far below what would be expected for a level playing field, studies in social psychology suggest that it may be high enough to provide social stability. These experimental studies demonstrate that the inclusion of a small number of members from previously excluded out-groups, as few as 2 percent in some instances, undercuts the impetus for collective action by the excluded group.[22] If these studies are right, then the tiny percentage of prominent African American executives at or near the top in the corporate world may serve as a buffer to the kind of collective action that leads to systemic change.

More generally, the corporate-mediated programs that feed the corporate pipeline demonstrate the complexity of the relationship between powerful elites and previously excluded people of color. On the one hand, moderates and centrists in the corporations, foundations, and government have to do battle with the conservatives and ultra-conservatives in their midst to maintain programs that only slightly compensate for ongoing discrimination and exclusionary practices, but nonetheless provide real opportunities for individual members of the excluded groups. On the other hand, these programs actually strengthen the power structure so fiercely defended by the conservatives by increasing the percentages and visibility of these previously excluded people of color, thereby reducing the possibility of collective protest that might destabilize the overall social system. This, indeed, is one of the ironies of collective success: the increase in individual mobility decreases the likelihood of further collective action. Class stratification, even with the class conflict that sometimes breaks out in the form of strikes or liberal-labor political programs, may unexpectedly work to the benefit of those at the top.[23]

Despite the reasons we have set forth for doubting that there will be an increasing percentage of African Americans at the highest levels of the professional and corporate worlds, there is still the possibility that the picture may continue to improve. Perhaps the recent corporate successes of high-level blacks will make a difference by ensuring the enforcement of fairness within the corporations and by providing role models and renewed hope for younger black executives. Or perhaps the market has become more color blind than we believe to be the case. Either way, the next few years are likely to be crucial ones in terms of evaluating the relative merits of the market-mediated and politically mediated perspectives that we have supplemented with the evidence for corporate mediation. Indeed, we think that the next ten years will tell the tale. There is thus a need for many specific studies of elite private schools, business and law schools, and the corporate world over the next decade to see if the progress is to continue, or whether it has hit its upper limit.

In the meantime, let there be no mistake, the exceptional life journeys of Vest Monroe, Cher Lewis, Eric Coleman, Linda Hurley Ishem, Bill Lewis, Bobette Reed Kahn, and many others like them serve as a constant reminder of what is possible when black Americans are provided with some of the same opportunities as the sons and daughters of the white elite.

NOTES

1. See Pierre Bourdieu, *Outline of a Theory of Practice* (Cambridge: Cambridge University Press, 1977). See also Richard L. Zweigenhaft, "The Application of Cultural and Social Capital: A Study of the 25th Year Reunion Entries of Prep School and Public School Graduates of Yale College," *Higher Education* 23 (1992): 311–320; "Prep School and Public School Graduates of Harvard: A Longitudinal Study of the Accumulation of Social and Cultural Capital," *Journal of Higher Education* 64, no. 2 (1993): 211–225; "Accumulation of Cultural and Social Capital: The Differing College Careers of Prep School and Public School Graduates," *Sociological Spectrum* 13 (1993): 365–376; and Caroline Persell and Peter Cookson, Jr., "Microcomputers and Elite Boarding Schools: Educational Innovation and Social Reproduction," *Sociology of Education* 60 (1987): 123–134.

2. Melvin L. Oliver and Thomas M. Shapiro, *Black Wealth/White Wealth: A New Perspective on Racial Inequality* (New York: Routledge, 1995), 86.

3. Dalton Conley, *Being Black, Living in the Red: Race, Wealth and Social Policy in America* (Berkeley: University of California Press, 1999), especially chap. 3, "From Financial to Social to Human Capital: Assets and Education," 55–81. See also, Robert B. Avery and Michael S. Rendall, "Lifetime Inheritances of Three Generations of Whites and Blacks," *American Journal of Sociology* 107, no. 5 (2002): 1300–1346.

4. Ronald F. Ferguson, "A Diagnostic Analysis of Black-White GPA Disparities in Shaker Heights, Ohio," in *Brookings Papers on Education Policy 2001*, edited by Diane Ravitch (Washington, D.C.: Brookings Institution Press, 2001), 347–414; Jason W. Osborne, "Unraveling Underachievement Among African American Boys from an Identification with Academics Perspective," *Journal of Negro Education* 68, no. 4 (1999): 555–565; William G. Bowen and Derek Bok, *The Shape of the River: Long-term Consequences of Considering Race in College and University Admissions*, 2nd ed. (Princeton, N.J.: Princeton University Press, 2000), xvi.

5. In her research comparing black and white middle-class adults, Karyn Lacey found that those in the black middle class defined themselves as different in terms of values (which she refers to as "moral boundaries"). Karyn Lacey, "'We Should Fall in the Middle:' Middle-Class Blacks and the Construction of a Class-Based Identity,"

paper presented at the annual meetings of the American Sociological Association, Chicago, August 16, 2002.

6. Thomas F. Pettigrew and Joanne Martin, "Shaping the Organizational Context for Black American Inclusion," *Journal of Social Issues* 43, no. 1 (1987): 41–78.

7. Margaret Bigger, "Willie Ratchford Tries to Give as Good as He Got," *Charlotte Observer*, April 14, 1983, 1D and 3D.

8. "Affirmative Action without Fear," *New York Times*, September 19, 1994, A10; "Civil Rights Chief Is Resigning," *New York Times*, November 15, 1996, A14.

9. Roger Catlin, "Chapman: A Class of '82 Act in Danbury," *Hartford Courant*, November 1, 1988, G1.

10. Bowen and Bok, *The Shape of the River*, 258.

11. See Sharon Collins, *Black Corporate Executives: The Making and Breaking of a Black Middle Class* (Philadelphia: Temple University Press, 1997), chap. 9, "Bursting the Bubble: The Failure of Black Progress," 155–168.

12. Cora Daniels, "50 Most Powerful Black Executives in America," *Fortune* (July 22, 2002): 63.

13. Roderick J. Harrison and Cassandra Cantave, "Earnings of African Americans," Joint Center for Political and Economic Studies (June 1999) available at www.jointcenter.org/DB/factsheet/earnings.htm.

14. For a discussion of "symbolic," "modern," and "aversive racism, see James M. Jones, *Prejudice and Racism*, 2nd ed. (New York: McGraw Hill, 1997), 124–130. For a summary of the work on aversive racism over the past two and a half decades, see John F. Dovidio, "On the Nature of Contemporary Prejudice: The Third Wave," *Journal of Social Issues* 57, no. 4 (2001): 829–849. See also Susan T. Fiske, "What We Know Now About Bias and Intergroup Conflict, the Problem of the Century," *Current Directions in Psychological Science* 11, no. 4 (2002): 123–128.

15. Roderick J. Harrison, "The Status of Residential Segregation: Despite Decades of Change, African Americans Remain the Nation's Most Segregated Racial Group," *Focus* 29, no. 7 (2001): 3–4.

16. Douglas S. Massey and Nancy A. Denton, *American Apartheid: Segregation and the Making of the Underclass* (Cambridge: Harvard University Press, 1993).

17. Gary Orfield and Michael Kurlaender, *Diversity Challenged: Evidence on the Impact of Affirmative Action* (Cambridge, Mass.: Harvard Education Publishing Group, 2001); and "Resegregation in American Schools," The Civil Rights Project, Harvard University (June 1999).

18. Richard L. Zweigenhaft and G. William Domhoff, *Diversity in the Power Elite: Have Women and Minorities Reached the Top?* (New Haven, Conn.: Yale University Press, 1998), 182–183.

19. See G. William Domhoff, *Who Rules America: Power and Politics*. 4th ed. (New York: McGraw Hill, 2002), chaps. 4 and 5, for a discussion of how the closely knit major corporations create overlapping policy-planning and opinion-shaping networks that include the major foundations—Ford, Rockefeller, Carnegie, Mellon—as well as think tanks, policy discussion groups, and nonprofit organizations that reach out to middle-class voluntary associations and the mass media. The "corporate foundations," those that receive new funding each year from their parent corporation, are

directly controlled by the corporations that fund them. Sixteen of the one hundred largest foundations in 2000 in terms of actual donations—not assets—were corporate foundations (see fdncenter.org/research/trends_analysis/top100giving.html). For more information on the important role of corporate foundations in supporting a wide range of non-profit organizations, see Jerome Himmelstein, *Looking Good and Doing Good: Corporate Philanthropy and Corporate Power* (Bloomington, Ind.: Indiana University Press, 1997).

20. These data can be found on the Web site of the National Center for Education Statistics, nces.ed.gov/edstats.

21. Elizabeth Chambliss (Research Director), "Miles to Go 2000: Progress of Minorities in the Legal Profession," American Bar Association Commission for Minorities in the Profession. See also "Bar Association Study Finds Little Diversity," *New York Times*, July 9, 2000, 19.

22. See Stephen Wright, Donald M. Taylor, and Fathali M. Moghaddam, "Responding to Membership in a Disadvantaged Group: From Acceptance to Collective Protest," *Journal of Personality and Social Psychology* 58, no. 6 (1990): 994–1003; Bruce R. Hare, "On the Desegregation of the Visible Elite: Or, Beware of the Emperor's New Helpers: He or She May Look Like You or Me," *Sociological Forum* 10, no. 4 (1995): 673–678; and Stephen C. Wright, "Restricted Intergroup Boundaries: Tokenism, Ambiguity, and the Tolerance of Injustice," in *The Psychology of Legitimacy: Emerging Perspectives on Ideology, Justice and Intergroup Relations*, edited by John T. Jost and Brenda N. Majors (New York: Cambridge University Press, 2001), 223–254.

23. For a more complete discussion of the ironies of diversity, see the final chapter in Zweigenhaft and Domhoff, *Diversity in the Power Elite*, 176–194.

Appendix 1

The Sample and Our Methods

This project is our current report on seventeen years of research on early graduates of the ABC program. In this work, we have used a variety of methods. For this updated edition of our 1991 book we have enjoyed the benefits of some of the newer Internet technologies that have allowed us to find people and information about people.

In October 1985, an informant who worked for ABC provided us with the names and addresses of sixty early graduates of the program. Because we had emphasized our interest in examining how ABC graduates were doing in the corporate world, the list we were given included men and women who, according to ABC records, had worked in one of nineteen different corporate-oriented occupational categories.

This list provided us with a way into the larger network of ABC graduates. We sent a letter to each of the sixty people explaining our general interest in the ABC program, and more particularly, in conducting face-to-face interviews. Twenty-three of the sixty responded, indicating a willingness to be interviewed. None wrote to say that he or she was not willing, and our subsequent attempts to contact those who did not respond led us to believe that most of the nonrespondents were no longer living at the addresses on the mailing list. Over the course of the next year, the first author traveled to the cities in which twelve of the twenty-three lived and interviewed them. In addition, a colleague put him in touch with an early ABC graduate living in a nearby city, and she was also interviewed.

We increased the size of our sample by using the technique known as "snowball sampling." At the conclusion of each interview, he asked for the names and, if possible, addresses and phone numbers of other graduates.

Many knew the general whereabouts of other ABC students whom they had met in the summer program, in prep school, in college, or in the cities in which they currently lived, though many had lost touch with friends they had made in the program fifteen to twenty years earlier. Some knew specifically how to contact ABC friends, and all but one were willing to provide names, addresses, and phone numbers. (The one who was unwilling said he would do so, but only after first obtaining his friends' permission.) After certain preliminaries (an introductory letter, then a follow-up phone call), these ABC graduates were interviewed, as were ABC alumni whom they, in turn, recommended. Using this snowball technique, between the fall of 1985 and the fall of 1987 he interviewed twelve more alumni of the ABC program.

Formally speaking, snowball sampling is a method of developing a research sample on the basis of referrals made by people who "know of others who possess some characteristics that are of research interest."[1] Some have even argued that it is an ideal method for some forms of sociological research "because it allows for the sampling of natural interactional units," the very stuff of which cliques, groups, classes, and other networks are constructed.[2] However, in practice, the method is usually used with difficult-to-reach populations or esoteric groups where the knowledge of insiders is necessary to locate members. ABC alumni are not an inherently esoteric group, of course, but they became so for us when we could not obtain a full list of the alumni.

Not all the problems of developing a snowball sample pertained to our work. For example, we had no trouble finding some respondents through the list our ABC informant provided to start the referral chains or in verifying the "eligibility" of those who were referred for inclusion in our study. It did make sense, however, to pursue as many new chains as we could to avoid becoming focused on one part of the overall ABC group. It also helped to ask explicitly for types of ABC participants who might not naturally be thought of; for example, we asked about those who had failed, dropped out, or somehow "fouled up."[3] At the same time, we also sought some duplication of key types of interviewees, such as those who had become highly successful in large corporations, to see if the new interviews confirmed the analysis we were developing.

By October 1987 the chains we had developed were based almost entirely on interviews conducted in large cities along the East Coast. When we arranged a trip to Cleveland to interview another link in one of our chains, we were able to convince our ABC informant to provide us with ABC alumni lists for Cleveland and for Chicago. Using the same technique we had used previously—a letter followed by a phone call—we were able to schedule and conduct an additional two interviews in Cleveland and four in Chicago. Finally, a few months later, our ABC informant provided us with the ABC alumni list for the state of North Carolina. Again using the same procedure, we conducted another six interviews.

By the end of 1988, the first author had conducted thirty-eight interviews: one with a person recommended by a colleague; thirteen with individuals on the first list our informant sent us; another twelve with people located through the "snowball technique"; and another twelve with people on the Cleveland, Chicago, and North Carolina lists our informant subsequently sent to us. The interviews, all but one of which were recorded, lasted between forty-five minutes and three hours. They took place in the offices and homes of ABC graduates, in indoor restaurants and outdoor cafes, and in hotel lobbies.

It is, of course, never clear how many interviews are "necessary" in a study like this. Barney Glaser and Anselm Strauss, two major figures in the use of interviewing to gain new sociological insights, suggest that there is no one right number. They believe interviews should stop when no new information is being uncovered. They use the term *saturation* to refer to the point at which "no additional data are being found whereby the sociologist can develop properties of the category."[4] Using this framework, Susan Ostrander found that interviews with thirty-six upper-class women in a large Midwestern city were enough to give her a very clear picture of the main concerns and routines in the lives of these women. The great emphasis they put on their careers as "volunteers" who run a wide range of social agencies, and the fact that they saw this work partly in terms of limiting government involvement in social welfare, permeated the interviews. So did their deference to their husbands and their pride in being good homemakers.[5] Ostrander's findings were supported by subsequent interview and observational studies in cities on the East and West Coasts.[6]

Similarly, by the time we had completed thirty interviews with wealthy Jewish businessmen for one of our previous books, the main patterns in their experiences had emerged, including the differences in their European origins and in the number of generations their families had been wealthy. Their assimilation into certain social and economic institutions had become clear, as had their exclusion from most social clubs.[7] Subsequent studies of Jews in the corporate elite in the late 1970s and 1980s reported similar findings.[8]

For the interviews we used a semistructured set of questions that moved chronologically from the time they first heard about A Better Chance through their recollections of their participation in the summer orientation program, their prep school experiences, their years in college, their careers, and their personal relationships.

Although we closely followed our interview schedule, in some cases our respondents gave long answers to early items that anticipated later questions; we therefore did not have to ask each and every question explicitly. Also, in some cases particular answers led us to ask a series of questions that were not on our list. When we spoke with Ed McPherson, a former president of his class at Andover, for example, we spent considerable time asking about student politics in 1969 because he had been one of three black class presidents elected at that school in that year (see chapter 3). And again guided by the work of Glaser and Strauss, Ostrander, and other researchers using interviews as an inductive method of discovery, we shifted the emphasis within our interviews as we came to understand some issues and saw the need to learn more about issues we did not fully understand or had not fully envisaged at the outset.

The thirty-eight people in our original sample may not be a perfectly representative sample of the hundreds of early black graduates of the ABC program, but they are similar in a number of respects to those who entered the program in the 1960s and early 1970s. Most of those we interviewed grew up in inner cities along the East Coast or in the Midwest; the hometowns represented included New York, New Haven, Boston, Chicago, Cleveland, Detroit, Philadelphia, Washington, D.C., Richmond, and Atlanta; some were from smaller towns in the Midwest (such as Steubenville, Ohio) and in the South (such as Henderson, North Carolina, and Clarksdale, Mississippi). A handful had parents or grandparents who had attended college, but most were the first in their family to obtain a college education. The parents of approximately a third of our interviewees never started high school, and many of the others had not graduated.

During the course of the interviews, we also asked about the experiences of other ABC students they had known (some of whom they were still in touch with, some of whom they were not). This provided us, in an indirect way, with a broader sample of ABC students. The results from this indirect sample were very similar to what we learned from the direct sample.

In addition to these interviews with ABC graduates in the late 1980s, the first author also interviewed, either in person or by phone, scores of individuals who had worked for or with ABC, including all of the former heads of the program, two of three headmasters who had founded the program (the third died in 1971), people who had recruited ABC students in the early years, people who had worked in the summer orientation programs, and many administrators at independent schools and colleges.

Interviews, however, were not our only source of information. We were also able to draw on a number of studies of ABC students performed in the late 1960s and early 1970s. Some of these, especially those by Alden Wessman and George Perry, were carefully controlled research efforts that included the testing and retesting of ABC students, control groups of white students in the same prep schools, and control groups of black students in public schools.[9] In addition to their considerable value in and of themselves, these studies confirm our belief that our interview sample is a representative one.

There were additional sources of archival, journalistic, and anecdotal data from which to draw. This material included the annual reports published by the ABC program, local histories of prep schools, books about prep schools, books about the upper class that included discussions of prep school life, articles appearing in magazines as diverse as *Reader's Digest*, the *Atlantic Monthly*, the *Independent Schools Bulletin*, the *Journal of Negro Education*, *Ebony*, and *Mother Jones*, and letters received from teachers and students who had participated in the ABC program. We also drew on interviews conducted with an ABC student at Stanford University in 1974 by one of the second author's research assistants.

In the summer of 1994, the first author reinterviewed seven of the ABC graduates he had interviewed in the late 1980s. At this time he also established and maintained email contact with most of the seven. Then, beginning in the late spring of 2001 and continuing through the early summer of 2002, he conducted face-to-face interviews in Washington, D.C., San Jose, California, Hartford and Middletown, Connecticut, New York City, Philadelphia, Greensboro and Winston-Salem, North Carolina, and Danbury, Virginia, with ten more of the original interviewees (and one, in New York City, with a 1995 ABC graduate). He conducted phone interviews with eight more, and communicated via email with many of these same graduates and with two he did not speak to face-to-face or by phone. Moreover, by this time, the Internet provided a way to obtain information about many of the ABC graduates in the original sample, both those he had reinterviewed face-to-face, by phone or via email, and some who had moved many times and with whom he had lost contact. All in all, twenty-three of the original thirty-eight were reinterviewed, and we were able to obtain information about three of the other fifteen.

For this update, we also drew on contacts with ABC graduates that we made in a variety of ways. For example, a number of people who read the first edition of this book wrote us about it, and we developed ongoing correspondences with them. Our letters and emails from several people, and especially Byron Haskins, were quite valuable for the insights they provided, but also because they led us to useful articles and to other ABC alumni with whom we then communicated. Thus, at times, we found ourselves using snowball-like techniques via email, in which one ABC graduate suggested others we might contact. Similarly, using the various search engines on the Internet, we were able to obtain information about, and make contact with, many recent graduates of the ABC program. Therefore, throughout the text there is information about many alumni of the ABC program over and beyond our original thirty-eight interviewees.

NOTES

1. Patrick Biernacki and Dan Waldorf, "Snowball Sampling: Problems and Techniques of Chain Referral Sampling," *Sociological Methods and Research* 10, no. 2 (1981): 141–163.

2. James S. Coleman, "Relational Analysis: The Study of Social Organizations with Survey Methods," *Human Organizations* 17, no. 4 (1958): 28–36 (as summarized by Biernacki and Waldorf, "Snowball Sampling," 141).

3. Biernacki and Waldorf, "Snowball Sampling," 155.

4. Barney G. Glaser and Anselm L. Strauss, *The Discovery of Grounded Theory: Strategies for Qualitative Research* (Chicago: Aldine, 1967), 61.

5. Susan A. Ostrander, *Women of the Upper Class* (Philadelphia: Temple University Press, 1984), 11.

6. Arlene Kaplan Daniels, *Invisible Careers* (Chicago: University of Chicago Press, 1988); Teresa Odendahl, *Charity Begins at Home* (New York: Basic Books, 1990); Margo MacLeod, "Influential Women Volunteers: Reexamining the Concept of Power," paper presented at the annual meetings of the American Sociological Association, San Antonio, 1984.

7. Richard L. Zweigenhaft and G. William Domhoff, *Jews in the Protestant Establishment* (New York: Praeger, 1982).

8. Richard L. Zweigenhaft, "Women and Minorities of the Corporation: Will They Make It to the Top?" in *Power Elites and Organizations*, edited by G. William Domhoff and Thomas R. Dye (Beverly Hills, Calif.: Sage, 1987), 37–62; and Abraham Korman, *The Outsiders: Jews and Corporate America* (Lexington, Mass.: Lexington, 1988).

9. Alden E. Wessman, "Evaluation of Project ABC (A Better Chance): An Evaluation of Dartmouth College—Independent Schools Scholarship Program for Disadvantaged High School Students," final report, Office of Education, Bureau of Research, April 1969, ERIC Document 031549; and George Perry, "A Better Chance: Evaluation of Student Attitudes and Academic Performance, 1964–1972," study funded by the Alfred R. Sloan Foundation, the Henry Luce Foundation, and the New York Community Trust, 1973, ERIC Document 075556.

Appendix 2

The Creation, Funding, and Evolution of A Better Chance

Before the civil rights movement created a crisis atmosphere and generated the concern that led to the ABC program, only a miniscule number of blacks attended prep school. Many of those few who did so were the sons and daughters of highly successful athletes and entertainers, such as Jackie Robinson's son, Lena Horne's daughter, and Nat King Cole's famous daughter Natalie. When Choate, the alma mater of John F. Kennedy (class of 1935), accepted its first black student in 1959, some students, some faculty, and many alumni protested that the school had "no business taking Negroes."[1] At about the same time, when Groton decided to enroll its first black student, one alumnus was so outraged that he sent a letter to all alumni falsely claiming that there was a new admissions policy that would reserve half the school's places for blacks. He forged the rector's signature at the end of the letter, setting off what one prominent Groton graduate refers to as "one of the most wretched scandals in Old Money history."[2] And, according to a 1960 graduate of the Pomfret School, when the headmaster there advocated accepting black students, he was figuratively dismissed by the board of trustees as "possibly Bolshevik" and, not long thereafter, literally dismissed from his position.[3]

Reluctant or not, by the early 1960s many private schools had accepted their first black students, though few schools had more than two or three at once. A survey of twelve private schools in Boston revealed that during the 1962–63 academic year they had a total of "23 Negro students."[4] The decision to accept blacks at these schools, where the students were exclusively, or almost exclusively, from upper-class white families, led to many problems. Perhaps the most immediate was finding black students. Elite boarding schools had established recruiting networks in upper-class communities throughout the country, but they had little experience and few contacts in

Harlem, south Philadelphia, or the inner city of Chicago. Furthermore, the black students who decided to go to prep school at this time often did not enjoy the experience, and many did not stay.

Despite these problems, a handful of well-connected or well-heeled men wanted to integrate elite schools more rapidly, more systematically, and more effectively. They were led by an unlikely but formidable trio of boarding school headmasters: the son of a military man, a psychologist, and a Merrill Lynch scion. John Kemper, headmaster at Andover, was the son of a career officer from West Point, and himself a graduate of West Point. Howard Jones was the head of Northfield and Mount Hermon schools. The son of an executive of the Boy Scouts of America and a graduate of a public high school, he had been an all-American goalie on the Colgate hockey team, flown airplanes in World War Two, and earned a doctorate in adolescent psychology from Syracuse.

The most unlikely of the three in many ways was Charles Merrill, whose wealth made it possible for him to establish his own prep school and become the legitimator and financial backer of the ABC program. Merrill was the unpredictable and at times eccentric son of the Merrill who founded what was to become Merrill Lynch. After attending Deerfield Academy and Harvard, he served in the army during World War Two. When the war ended, he accepted a teaching position at the Thomas Jefferson School in St. Louis, where he taught the sons of wealthy Midwestern businessmen who would go East to Harvard, Yale, and Wesleyan and then "return to run their fathers' businesses and communities in a disciplined and civilized way."[5] After nine years at Thomas Jefferson, and two years as an unpublished novelist in Paris, he moved his family to Boston and started his own school in the fall of 1958.

It was Jones who initiated the process in 1962. As he told an interviewer in the early 1970s: "I called Johnnie Kemper of Andover, probably the most respected headmaster in the country, and I shared with him . . . my new enthusiasm for trying to get a number of schools involved in providing an education for a significant number of Negro students. Johnnie was very supportive, saying that he had been having some of these same feelings."[6]

In late February 1963, Kemper invited the heads of twenty-three prep schools to meet at Andover. At this point Jones and Kemper were able to bring Merrill into their planning by putting him on the executive committee to create a new program, first known by the awkward and soon-abandoned name, Independent Schools Talent Search Program (ISTSP).

The committee submitted a request to the Merrill Foundation for a grant, which was as good as money in the bank due to Charles Merrill's position on its executive committee. They also sent letters to fifty prep schools "known to be particularly concerned for the welfare of promising Negro students," asking them to support the new program with one dollar for every student they currently enrolled in their schools.[7]

Thirty responded favorably, and sixteen actually joined. The list reads like a who's who of elite independent private schools: Choate, Commonwealth School, Deerfield Academy, Emma Willard, George School, Groton, The Gunnery, Hotchkiss, Northfield-Mount Hermon, Phillips Academy (Andover), Pomfret, The Putney School, St. George's, St. Paul's, Taft, and Western Reserve Academy. With their combined 1963 enrollment of about nine thousand students, the member fees generated $9,000 to support the program. The board hired James S. Simmons, a black graduate of Hampton Institute, who was about to complete his MA in education from Harvard, as its first director. Working out of an office in New York City, Simmons began to recruit students.

From the earliest discussions of what the prep schools needed, Jones and the other headmasters believed that in order to succeed, inner city black students recruited by ISTSP would require a thorough orientation program. The opening for funding such an orientation program came on July 1, 1963, when the president of Dartmouth College, John Sloan Dickey, gave a speech at Mount Hermon. That night, in Jones's living room, the discussion turned to the need for a summer program to prepare black students for their prep school placements.

Jones raised this topic with Dickey at an especially fortuitous time. Dickey was feeling pressure to demonstrate Dartmouth's commitment to equal educational opportunity. During the very week when he spoke at Mount Hermon, two Dartmouth deans and a member of the English department had proposed that Dartmouth establish a small secondary school on campus for "bright Negro boys" from poor backgrounds. Dickey immediately said that Dartmouth would house an orientation program, and that he would find the funds for it.

It was not hard for Dickey to keep his word. Because he sat on the board of trustees of the Rockefeller Foundation, he had no difficulty convincing the other members of the board to fund the proposal for the summer program that he himself wrote.[8] The summer program was to be known as Project A. B. C. (A Better Chance).[9] Meanwhile, it soon became apparent that the awkward name of the program—Independent Schools Talent Search Program—was creating confusion because it was attracting performing artists.[10] At the same time, it became increasingly clear that "A Better Chance" was an ideal name. It resonated with the root American value of "equal opportunity" and it had a catchy educational acronym (ABC).[11]

THE CHALLENGE OF FUNDING ABC THROUGH THE YEARS

Although ABC started with money from independent schools and foundations, it received a major financial boost in 1965 from an unlikely source, federal government poverty funds, but it was once again elite networks that played the key role. When Howard Jones, the head of Northfield and Mount

Hermon, had served as chairman of the Commission on Higher Education for the Virgin Islands in the early 1960s, he had recruited a famous Kennedy in-law, Sargent Shriver, whose daughter, Maria, is now a well-known television news personality and the wife of Arnold Schwarzenegger, to assist the commission in its work. As a Kennedy in-law and the former director of the Peace Corps, as well as the current director of the Office of Economic Opportunity, the government's newly founded poverty agency created in response to ghetto unrest in 1964, Shriver was as thoroughly entrenched in the most important networks of the upper class and government as anyone could be in the 1960s.

When the Office of Economic Opportunity began deliberations on what to do with the considerable amount of money it had been budgeted, Shriver quickly thought of his friend Jones and the ABC program. The result was a four-year grant of $10 million, the equivalent of about $57 million in 2002 dollars. Shriver had such high hopes for the program that he wanted it to place one thousand students in the summer of 1966, but the program was not prepared to process that many students immediately; instead, ABC agreed to do so over a four-year period. Within a month of receiving the grant, Simmons had hired three associate directors, all of whom were white. Simmons spent most of his time at the white prep schools, selling the program to the schools, while the three white associate directors spent their time at black junior high schools selling the program to black faculty, staff, counselors, and teenagers.

Since the earliest days of the Reagan administration, many conservatives, and especially many conservative religious fundamentalists, have advocated voucher plans whereby parents can draw on public funds to send their children to private schools. Liberal critics have opposed this idea because they believe it is unconstitutional for public funds to pay for students to attend private religious schools. This debate still goes on (a 2002 Supreme Court decision allowed for the use of vouchers in private religious schools in Cleveland). Notably, this is, in effect, what ABC did with OEO funds in the 1960s. It sent needy students to expensive private (and, often, religiously affiliated) schools with government money. From the outset, at least some ABC leaders realized this could lead to serious legal controversy. As William Berkeley, who took over from Simmons in 1966 and remained president of the organization until 1974, recalled when we interviewed him in 1987: "We always questioned while we were there the very constitutionality of public money going to us. Why should the public sector pay for a poor kid to go to Groton? So, in a way, you can say we were almost an accident to be where we were at the time we were, and if the money hadn't dried up on its own, probably someone would have blown the whistle somewhere down the line. . . . Total inappropriate use of money, and the only reason we were willing to take it is we were using it darn well; at least we were achieving results. Even though the cost per student, per person, was enormous, there were real achievements there."[12]

Not surprisingly, the OEO grant gave the ABC program more clout with the prep schools. The number of ABC students rose dramatically from the original 55 males in the fall of 1964 to 200 male and female students in the fall of 1965, and to 430 in the fall of 1966; the number of schools participating increased from the original 16 charter members, mostly in New England, to more than 100 independent schools across the country. The OEO grant also enabled ABC to provide substantial support for each ABC student: $2,500 for tuition, room and board, plus $250 for pocket money, travel costs, and medical expenses. Since many schools wanted black students anyway, this money provided a strong incentive for the schools to join ABC: ABC would not only find the students, it would pay the bulk of their costs.[13] To keep schools from seeing ABC students as mere moneymaking acquisitions, ABC instituted a sliding scale designed to encourage financial commitments. If a school took only one ABC student, the school had to pay all the costs for that student. But if the school took additional ABC students, ABC picked up increasing portions of the costs for each student.

Then, in an unexpected turn of events, the funds from OEO were cut in 1967. According to Berkeley, the OEO had developed many new programs, including Upward Bound, and decided that providing funding for impoverished students to attend elite boarding schools was not the best use of its money. Students who had already started in the ABC program were allowed to continue to receive support, but no more OEO money could be used for new students to enter the program. Ultimately, ABC received $4,319,848 (the equivalent of about $24.7 million in 2002 dollars), but by 1970 the program was receiving no public funds.[14]

From 1969 through 1974, ABC raised an average of $975,000 a year from private sources, especially foundations and corporations. As Berkeley recalled: "The funding base for ABC was terribly narrow. If you took away about ten foundations out of ABC's history, you'd cut out about 90 percent of the private funding we were able to attract." Among the largest donors during this period were the Vincent Astor Foundation ($530,000 in 1969), the Edward E. Ford Foundation ($125,000 in 1969, $150,000 in 1970), and the Andrew W. Mellon Foundation ($100,000 in 1971).

By the early 1970s, as the civil rights movement faded and the Vietnam War lingered on, Berkeley was starting to burn out. As is often the case with nonprofit organizations, ABC was kept on a short tether by the foundations and the corporations despite its proven success. "It was all fund-raising at that point," he recalls, "and it was just exhausting. I mean, there's a limit to how many times you can go back to the same old people. There was no base, no financial base . . . and so you're starting from scratch every year. I mean, Mike [Zoob, my assistant] and I used to laugh. Every July 1, we would say 'Well, as good as we were last year, it doesn't help us at all this year. We'd better start from scratch.'"

Almost every measure of black participation in elite educational institutions—prep schools, colleges, the Harvard Business School, or medical schools—reveals that the percentage of black students declined after a peak in the mid-1970s.[15] Moreover, there was a sharp decline in the willingness of foundations to fund social movement organizations; from the early 1960s through 1971, such funding increased, but the 1970s saw a 55 percent decrease. "The funding peak," sociologist Craig Jenkins writes, "followed closely on the upsurge of the mass movements, and then, after the movements declined, funding gradually tapered off."[16]

The change in the fundraising climate was exacerbated by internal problems at ABC. Berkeley's successor, William Boyd, who took office in December 1974, was the first black graduate of Deerfield Academy, received his BA from Williams College and his Ph.D. in political science from the University of California, Berkeley. He worked for the ABC summer program at Williams in 1966, and joined the ABC board of directors in 1971. He appeared to be the ideal person for the job, but he soon attracted critics. As one administrator who worked for many years in the world of private independent schools put it: "I think their funding was dicey during his era, and management and administration even dicier."

It was a troubled time for ABC. More than fifty employees quit between 1978 and 1981, and by 1981 only four people had been with the organization for more than three years. The alarmingly high turnover rate, low morale, and general confusion about roles and internal organization convinced the board of directors to hire James H. Lowry and Associates, a black-owned management consulting firm, to conduct a study of ABC and suggest ways that it could function more effectively. The company's thirty-one-page report, titled "Improving the Overall Effectiveness of A Better Chance, Inc., in a Changing Environment," identified many problems and called for many changes. The report made clear that the high turnover rate and low morale stemmed, at least in part, from "inadequate supervision from the President." "Unless radical changes are made," the report concluded, "ABC as an institution will suffer irreparable damage."[17] Soon thereafter, William Boyd left to become a vice president at the World Institute for Computer Training (WICAT), a firm in Utah he helped start.[18]

With reduced funding, and internal problems, the ABC program was in serious trouble in February 1982, when Judith Berry Griffin took over. The daughter of Leonidas H. Berry, an eminent Chicago physician who was an authority on digestive diseases and endoscopy (he had been the first black internist at Cook County Hospital, where he retired in 1975 as chief of endoscopy and senior attending physician), Griffin was an educator with degrees from the University of Chicago and Columbia, and the author of an award-winning children's book, *Phoebe and the General.*[19] As one of those we interviewed put it, "It fell in her lap to try to save the organization from collapse." Griffin kept the program going primarily through the elimination of all funding assistance to the schools that took ABC students. As she explained in the 1984 annual report: "The ending of the federal funding that allowed ABC to pay partial tuition to schools created a painful dilemma. Given fundraising realities, we could either end these tuition payments or severely limit the number of students recruited and placed in our member schools. In 1984 the Board of Directors made the difficult decision to end payments."[20]

Based on interviews we have conducted with a number of people in the independent school world, we conclude that this difficult decision cost ABC a great deal of clout with prep schools. Meanwhile, as we show in chapter 9, various new programs were created in the 1980s and 1990s to identify, prepare, and provide funding for students of color at private schools. In particular, city and state associations of independent schools aided in the creation of their own minority recruiting networks by paying extra dues to help fund such programs. A November 2000 *New York Times* article on "diversity at prep schools today" referred to "a dozen diversity programs that open the doors to boarding schools for academically talented minority students."[21]

As early as the mid-1970s, ABC had expanded its activities to include some students from middle-class backgrounds. Veronica Dunning-Alami and Susan Boiko, associate directors of research at ABC, explained the rationale for this in a 1977 article in *Independent School*:

> The growing proportion of the minority population in middle and higher income categories should be reflected in independent school enrollments. In addition, economic barriers to increasing minority enrollment can be lowered if schools admit students who need smaller amounts of financial assistance. ABC has therefore begun to expand its activities to include middle-income minority students. Approximately a dozen such students were placed last September, and two dozen or more should be placed next fall. If the interest of member schools is sustained, this effort will grow, making possible the first real advance in the number of minority students attending ABC member schools since the early 1970s.[22]

It became the erroneous perception of some that ABC had changed its mission. For example, one of the ABC graduates we interviewed in Atlanta in the 1980s expressed concern that the program seemed to have changed in this respect:

> They're getting away from the real, true, I guess basic beginnings of the program. Those people who really need it. When we had our parents' group meeting, there were people who live in southwest Atlanta who could well afford to send their kids to these schools, or at least partially pay for it. The kids who were really in need—what do you do about them? My husband and I may be able to afford to send our kids there. If it is going to take it away from some other kid, we wouldn't want to do it. We would find means or whatever to try to send them on our own. That's just the way I feel about it.

However, even though ABC does assist middle-class families who seek independent schools for their children, its primary mission continues to be the placement of minority students from low-income families.[23]

ABC IN THE 1990S AND INTO THE 2000S

By the early 1990s, ABC was clearly not able to do as much as it did at its peak, when it placed more than five hundred students per year, provided each with an intense eight-week orientation, and paid a substantial portion of each student's room, board, and tuition. In 1971 the program had revenues of $1,248,359, but by 1991 its revenues were the equivalent of only $487,108 in 1971 dollars.[24] The funding efforts had not been able to keep up with inflation.

By the late 1990s, however, as we've indicated in chapter 1, the ABC program had turned things around financially. The revenues for 1998 were $3,928,523, an increase of 250 percent from the amount ten years earlier. Along with the increase in funding came an increase in student placements and the addition of another program called "Pathways to College," an after-school curriculum in public schools to reach students unable to participate in the prep school program.

The resurgence in funding did not come from foundations and corporations, the key sources of ABC funds for many years. In fact, comparative figures for 1988 and 1998 fundraising indicate that income from foundations dropped from $758,257 to $463,508, a decline of 39 percent. Income from corporations increased, but only from $416,050 in 1988 to $633,508 in 1998. The dramatic increase came from contributions from individuals. As the program noted in its *A Better Chance News*, a newsletter mailed to alumni and supporters every few months, "over 50 percent of our annual revenue is now provided by individuals, who, with their strong bonds to the organization, are our most stable long-term funding sources."[25] Among those with strong bonds are ABC alums themselves, many of whom by the late 1990s had earned significant sums of money and wished to express their gratitude to the program that was so central in contributing to their upward mobility. As we noted in chapter 1, ABC has also managed to establish relationships with highly visible African Americans in the entertainment industry, the most significant of whom is Oprah Winfrey, with over $12,300,000 in total gifts and pledges as of 2000. ABC, therefore, seems to be on solid financial ground as it approaches its fifth decade of helping low-income students, and especially low-income African Americans, to attend elite private schools and suburban high schools that often serve as a steppingstone to upward mobility.

NOTES

1. Peter S. Prescott, *A World of our Own: Notes on Life and Learning in a Boys' Preparatory School* (New York: Coward-McCann, 1970), 244.

2. Nelson W. Aldrich, Jr., *Old Money: The Mythology of America's Upper Class* (New York: Knopf, 1988), 278.

3. Adam Hochschild, *Half the Way Home* (New York: Viking, 1986), 97–98.

4. Charles Merrill, "Negroes in the Private Schools," *Atlantic Monthly* (July 1967): 37.

5. Charles Merrill, *The Walled Garden: The Story of a School* (Boston: Rowan Tree Press, 1982), 12.

6. "No reason . . . Except Faith: 10 Years of ABC," unpublished and undated report, 1.

7. This quote is drawn from an undated and anonymously written internal ABC document titled "Origins of ABC-ISTS or How the Hell Did We Get This Way?"

8. "No Reason . . . Except Faith," 3.

9. "Dartmouth Aids Gifted Negroes," *New York Times*, December 29, 1963, 26.

10. Howard Jones, interview with Richard L. Zweigenhaft, Roanoke, Virginia, July 12, 1986.

11. Linda R. McLean, "The Black Student in the White Independent School," *Independent School Bulletin* (1969): 68.

12. This, and all the subsequent quotes from William Berkeley, are drawn from an interview conducted by Richard L. Zweigenhaft in Boston, May 1, 1987.

13. Merrill, "Negroes in the Private Schools," 38.

14. George Perry, the author of "A Better Chance: Evaluation of Student Attitudes and Academic Performance, 1964–1972," funded by the Alfred P. Sloan Foundation, the Henry Luce Foundation and the New York Community Trust (published in 1973, and available as ERIC Document ED075556), writes: "OEO had encouraged ABC to expect that funding for new students (who would enter in September 1967) would continue at the high 1966 level. However, late in the spring of

1967, ABC was suddenly notified that OEO could not fund any new students" (6). The $10 million and $4,319,848 figures were provided by William Berkeley in an email, August 15, 2002.

15. See Edward B. Fiske, "Colleges Open New Minority Drives," *New York Times* November 18, 1987, 12; Meg Dooley, "Minorities in Higher Education: Bridging the Access Gap," *Columbia Magazine* (June 1987): 27–35; Keith B. Richburg, "Blacks Forgoing Academic Life," *Washington Post*, December 16, 1985, A3; Richard L. Zweigenhaft, *Who Gets to the Top?: Executive Suite Discrimination in the Eighties* (New York: Institute of Human Relations, 1984), 25; Martin Carnoy, *Faded Dreams: The Politics and Economics of Race* (New York: Cambridge University Press, 1994), especially chap. 3, "Politics and Black Educational Opportunity," 127–149. One of the many special features of the class of 1973 at Harvard, which included Sylvester Monroe, and about whom he is writing a book, is that Harvard had never before had as many African American students, and, according to Monroe, has not had that many again since then.

16. J. Craig Jenkins, "Nonprofit Organizations and Public Advocacy," in Walter W. Powell, ed., *The Non-Profit Sector: A Research Handbook* (New Haven, Conn.: Yale University Press, 1987), 312–313; see also, J. Craig Jenkins, "Social Movement Philanthropy and American Democracy," in *Philanthropic Giving*, edited by Richard Magat (New York: Oxford University Press, 1989), 292–314.

17. James H. Lowry and Associates, "Improving the Overall Effectiveness of A Better Chance, Inc., in a Changing Environment" (September 9, 1981), photocopy.

18. William Boyd, telephone interview with Richard L. Zweigenhaft, March 18, 1987.

19. Joy Bennett Kinnon, "A Better Chance: National Program Produces Students Who Can Compete With the Best," *Ebony* (May 1997): 44ff.

20. "ABC Annual Report, 1984–1985," 3.

21. Victoria Goldman and Catherine Hausman, "Less Austerity, More Diversity at Prep School Today, Education Life, *New York Times*, November 12, 2000, 30.

22. Veronica Dunning-Alami and Susan Boiko, "A Better Chance: A Program that Works," *Independent School* 36 (May 1977): 26–28.

23. In some cases, the placement of middle-class African American youngsters into private schools through the ABC program may have sentimental or symbolic motives. For example, when Sylvester Monroe told ABC president Judith Griffin that his son was going to attend St. George's, she wanted him to apply through the ABC program. When he said to her "He can't be, he's not a disadvantaged kid," she explained: "It doesn't matter. He should be an A Better Chance student." He therefore applied through ABC, but unlike other ABC applications, he only applied to the school that he already had decided to attend. Perhaps such exceptions to the general rule should be seen as a way of building an ABC community.

24. These figures are from the annual reports in 1971 and 1991. In 1981 the program reported revenues of $1,656,170; the 1991 revenues are the equivalent of $1,031,298 in 1981 dollars.

25. "1998: Best Year Ever for Fundraising," *A Better Chance News* 1, no. 2 (Spring 1999): 1.

References

Abdul-Jabbar, Kareem, and Peter Knobler. 1983. *Giant Steps: The Autobiography of Kareem Abdul-Jabbar*. New York: Bantam Books.

Aldrich, Nelson W., Jr. 1988. *Old Money: The Mythology of America's Upper Class*. New York: Knopf.

Allis, Frederick S., Jr. 1979. *Youth from Every Quarter: A Bicentennial History of Phillips Academy, Andover*. Hanover, N.H.: Phillips Academy, Andover.

Allport, Gordon W. 1958. *The Nature of Prejudice*. Garden City, N.Y.: Doubleday.

Anson, Robert Sam. 1987. *Best Intentions: The Education and Killing of Edmund Perry*. New York: Random House.

Archibold, Randal C. 1999. "Minority Growth Slips at Top Private Schools." *New York Times*. December 12: A1.

Astin, Alexander W. 1982. *Minorities in American Higher Education*. San Francisco: Jossey-Bass.

Avery, Robert B., and Michael S. Rendall. 2002. "Lifetime Inheritances of Three Generations of Whites and Blacks." *American Journal of Sociology*, 107, no. 5: 1300–1346.

Baltzell, E. Digby. 1958. *Philadelphia Gentlemen: The Making of a National Upper Class*. Glencoe, Ill.: Free Press.

Bennett, Andrea. 1985. "Building Up Bank Unity for Big Business Bids: Linda Hurley Harnesses Minority Bank Power." *American Banker* (August 23): 25.

Biernacki, Patrick, and Dan Waldorf. 1981. "Snowball Sampling: Problems and Techniques of Chain Referral Sampling." *Sociological Methods and Research* 10 (2): 141–163.

Bigger, Margaret. 1983. "Willie Ratchford Tries to Give as Good as He Got." *Charlotte Observer*. April 14.

Bourdieu, Pierre. 1977. *Outline of a Theory of Practice*. Cambridge: Cambridge University Press.

Bowen, William G., and Derek Bok. 2000. *The Shape of the River,* 2nd ed. Princeton, N.J.: Princeton University Press.

Boyd, William M. II. 1974. *Desegregating America's Colleges: A Nationwide Survey of Black Students, 1972–73.* New York: Praeger.

Brady, Lois Smith. 2000. "Vows: Althea Beaton and Malik Ducard." *New York Times.* August 20: 37.

Branch, Shelley. 1998. "What Blacks Think of Corporate America." *Fortune* (July 6): 140–143.

Brodkin, Karen. 1998. *How Jews Became White Folks and What that Says about Race in America.* New Brunswick, N.J.: Rutgers University Press.

Buckley, Gail Lumet. 1986. *The Hornes: An American Family.* New York: Knopf.

Butterfield, Fox. 1993. "At Milton, a Headmaster with a Difference," *New York Times,* January 10: Sec. 4A, 37ff

Carnoy, Martin. 1994. *Faded Dreams: The Politics and Economics of Race.* New York: Cambridge University Press.

Cary, Lorene. 1992. *Black Ice.* New York: Knopf.

Catlin, Roger. 1988. "Chapman: A Class of '82 Act in Danbury." *Hartford Courant.* November 1: Gl.

Chambliss, Elizabeth (Research Director). 2000. "Miles to Go 2000: Progress of Minorities in the Legal Profession." American Bar Association Commission for Minorities in the Profession.

Clarke, Caroline V. 2001. *Take a Lesson: Today's Black Achievers on How They Made It & What They Learned Along the Way.* New York: John Wiley and Sons.

"Clifton R. Wharton, Jr." 1987. *Current Biography Yearbook.* New York: H. W. Wilson Co., pp. 597–601.

Clines, Frances X. 1969. "Caseworkers Pool Funds to Aid Groton-Bound Harlem Student." *New York Times.* August 2: 17.

Cohen, Jordan, Barbara Gabriel, and Charles Terrell. 2002. "The Case for Diversity in the Health Workforce." *Health Affairs* 21 (5): 90–102.

Coleman, James S. 1958. "Relational Analysis: The Study of Social Organizations with Survey Methods." *Human Organizations* 17 (4): 28–36.

Collins, Sharon M. 1989. "The Marginalization of Black Executives." *Social Problems* 36 (4): 317–331.

Collins, Sharon M. 1997. *Black Corporate Executives: The Making and Breaking of a Black Middle Class.* Philadelphia: Temple University Press.

Conley, Dalton. 1999. *Being Black, Living in the Red: Race, Wealth and Social Policy in America.* Berkeley: University of California Press.

Cookson, Peter, W., Jr., and Caroline H. Persell. 1985. "English and American Residential Secondary Schools: A Comparative Study of the Reproduction of Social Elites." *Comparative Education Review* 29 (3): 283–298.

Cookson, Peter W., Jr., and Caroline H. Persell. 1985. *Preparing for Power: America's Elite Boarding Schools.* New York: Basic Books.

Cookson, Peter W., Jr., and Caroline H. Persell. 1991. "Race and Class in America's Elite Preparatory Boarding Schools: African Americans as the 'Outsiders Within.'" *Journal of Negro Education* 60 (2): 219–228.

Cowan, Paul. 1967. *The Making of an Un-American*. New York: Viking.

Daniels, Arlene Kaplan. 1988. *Invisible Careers*. Chicago: University of Chicago Press.

Daniels, Cora. 2002. "50 Most Powerful Black Executives." *Fortune* (July 22): 60–80.

Daniels, Lee A. 1994. "Abrupt Exit: Racism, Leaks, and Isolation Drove Clif Wharton to Resign from State Department." *Emerge* (February): 28–33.

Datnow, Amanda, and Robert Cooper. 1997. "Peer Networks of African American Students in Independent Schools: Affirming Academic Success and Racial Identity." *Journal of Negro Education* 66 (1): 56–72.

Deutsch, Claudia H. 2001. "Xerox Moves Up an Insider to Be Its Chief." *New York Times*. July 27: C4.

Domhoff, G. William. 2002. *Who Rules America: Power and Politics?* 4th ed. New York: McGraw Hill.

Dooley, Meg. 1987. "Minorities in Higher Education: Bridging the Access Gap." *Columbia Magazine* (June): 27–35.

Dovidio, John F. 2001. "On the Nature of Contemporary Prejudice: The Third Wave." *Journal of Social Issues* 57 (4): 829–849.

Dunning-Alami, Veronica, and Susan Boiko. 1977. "A Better Chance: A Program that Works." *Independent School* (May): 26–28.

Feagin, Joe R. 1989. *Race and Ethnic Relations*. 3rd ed. Englewood Cliffs, N.J.: Prentice-Hall.

Fenton, John H. 1965. "Dartmouth Greets 140 Studying in Talent Project." *New York Times*. August 16: 27.

Ferguson, Ronald F. 2001. "A Diagnostic Analysis of Black-White GPA Disparities in Shaker Heights, Ohio." In *Brookings Papers on Education Policy 2001*, edited by Diane Ravitch, pp. 347–414. Washington, D.C.: Brookings Institution Press.

Fernandez, John R. 1975. *Black Managers in White Corporations*. New York: Wiley.

Fernandez, John R. 1981. *Racism and Sexism in Corporate Life: Changing Values in American Business*. Lexington, Mass.: Lexington.

Fernandez, John R. 1988. "Racism and Sexism in Corporate America: Still Not Color- or Gender-Blind in the 1980s." In *Ensuring Minority Success in Corporate Management*, edited by Donna E. Thompson and Nancy DiTomaso, pp. 71–99. New York: Plenum Press.

Fiske, Edward B. 1987. "Colleges Open New Minority Drives." *New York Times*. November 18: 12.

Fiske, Susan T. 2002. "What We Know Now About Bias and Intergroup Conflict, the Problem of the Century." *Current Directions in Psychological Science* 11 (4): 123–128.

Fordham, Signithia, and John U. Ogbu. 1986. "Black Students' School Success: Coping with the Burden of 'Acting White.'" *Urban Review* 8 (3): 176–206.

Forman, Tyrone A. 2002. "The Social Psychological Costs of Racial Segmentation: A Study of African Americans' Well-Being." Paper presented at the annual meetings of the American Sociological Association, Chicago.

Fredrickson, George M. 2002. *Racism: A Short History*. Princeton, N.J.: Princeton University Press.

Freeman, Richard B. 1976. *Black Elite: The New Market for Highly Educated Black Americans*. New York: McGraw-Hill.

Gaines, Richard L. 1972. *The Finest Education Money Can Buy*. New York: Simon and Schuster.

Gilbert, Dennis. 1998. *The American Class Structure: A New Synthesis*. 5th ed. Belmont, Calif.: Wadsworth.

Glaser, Barney G., and Anselm L. Strauss. 1967. *The Discovery of Grounded Theory: Strategies for Qualitative Research*. Chicago: Aldine.

Goffman, Erving. 1961. *Asylums: Essays on the Social Situation of Mental Patients and Other Inmates*. Garden City, N.Y.: Anchor Books.

Goldman, Victoria, and Catherine Hausman. 2000. "Less Austerity, More Diversity at Prep School Today." *New York Times*, Education Life Section, November 12: 30.

Graham, Lawrence Otis. 1995. *Member of the Club*. New York: HarperCollins.

Gunn, Eileen P. 1997. "No Boundaries." *Fortune* (August 4): 77.

Hare, Bruce R. 1995. "On the Desegregation of the Visible Elite: Or, Beware of the Emperor's New Helpers: He or She May Look Like You or Me." *Sociological Forum* 10 (4): 673–678

Harrison, Roderick J. 2001. "The Status of Residential Segregation: Despite Decades of Change, African Americans Remain the Nation's Most Segregated Racial Group." *Focus* 29 (7): 3–4.

Haskins, Byron. 2000. "A Mission Together: Establishing a Legacy." *Choate Rosemary Hall Alumni Magazine* (Winter/Spring): 50–51.

Heer, David. 1974. "The Prevalence of Black White Marriage in the U.S., 1960–1970." *Journal of Marriage and the Family* 35: 246–258.

Helms, Janet E., ed. 1990. *Black and White Racial Identity: Theory, Research and Practice*. Westport, Conn.: Greenwood.

Higginbotham, Elizabeth. 2001. *Too Much to Ask: Black Women in the Era of Integration*. Chapel Hill: University of North Carolina Press.

Himmelstein, Jerome. 1997. *Looking Good and Doing Good: Corporate Philanthropy and Corporate Power*. Bloomington, Ind.: Indiana University Press.

Hochschild, Adam. 1986. *Half the Way Home*. New York: Viking.

Holmes, Steven A. 1994. "Street Survivor via Harvard: Deval Laurdine Patrick." *New York Times*. February 2: A12.

Horvat, Erin M., and Anthony L. Antonio. 1999. "'Hey, Those Shoes Are Out of Uniform': African American Girls in an Elite High School and the Importance of Habitus." *Anthropology & Education Quarterly* 30 (3): 317–342.

Howard, Susan. 1986. "3 Legislators among 45 Arrested in Colt Protest." *Hartford Courant*. May 14: Al.

Hoy, John C. 1969. "The Price of Diversity." *Saturday Review* (February 15): 96–97, 104.

Jacobs, Jerry A., and Teresa Labov. 1995. "Asian Brides, Anglo Grooms: Asian Exceptionalism in Intermarriage." Unpublished paper, Department of Sociology, University of Pennsylvania (October).

Jacobs, Jerry A., and Teresa Labov. 1995. "Sex Differences in Intermarriage: Exchange Theory Reconsidered." Unpublished paper, Department of Sociology, University of Pennsylvania (September).

James, C. L. R. 1983 [1963]. *Beyond a Boundary*. New York: Pantheon.

Jenkins, J. Craig. 1987. "Nonprofit Organizations and Public Advocacy." In *The Non-Profit Sector: A Research Handbook*, edited by Walter W. Powell, pp. 296–318. New Haven, Conn.: Yale University Press.

Jenkins, J. Craig. 1989. "Social Movement Philanthropy and American Democracy." In *Philanthropic Giving*, edited by Richard Magat, pp. 292–314. New York: Oxford University Press.

Jones, Edward W., Jr. 1973. "What's It Like to Be a Black Manager?" *Harvard Business Review* 51 (4): 108–116.

Jones, Edward W., Jr. 1986. "Black Managers: The Dream Deferred." *Harvard Business Review* 86 (3): 84–93.

Jones, James M. 1988. "Racism in Black and White: A Bicultural Model of Reaction and Evolution." In *Eliminating Racism: Profiles in Controversy*, edited by Phyliss A. Katz and Dalmas A. Taylor, pp. 127–131. New York: Plenum Press.

Jones, James M. 1997. *Prejudice and Racism*. 2nd ed. New York: McGraw Hill.

Kantrowitz, Barbara. 1988. "Colorblind Love." *Newsweek* (March 7): 40–41.

Karen, David. 1985. "Who Gets into Harvard? Selection and Exclusion." Ph.D. dissertation, Harvard University.

Kaufman, Jonathan. 1998. "As Blacks Rise High in the Executive Suite, CEO Is Often Jewish." *Wall Street Journal*. April 22: 1.

King, Rosalind Berkowitz, and Jenifer L. Bratter. 2001. "The Path to Interracial Mate Selection: Choosing First Partners and Husbands Across Racial Lines." Paper presented at the annual meetings of the American Sociological Association, Anaheim, Calif. (August).

Kinnon, Joy Bennett. 1997. "A Better Chance: National Program Produces Students Who Can Compete With the Best." *Ebony Magazine* (May): 44ff.

Klitgaard, Robert. 1985. *Choosing Elites*. New York: Basic Books.

Knowles, John. 1959. *A Separate Peace*. New York: Macmillan.

Korman, Abraham. 1988. *The Outsiders: Jews and Corporate America.* Lexington, Mass.: Lexington.

Kurtz, Howard. 2001. "Newsroom Versus Boardroom: Ex-Publisher Decries Emphasis on Profits." *Washington Post*. April 7: C1, C14.

Lacey, Karyn. 2002. "'We Should Fall in the Middle:' Middle-Class Blacks and the Construction of a Class-based Identity." Paper presented at the annual meetings of the American Sociological Association, Chicago (August 16).

Landry, Bart. 1987. *The New Black Middle Class*. Berkeley: University of California Press.

Lasch-Quinn, Elisabeth. 2001. *Race Experts: How Racial Etiquette, Sensitivity Training and New Age Therapy Hijacked the Civil Rights Movement*. New York: Norton.

Leo, John. 1969. "Negroes Elected President of Three Classes at Andover." *New York Times*. June 11: 33.

Lyles, Charlise. 1994. *Do I Dare Disturb the Universe? From the Projects to Prep School*. Boston: Faber and Faber.

MacLeod, Margo. 1984. "Influential Women Volunteers: Reexamining the Concept of Power." Paper presented at the annual meetings of the American Sociological Association, San Antonio, Tex.

Macpherson, Pat, and Rita Goldman. 2002. "Schooled in Diversity: How Do Schools Change?" In *Schooled in Diversity: Stories of African-American Alumni*, edited by Pat Macpherson. Philadelphia: Friends Council on Education.

Macpherson, Pat, Irene McHenry, and Sarah Sweeney-Denham, eds. 2001. *Schooled in Diversity: Readings on Racial Diversity in Friends Schools*. Philadelphia: Friends Council on Education.

Maeroff, Gene I. 1982. *Don't Blame the Kids: The Trouble with America's Public Schools*. New York: McGraw-Hill.

Massey, Douglas S., and Nancy A. Denton. 1993. *American Apartheid: Segregation and the Making of the Underclass*. Cambridge: Harvard University Press.

McBride, James. 1996. *The Color of Water: A Black Man's Tribute to His White Mother*. New York: Riverhead Books.

McLean, Linda R. 1969. "The Black Student in the White Independent School." *Independent School Bulletin* (February): 68–72.

McMillon, Doris, with Michele Sherman. 1985. *Mixed Blessings: The Dramatic True Story of a Woman's Search for Her Real Mother*. New York: St. Martin's Press.

McPherson, Edward. 1999. "Heartfelt Reflections: Thoughts on Af-Lat-Am's 30th Anniversary." *Prism: The Newsletter of the Multicultural Affairs Committee of the Phillips Academy Alumni Council* (March): 4.

Merrill, Charles. 1967. "Negroes in the Private Schools." *Atlantic Monthly* (July): 37f.

Merrill, Charles. 1982. *The Walled Garden: The Story of a School*. Boston: Rowan Tree Press.

Mickelson, Roslyn A. 1990. "The Attitude-Achievement Paradox Among Black Adolescents." *Sociology of Education* 63: 44–61

Mickelson, Roslyn A. 2002. "The Contributions of Abstract, Concrete, and Oppositional Attitudes to Understanding Race and Class Differences in Adolescents' Achievement." Paper presented at the annual meetings of the American Sociological Association, Chicago.

Monroe, Sylvester. 1973. "Guest in a Strange House: A Black at Harvard." *Saturday Review of Education* (February): 45–48.

Monroe, Sylvester. 1993. "Diversity Comes to Elite Prep Schools." *Emerge* (October): 50–53.

Monroe, Sylvester, and Peter Goldman with Vern E. Smith, Terry E. Johnson, Monroe Anderson, and Jacques Chenet. 1988. *Brothers: Black and Poor—A True Story of Courage and Survival*. New York: William Morrow.

Moore, Mignon R., and Sandra S. Smith. 2002. "'We Need to Know Who's With Us and Who's Not.' Intraracial Conflict, Race Consciousness, and What It Means to Be Black." Paper presented at the annual meetings of the American Sociological Association, Chicago (August 16).

Neary, John. 1971. *Julian Bond: Black Rebel*. New York: William Morrow.

Odendahl, Teresa. 1990. *Charity Begins at Home.* New York: Basic Books.

O'Hearn, Claudine Chiawei, ed. 1998. *Half and Half: Writers on Growing Up Biracial and Bicultural.* New York: Pantheon.

Oliver, Melvin L., and Thomas M. Shapiro. 1995. *Black Wealth/White Wealth: A New Perspective on Racial Inequality.* New York: Routledge.

Orfield, Gary, and Michael Kurlaender. 2001. *Diversity Challenged: Evidence on the Impact of Affirmative Action.* Cambridge, Mass.: Harvard Education Publishing Group.

Osborne, Jason W. 1999. "Unraveling Underachievement Among African American Boys from an Identification with Academics Perspective." *Journal of Negro Education* 68 (4): 555–565.

Ostrander, Susan A. 1980. "Upper-Class Women: Class Consciousness as Conduct and Meaning." In *Power Structure Research*, edited by G. William Domhoff, pp. 73–96. Beverly Hills, Calif.: Sage.

Ostrander, Susan A. 1984. *Women of the Upper Class.* Philadelphia: Temple University Press.

Patillo-McCoy, Mary. 1999. *Black Picket Fences: Privilege and Peril Among the Black Middle Class.* Chicago: University of Chicago Press.

Pennington, Gregory. 1983. "The Minority Student Experience in Predominantly White High Schools." Report for the Whitney M. Young Foundation and A Better Chance.

Perry, George. 1973. "A Better Chance: Evaluation of Student Attitudes and Academic Performance, 1964–1972." Study funded by the Alfred R. Sloan Foundation, the Henry Luce Foundation, and the New York Community Trust. ERIC Document 075556.

Persell, Caroline H., and Peter W. Cookson, Jr. 1985. "Chartering and Bartering: Elite Education and Social Reproduction." *Social Problems* 33 (2): 114–129.

Persell, Caroline H., and Peter W. Cookson, Jr. 1987. "Microcomputers and Elite Boarding Schools: Educational Innovation and Social Reproduction." *Sociology of Education* 60: 123–134.

Pettigrew, Thomas F. 1988. "Integration and Pluralism." In *Eliminating Racism: Profiles in Controversy*, edited by Phyliss A. Katz and Dalmas A. Taylor. New York: Plenum Press.

Pettigrew, Thomas F., and Joanne Martin. 1987. "Shaping the Organizational Context for Black American Inclusion." *Journal of Social Issues* 43 (1): 41–78.

Pierson, George. 1969. *The Education of American Leaders.* New York: Praeger.

Prescott, Peter S. 1970. *A World of Our Own: Notes on Life and Learning in a Boys' Preparatory School.* New York: Coward-McCann.

Raymond, Ronald. 1980. *Grow Your Roots Anywhere, Anytime.* Ridgefield, Conn.: Wyden.

Raymond, Ronald. 1985. "On Becoming Uprooted: The Beinecke Symposium." *WoosterNews* (Spring): 19–32.

Richburg, Keith B. 1985. "Blacks Forgoing Academic Life." *Washington Post.* December 16: A3.

Robinson, James H. 1950. *Road Without Turning: The Story of Rev. James H. Robinson.* New York: Farrar, Straus.

Rodriguez, Richard. 1982. *Hunger of Memory: The Education of Richard Rodriguez: An Autobiography*. Boston: D. R. Godine.

Rohrlich, Marianne. 1998. "Feeling Isolated at the Top, Seeking Roots: Jack and Jill Clubs for Middle-class Black Children Are Newly Fashionable, as Families Feel Cut Off in Nearly All-White Suburbs." *New York Times*. July 19: 1

Romero, Simon. 2002. "Lucent Finally Chooses a Chief Executive." *New York Times*. January 8: C1.

Root, Maria P. P., ed. 1992. *Racially Mixed People in America*. Newbury Park, Calif.: Sage.

Rosen, Gerald H. 1992. "TIAA-CREF: Declining Returns," *Academe* 78 (1): 8–12.

Rubin, Zick. 1973. *Liking and Loving*. New York: Holt, Rinehart and Winston.

Sedgwick, John. 1988. "World without End," *New England Monthly* 5 (9): 53–57, 106.

Sennett, Richard, and Jonathan Cobb, 1972. *The Hidden Injuries of Class*. New York: Random House.

Shea, Daniel J. 1987. "The Rebuilding of Frank Borges," *Bond-Buyer* (June 1): 1.

Simpson, George E., and J. Milton Yinger. 1985. *Racial and Cultural Minorities: An Analysis of Prejudice and Discrimination*. 5th ed. New York: Plenum Press.

Smith, Sandra S., and Mignon R. Moore. 2000. "Intraracial Diversity and Relations Among African-Americans: Closeness Among Black Students at a Predominantly White University." *American Journal of Sociology* 106 (1): 1–39.

Strauss, Anselm L. 1987. *Qualitative Analysis for Social Scientists*. New York: Cambridge University Press.

Tatum, Beverly Daniel. 1999. *"Why Are All the Black Kids Sitting Together in the Cafeteria?" and Other Conversations About Race*. Rev. ed. New York: Basic Books.

Teachman, Jay D., Karen A. Polonko, and Geoffrey K. Leigh. 1987. "Marital Timing: Race and Sex Comparisons." *Social Forces* 66 (1): 239–268.

Tinto, Vincent. 1980. "College Origin and Patterns of Status Attainment." *Sociology of Work and Occupations* 7: 457–486.

Unger, Henry. 2001. "Ex-Coke President Got $3.5 Million; Stahl's Separation Deal Also Gave Stock Access." *Atlanta Journal and Constitution*. May 2: 1C

Useem, Michael, and Jerome Karabel. 1986. "Pathways to Corporate Management." *American Sociological Review* 5: 184–200.

Van Duch, Darryl. 1999. "Minority GCs are Few, Far Between." *National Law Journal* (October 18): 1ff.

Washington, Joseph R., Jr. 1970. *Marriage in Black and White*. Boston: Beacon Press.

Wells, Amy Stuart, and Robert L. Crain. 1997. *Stepping Over the Color Line: African American Students in White Suburban Schools*. New Haven, Conn.: Yale University Press.

Wessman, Alden E. 1969. "Evaluation of Project ABC [A Better Chance]: An Evaluation of Dartmouth College—Independent Schools Scholarship Program for Disadvantaged High School Students." Final report, Office of Education, Bureau of Research (April), ERIC Document 031549.

Wessman, Alden E. 1971–1972. "Scholastic and Psychological Effects of a Compensatory Education Program for Disadvantaged High School Students: Project ABC." In *Educating the Disadvantaged*, edited by Edwin Flaxman, pp. 269–278. New York: AMS Press.

Witcher, Gregory B. 1980. "A Journey from Anacostia to the Elite White World." *Independent School* (May): 31–33.

Wright, Stephen C. 2001. "Restricted Intergroup Boundaries: Tokenism, Ambiguity, and the Tolerance of Injustice." In *The Psychology of Legitimacy: Emerging Perspectives on Ideology, Justice and Intergroup Relations*, edited by John T. Jost and Brenda N. Majors, pp. 223–254. New York: Cambridge University Press.

Wright, Stephen, Donald M. Taylor, and Fathali M. Moghaddam. 1990. "Responding to Membership in a Disadvantaged Group: From Acceptance to Collective Protest." *Journal of Personality and Social Psychology* 58 (6): 994–1003.

Yaqub, Reshma Memon. 2002. "Getting Inside the Ivy Gates." *Worth* (September): 97–104.

Zweigenhaft, Richard L. 1984. *Who Gets to the Top?: Executive Suite Discrimination in the Eighties*. New York: Institute of Human Relations.

Zweigenhaft, Richard L. 1987. "Women and Minorities of the Corporation: Will They Make It to the Top?" In *Power Elites and Organizations*, edited by G. William Domhoff and Thomas R. Dye, pp. 37–62. Beverly Hills, Calif.: Sage.

Zweigenhaft, Richard L. 1992. "The Application of Cultural and Social Capital: A Study of the 25th Year Reunion Entries of Prep School and Public School Graduates of Yale College." *Higher Education* 23: 311–320.

Zweigenhaft, Richard L. 1993. "Accumulation of Cultural and Social Capital: The Differing College Careers of Prep School and Public School Graduates." *Sociological Spectrum* 13: 365–376.

Zweigenhaft, Richard L. 1993. "Prep School and Public School Graduates of Harvard: A Longitudinal Study of the Accumulation of Social and Cultural Capital." *Journal of Higher Education* 64 (2): 211–225.

Zweigenhaft, Richard L. 2000. "The African Americans in the White Establishment: How and Why Did They Get There?" Paper presented at the annual meetings of the American Sociological Association, Washington, D.C. (August 14).

Zweigenhaft, Richard L., and G. William Domhoff. 1982. *Jews in the Protestant Establishment*. New York: Praeger.

Zweigenhaft, Richard L., and G. William Domhoff. 1998. *Diversity in the Power Elite: Have Women and Minorities Reached the Top?* New Haven, Conn.: Yale University Press.

Index

About the Authors

Richard L. Zweigenhaft is Dana Professor of Psychology and director of the Communications Concentration at Guilford College in Greensboro, North Carolina.

G. William Domhoff is research professor at the University of California, Santa Cruz. They are the coauthors of three previous books: *Jews in the Protestant Establishment* (Praeger, 1982), *Blacks in the White Establishment? A Study of Race and Class in America* (Yale, 1991), and *Diversity in the Power Elite* (Yale, 1998).